Quick and Fun Activities for Every Day of the Year

Written by Tim Tuck
Revised and Rewritten by Karen Tam Froloff and Wanda Kelly
Edited by Karen Tam Froloff

Editor-in-Chief
Sharon Coan, M.S. Ed.

Art Director
CJae Froshay

Product Manager
Phil Garcia

Imaging
James Edward Grace

Cover Design
Denise Bauer

Publisher

Mary D. Smith, M.S. Ed.

Blake Staff

Publisher: Sharon Dalgleish

Editor: Tricia Dearborn

Original cover and internal illustrations by Jobi Murphy

This edition published by

Teacher Created Resources, Inc.
6421 Industry Way
Westminster, CA 92683
www.teachercreated.com
ISBN: 978-0-7439-3626-2
©2001 Teacher Created Resources, Inc.
Reprinted, 2008
Made in U.S.A.
with permission from
Blake Education
Locked Bag 2022
Glebe NSW 2037

Using the Book

As a famous person once said, "Most modern calendars mar the sweet simplicity of our lives by reminding us that each day that passes is the anniversary of some perfectly uninteresting event."[1] This book is here to spice up the sweet simplicity of our lives with perfectly interesting events for every day of the year. You can turn to any given page and find out something new. For example, on March 30 in 1867, Alaska was sold to the United States for a mere 7.2 million dollars. Or, a giant squid dragged a ship to the ocean's depths on May 10, 1874. And, on October 5, 1964, Janice Salt married Francis Pepper.

Is it trivia? For sure! Useless trivia? No, not when we combine the event with other thematically-related sections:

- **Word of the Day** contains the word's definition and origin.
- **Imagine . . .** is a creative springboard for writing, design, drama, and art.
- **Quote of the Day** is a thought-provoking quote, one-liner, or lyric.
- **Activity of the Day** is a puzzle, game, or a recipe for fun.

Using the Activities

Yes, you can just photocopy the pages from *Activities for Every Day of the Year* and give them to the students. But here are some ideas for getting more out of the book.

Today in . . .

Births, deaths, trivia, record attempts, historic firsts, special days, celebrations, and holidays all make appearances in this section on each page. The format is consistent throughout the book: first a statement of fact about an event that occurred on that calendar date in history, then either further information about the event, related trivia, or thematically relevant (and often irreverent) facts. Students will have knowledge of some of the featured events (December 17: first powered airflight), people (August 4: Hans Christian Andersen), or celebrations (January 1: New Year's Day). You may, however, need to provide additional information on lesser-known historical figures such as Yuri Gagarin (April 12) or the importance of some events (February 12: the gold rush).

If used as a class exercise:

- Read through and discuss the details of the day's entry.
- Have students share their knowledge of the subject.
- If the focus is a person, what else is known of his/her life? Why is the person well-known? What were his/her achievements?

[1]Oscar Wilde, March 21

- If an invention, discuss how it changed people's lives. How would life be different without it?
- If an event, discuss similar events held in other countries, the state, or locally.
- Look up place names in an atlas. Keep track of locations on a large map of the world.

Individually or in groups, students could also do the following:

- Research the topic further in the encyclopedia, in the library, or on the Internet.
- Investigate similar records. For example, Robert Wadlow (April 22) was one of the world's tallest people. Who was the shortest? (See May 21 for ideas.)
- Make their own almanacs[2] of interesting information.
- Collect newspaper clippings for each day of the year.
- Visit online almanacs[3] for additional "Today in . . ." information.

Word of the Day

The "Word of the Day" section defines and gives the etymology[4] of a word included on the page or related to the page's theme. Students can do the following:

- Add the word to their weekly spelling lists.
- Look up the word to find additional definitions.
- Discuss how the word evolved from the given source. Why, for instance, did the word "capital" come from the Latin word caput, meaning "head"?
- Find other words that might be related to the original, for example, "cap" (a head covering), "capsize" (to tip head-over), or "cape" (the headland).
- Investigate the Roman (Latin) and Greek cultures that supplied many of our words.
- Invent new words by joining existing words together. Use "tele-vision," "micro-scope," or "micro-phone" as examples.
- Make a class dictionary of "Word of the Day" words and meanings. Add other words and phrases as they appear in class discussions and activities.
- Investigate the origins of other words. Most larger dictionaries (book and online)[5] include etymological information.

Imagine . . .

The "Imagine . . ." section takes an imaginative leap from "Today in . . ." to stimulate creative expression. Many of the "Imagine . . ." entries encourage a written response (e.g., October 1), some are design projects (e.g., July 1), while others are open-ended (e.g., April 11). Don't feel restrained by the suggested "creative medium." Encourage students to respond with scripts, screenplays, shopping lists, menus, recipes, top-ten lists, codes, songs, lyrics, drawings, designs, models, or poetry.

[2]A calendar-like publication containing astronomical, meteorological, and miscellaneous information.

[3]To find many almanacs online go to www.infoplease.com/almanacs.html

[4]The original source or derivation of a word.

[5]Try the *Collins Concise Dictionary*, the *Encarta Encyclopedia*, or the *Webster Miriam* Web site at www.m-w.com/

Quote of the Day

The "Quote of the Day" section is the highbrow section of the book; it's the witty one-liner, the clever cliché, or the amusing apothegm.[6]
Here are some suggestions for using the quotes:

- Discuss what the quote is saying. (The interpretations are always open-ended so respect all of them.)
- Who is the epigrammatist?[7] Try the encyclopedia for a short biography.
- Find other quotes from the same person. Collections of quotes[8] are a useful place to start.
- Make posters or banners of the more inspiring quotes.
- Collect quotes and sayings from the class and publish them in your own class book of quotes.
- Find and read the texts the quotes come from.

Activity of the Day

Each day's activity is related (sometimes tenuously) to the "Today in . . ." event. Activities include word puzzles, math problems, recipes, art, and things to make. Many activities can be completed individually by students at their desks, but some will need materials prepared beforehand and/or directions given to the whole class step by step.

After the students have completed activities:

- Have them make puzzles for their friends to try.
- Challenge them to create similar puzzles on different themes.
- Have them research further aspects of the activity.

Themes

Each day is based on a theme. Good examples include February 27 (Halley's comet), April 3 (jeans), and October 1 (postcards). The factual, creative, research, and entertaining aspects of the theme make it a useful starting point for an entire theme day.

Here are some ideas for a theme day based on October 10 (Tutankhamen's treasures photographed for the first time). Other days' events can be expanded in a similar way.

- Read through "Today in . . ." and discuss. Who was Tutankhamen? Why was he important? What does the class know of Pharaohs, Egypt, and archaeology?
- In small groups, act out the opening of the tomb. (drama)
- Stop at the point where the noise is heard. Have the class write the remainder of the story. (language arts)
- Look at the "Word of the Day." Look up the word "Pharoah" and investigate its history. Make a list of related Egyptian words.
- Find out when Tutankhamen lived. Make a time line that includes his birth and the discovery of the tomb.

[6]A short, pithy instructive saying, maxim, or proverb.

[7]A writer of pigrams (witty sayings).

[8]*The Everyman Dictionary of Quotations and Proverbs*, compiled by D. C. Browning (Chancellor Press) is a good source. You can also go online to the Quotation Center at www.cynernation.com/victory/quotations/ which has over 13,000 quotations.

Themes *(cont.)*

- What shape can be folded into a pyramid? (a diamond) Make some cards and on the inside write some basic facts problems using Egyptian symbols instead of numbers. (math)
- Locate Egypt and the Valley of the Kings in an atlas. How does Tutankhamen's burial differ from burial customs in other cultures/ countries? Research burial traditions and rituals in different countries. What other discoveries have been made in Egypt? How did ordinary people live in Tutankhamen's time? (social studies)
- Use the hieroglyphics in the activity section and paint Egyptian murals. Have the students write their own names in hieroglyphics. (art)
- Re-create an archaeological dig in sand. Bury small items and then discuss how archaeologists work. Give students small brushes and have them find the items. Research Howard Carter and other famous archaeologists.

And Even More Uses

- Use the day's sheet for work for more able students. When students finish their work, direct them to the sheet for the day. Encourage them to investigate the theme and research further aspects themselves.
- Use it for homework. Have students complete a whole sheet, certain sections, or use it as a starting point for research.
- Use it to fill those five-minute spots between lessons, before dismissal, or when a break is needed. Read through the sheet. Ask questions. Have a quiz. Look up the word of the day. Use "Imagine . . ." for an around-the-class story.[9]
- And for those who can't bear to see a good day go to waste, use any sheet on any day.[10]

[9]Each child contributes one sentence at a time.

[10]Thanks to Beth!

Today

is New Year's Day. It is a day of new beginnings and renewed commitment to beliefs.

- January is named after the Roman God Janus, God of all passages and the spirit of new beginnings.
- Many countries have special customs for celebrating this day. One popular custom is to make a New Year's resolution, a promise you make to yourself (to do) for the coming year.
- Famous birthdays in 1735 belong to notable American patriots Paul Revere, who rallied American colonists against the British and Betsy Ross, who made the first U.S. flag.
- In 1863, U.S. President Abraham Lincoln issued the Emancipation Proclamation, which freed all slaves in the northern states and proclaimed that no man can own another.

Word of the day

resolution A decision as to future action.

Imagine...

You've just inherited an island. It's a new beginning for your little society and you want it to be special. Laws, customs, holidays. There's a lot to think about . . . starting with the new year. How will you celebrate it? Decide on some laws and customs.

Quote of the day

"I am in earnest. I will not equivocate; I will not excuse; I will not retreat a single inch; and I will be heard."

William Lloyd Garrison
(*The Liberator*, 1832)

Activity of the day

What's Your Resolution?
Using the letters in the word "resolution," list things that you will resolve to do in the coming year. "R," for example, could mean "Read every day!"

R _____
E _____
S _____
O _____
L _____
U _____
T _____
I _____
O _____
N _____

Answer: Answers will vary

Today

is Science Fiction day, which commemorates the birth of Isaac Asimov, who helped to create science fiction.

- Born in Petrovichi, Russia in 1920, Asimov and his family moved to the U.S. when he was three years old. He taught himself to read before age 5, using street signs in Brooklyn, New York.

- He was an author, scientist, and astronomer who over his lifetime, wrote many articles, short stories, and more than 500 books.

- It is his 40 years of writing science fiction that he is best known for, elevating the genre from pulp-magazine adventure to a more intellectual, novel level.

- His first 100 books took him almost 20 years to write; his second 100 took 9 ½ years; his third 100 took 6 years.

Word
of the day

creature Anything created, animate or inanimate.

Quote
of the day

"Writing is more fun than ever. The longer I write, the easier it gets."
Isaac Asimov (in an 1984 interview)

Imagine...

It's a beautiful starry night and your parents have just given you that telescope you've been asking for. You peer up into the dark sky. Shooting stars abound. A fantastic shower of lights streaking across the sky. Then it happens . . . a shooting star brightens the surroundings like a floodlight, landing close by. You decide to investigate. What do you find? Is it a meteor? A space ship? Finish the story.

Activity
of the day

Sci-fi Character

Draw your own science fiction character. Perhaps use one from your "Imagine . . ." story. Or, look at creatures in sci-fi movies, television series, or books. Be creative. Invent and design a creature with unique traits.

Today in 1959

Norman Rockwell was born.

- He painted and drew realistic portraits of people living and working in small U.S. town and farms.
- His artwork graced more than 300 covers of the *Saturday Evening Post*.

Word of the day

realistic Picturing in art of people and things as they really appear.

Imagine...

If you could paint a picture of an everyday scene, what would you paint? Describe the people, place, and things you would include in your painting. Use detail to paint this "picture" with words.

Quote of the day

"I have nothing to declare but my genius."

Oscar Wilde (what he told a U.S. Customs Official)

Activity of the day

Be an Artist

All you need is a pen or pencil paper, and your surroundings. Go to the park, go to the store, or go to the mall. Sit and watch people go by and then sketch a scene like Norman Rockwell would do.

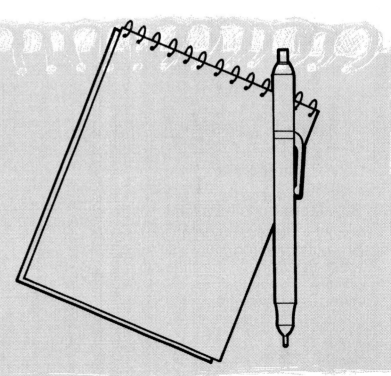

Answer: Answers will vary

Today in 1642

Sir Isaac Newton, mathematician and physicist, was born in Woolsthorpe, England.

- He grew up to discover the law of gravity when he saw an apple fall in his orchard (contrary to popular belief, not on his head). This simple event inspired him to deduce that what goes up must come down.
- He also found white light to be a mixture of infinitely colored rays.
- Other major contributions include writings on analytical geometry, alchemy and chemistry, philosophy, Judaeo-Christian prophecy, and Principia (*Mathematical Principles of Natural Philosophy*) which was published in 1687.
- Sir Isaac Newton died in 1927.

Word of the day

gravity The force that draws our bodies in the earth's sphere toward the center of the earth; from the Latin *gravis* (heavy).

Quote of the day

"By always thinking about them"
Isaac Newton (when asked how he came up with all of his brilliant ideas)

Imagine...

You wake up one morning and there is no gravity. How would you deal with everyday life? What adjustments would you need to make? What would you have to do to eat, sleep, travel, etc.?

Activity of the day

How Much Do You Weigh?
Weight is the force of gravity. Find out how much you would weigh in pounds on the different planets. Use the chart to calculate your weight.

My weight on Earth is:_____

Planet	Multiply Your Weight (in pounds) by:	My Weight Would Be
Mercury	.383	
Venus	.067	
Mars	.383	
Jupiter	2.533	
Saturn	1.067	
Uranus	.9	
Neptune	1.134	
Pluto	.067	

Answer: Answers will vary

Today

is a day for ideas that endure time.

- Henry Ford started a trend that continues to this day. He introduced the concepts of an eight-hour workday and a $5 a day minimum wage.

  He was labeled crazy, heretical, and subversive because of his new ideas.

- On this day in 1943, one-time slave, botanist, and inventor George Washington Carver died.

  His research created many new products for peanuts, potatoes, and wood.

  Most famous of his discoveries is peanut butter.

Word of the day

invent To think of or devise for the first time; from the Latin *invenire*: in (on) + *venire* (to come).

Imagine...

George Washington Carver gave the world 101 uses for peanuts. Did you know that peanuts are an ingredient in dynamite? Make up some uses of your own for his most popular use of the peanut—peanut butter. Would it be a good substitute for glue? Be wild about your answers. In other words, go nuts!

Quote of the day

"Opinion has caused more trouble on this little earth than plague or earthquakes."
Voltaire

"When nuts have thick shells, it will be a hard winter."
Old Proverb

Activity of the day

Shape Sandwiches
Celebrate the peanut with shape sandwiches.

You will need:
- peanut butter (or a suitable substitute if you are allergic)
- two slices of bread
- cookie cutters.

To make:
1. Spread the peanut butter on one slice of bread.
2. Cover with the other slice.
3. Use a cookie cutter to make a shaped sandwich.

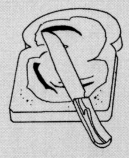

Today in 1941

U.S. President Franklin D. Roosevelt voiced his vision when he made his "Four Freedoms" speech.

- These four freedoms are: freedom of speech, freedom of worship, freedom from want, and freedom from fear.
- Freedom to travel anywhere in the world became reality in 1942 when a Pan Am passenger plane completed the first around the world commercial flight.

Word of the day

freedom The state or quality of being free; without hindrance.

Quote of the day

"... world founded upon four essential freedoms: freedom of speech and expression, freedom of every person to worship God in his own way, freedom from want, (and) freedom from fear."

President Franklin D. Roosevelt as he addressed the U.S. Congress

Imagine...

Freedom comes in many forms . . . . Can you make a case for freedom? How about freedom for zoo animals? Freedom for kids to stay up until midnight? Freedom to change your school to only four days a week? Be serious or be outrageous. Just remember to support your case for freedom.

Activity of the day

Freedom
How many words of three letters or more can you make from the word "freedom"?

_____

_____

_____

_____

_____

Answers: Here are thirteen: fed, for, red, rod, deem, deer, feed, free, mere, mode, reed, rode

Today in 1929

Tarzan first appeared in a comic strip.

- The cartoon was based on Edgar Rice Burroughs' character in his book *Tarzan of the Apes.*
- In this book, Tarzan lived in the jungle and could communicate with animals.
- Tarzan has been made into movies, television series, and most recently, a Disney animation.
- Tarzan's yell is famous.

Word of the day

communicate To give or exchange information as by talking or writing; from the Latin *communicare*.

Imagine...

You are a reporter and you have been sent out on assignment to interview none other than, who else? Tarzan! Write your interview with Tarzan in question and answer format. And don't forget to have a wild and swingin' time!

Quote of the day

"Yes, Jane. You? Jane. And you? You?"
"Tarzan, Tarzan."

From the Tarzan script (Not "[Me] Tarzan . . . [You] Jane.")

Activity of the day

Tarzan Scramble
Unscramble these words associated with Tarzan.

lgatliaor _____

yonmke _____

paamen _____

yhpton _____

larfweatl _____

nwnsgiig _____

ievns _____

naje _____

ietgr _____

alolgir _____

ugjnle _____

Answer: alligator, monkey, apeman, python, waterfall, swinging, vines, jane, tiger, gorilla, jungle

Today in 1859

Adventurer Fanny Bullock Workman was born in Worcester, Massachusetts.

- Fanny and her husband, Dr. William Hunter, traveled through many countries on bicycle, studying the places they visited and learning the language.
- Fanny gave many lectures about her explorations.
- In 1903, she was the first woman to climb Mount Koser Gunya in the Himalayas.

Word of the day

explore To travel in a region (previously unknown or little known) for discovery.

Quote of the day

"Twenty years from now you will be more disappointed by the things that you didn't do than by the ones you did do. So throw off the bowlines. Sail away from the safe harbor. Catch the trade winds in your sails. Explore. Dream. Discover."

Mark Twain

Imagine...

You are an adventurer like Fanny Bullock Workman. Brave and fearless, where in the world would you like to go—on a bicycle, of course? Why would you choose this place and what would you do to prepare for your trip?

Activity of the day

Cycle Words

Match up the definitions to these "cycle" words.

1. unicycle
2. bicycle
3. tricycle
4. bicycle-built-for-two
5. motorcycle

A. a vehicle consisting of a metal frame, mounted on two wheels, and equipped with handlebars, a saddle-like seat, and foot pedals

B. a two-wheeled vehicle propelled by an engine

C. a riding device with only one wheel and a seat which is straddled by the rider

D. a light, three-wheeled vehicle worked by pedals; especially good for children

E. a vehicle consisting of a metal frame, mounted on two wheels, and equipped with two sets of handlebars, seats, and foot pedals

Answer: 1. C, 2. A, 3. D, 4. E, 5. B

Today

is Aviation in America Day.

- On this day in 1793, Frenchman Jean Pierre Blanchard made the first hot air balloon flight in U.S. history. The flight took place in Philadelphia, Pennsylvania.
- President George Washington was present to witness the event.
- The Montgolfier brothers (Joseph and Etienne) were first to invent the hot air balloon in 1783. They called their invention the "aerostat."
- Today balloons are powered by propane gas and can fly to 10,000 ft. (3050 m) or higher. The most popular sized balloon (55 ft. [16.7 m] and 7 stories tall) uses 1,800 sq. yards (1,505 sq. m) of nylon fabric, 3 miles (5 km) of thread, a ½ mile (.8 km) of reinforced nylon webbing, and holds 90,000 sq. ft. (8,370 sq. m) of heated air.
- There are over 5,000 balloon pilots in the U.S. alone.

Word of the day

Balloon A large, airtight bag that rises above the earth when filled with a gas that is lighter than air; from the French *pallone* (a ball).

Imagine...

You're taking a hot air balloon ride over your neighborhood. Write about what you see from above, or draw an aerial view of what you see when you're looking down.

Quote of the day

"Get in a stock of taffeta and rope and you'll see one of the most astonishing sights in the whole world!"

Joseph Montgolfier, inventor of the hot air balloon

Activity of the day

Make a Hot Air Balloon

You will need:

- a small narrow-mouthed bottle
- a balloon that fits snugly over the top of the bottle
- a pan filled with ice water
- a pan filled with hot water

Directions:

1. Slip the end of the balloon over the top of the bottle and let the balloon hang down the side.
2. Place the bottle in cold water for five minutes.
3. Then place the bottle in the hot water and watch what happens to the balloon.
4. Repeat steps 2 and 3 again.

Did your balloon get larger when you put the balloon in the hot water?

As the air warms, it expands. Placing the bottle in the hot water warms the air in the bottle. The expanded air goes up into the balloon just like it would in a hot air balloon, but on a much smaller scale!

Answer: Answers will vary

Today in 1870

John D. Rockefeller incorporated Standard Oil Company.

- Standard Oil was the first major oil company.
- On this day in 1901, oil was discovered in Beaumont, Texas thus starting the Texas oil boom.
- An era of American prosperity resulted as oil was introduced as a new energy resource.

Word of the day

resource Something ready for use and available as needed.

Quote of the day

"A valuable resource is simply one which someone has found a good use for."

Imagine...

You were the one who discovered the oil in Texas. You are now rich beyond your wildest dreams. After spending only a fraction of your wealth on everything you've always wanted, now you want to use it to help others. Make a list of what you will do with your money. You are now a benefactor!

Activity of the day

Where's the Oil?
There are many words that have the word "oil" in them. How many can you come up with? Make a list.

_____ _____ _____
_____ _____ _____
_____ _____ _____
_____ _____ _____
_____ _____ _____
_____ _____ _____
_____ _____ _____

Answer: Here are a few words we came up with: boil, broil, broiler, coil, doilie, foil, oily, recoil, soil, spoil, toil, uncoil

Today in 1935

Amelia Earhart became the first woman to fly solo across the Pacific Ocean.

- She completed the flight from Honolulu, HI to Oakland, CA on January 12th.
- In 1929, she helped found the "Ninety-Nines," an international organization of women pilots that still exists today.
- In 1937, Amelia and a navigator tried to fly around the world. On the hardest leg of their journey, their plane vanished near Howland Island in the central Pacific Ocean.
- Some believe that they drowned. Others believe that they were killed or captured by the Japanese. No evidence of either event happening exists.

Word of the day

destiny The seemingly inevitable or necessary succession of events; fate; from the Old French and Latin *destinare*.

Quote of the day

"Please know I am quite aware of the hazards . . . I want to do it because I want to do it. Women must try to do things as men have tried. When they fail, their failure must be but a challenge to others."

Amelia Earhart
(in a letter to her publisher)

Imagine...

There is always a first for everything. What would you like to be the "first" at?

Activity of the day

"Firsts"

Make a list of famous "firsts." Here are a few to

#1

First base (in baseball)

First letter of the alphabet

Baby's first word

Today in 1628

Charles Perrault was born in France.

- For centuries, fairy tales were handed down through storytelling.

- In 1697, Charles Perrault published *The Tales of Mother Goose*. He wrote down these fairy tales to amuse his children and friends.

- He included such classics as "Sleeping Beauty," "Little Red Riding Hood," "Cinderella," and "Puss in Boots."

Word of the day

fairy tale A story about fairies, magic deeds, etc.

Quote of the day

"The age for hearing . . . fairy tales is three years to death. Our world can seem so technical and cold. All of us need these stories to warm our souls."

Elfriede Kleinhans, professional German storyteller

Imagine...

Many fairy tales end with " . . . and they lived happily ever after." But what do you think happens after the story ends? Continue your favorite fairy tale. For example, what happened to the Little Mermaid after she got her legs and married the prince.

Activity of the day

Match the Opposites
Most fairy tales have a good character and a wicked character. Can you match these fairy tale opposites?

Snow White	Malificent
Cinderella	Giant
Sleeping Beauty	Queen
Little Red Riding Hood	The Wolf
Jack	Stepmother and Stepsisters

Can you think of others?

Answer: Snow White/Queen; Cinderella/Stepmother and Stepsisters; Sleeping Beauty/Malificent; Little Red Riding Hood/The Wolf; Jack/Giant

Today in 1926

Michael Bond, creator of Paddington the Bear, was born in Newbury, Berkshire, England.

- On Christmas Eve in 1957, Bond was shopping for a present for his wife when he spotted an unsold stuffed bear sitting on a store shelf. He felt sorry for the bear and bought it for his wife.

- Bond lived near Paddington Station in London, England at the time. Hence, the name Paddington.

- The bear with the yellow hat, blue duffle coat, and Wellington boots has been the subject of Bond's many stories. Paddington's adventures have been published in 20 countries.

Word of the day

teddy bear A child's stuffed toy made to look like a bear cub; named after U.S. President Theodore (Teddy) Roosevelt.

Imagine...

Paddington always wears a coat with pockets so that he has a place to keep his things. Write about what you like to keep in your pockets. Is it loose change? A collection of rocks? Trash?

Quote of the day

"Writing is a lonely occupation, but it's also a selfish one. When things get bad, as they do for everyone from time to time, writers are able to shut themselves away from it, peopling the world with their characters, making them behave the way they want them to behave, saying the things they want to hear. . . . Sometimes I am Paddington walking down Windsor Gardens . . . to buy his morning supply of buns, . . . I wouldn't wish for anything nicer."

Michael Bond

Activity of the day

A New Outfit

Design a new outfit for Paddington the Bear to wear in each season. Remember what the weather will be like and remember the pockets!

Winter	Spring
Summer	Fall

Today in 1875

medical missionary, musician, and philosopher Albert Schweitzer was born in Alsace, then a part of Germany that later became a part of France.

- He became a doctor and opened a hospital in Lambarene, Gabon, a provence of French Equatorial Africa.
- He had a "reverence for life" and by stressing the interdependence and unity of all life, he was a forerunner of the environmental and animal welfare movements.
- In 1953 at the age of 78, he was awarded the Nobel Peace Prize for his humanitarian efforts.
- During the last 12 years of his life, he emphasized the dangers of nuclear energy, nuclear testing, and the nuclear arms race between the superpowers.
- He continued to oversee his hospital in Lambarene until his death in 1965 at age 90. He and his wife are buried on the hospital grounds.

Word of the day

missionary A person sent out by his church to preach, teach, and proselytize in a foreign country that is considered in need.

Quote of the day

"Example is not the main thing in influencing others. It is the only thing."
Dr. Albert Schweitzer

Imagine...

You have been chosen to take a ride on a time machine back into the past. You will be going back in time to spend the day with Dr. Albert Schweitzer. Make a journal detailing your experiences. You may have to do some research on this one!

Activity of the day

Draw the Quote
Dr. Albert Schweitzer left many thought-provoking quotes. Choose one of these quotes and turn it into a picture that represents its message.

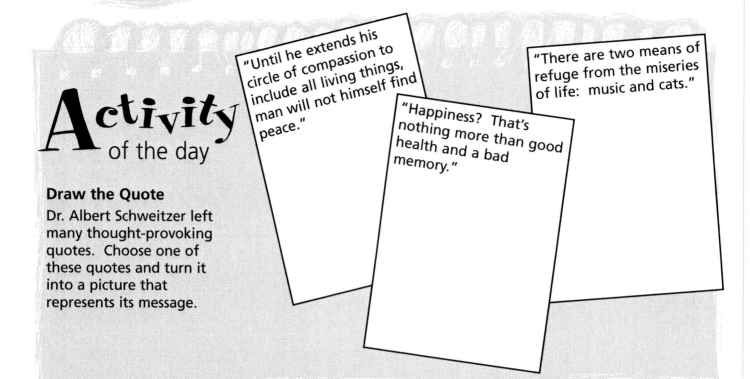

"Until he extends his circle of compassion to include all living things, man will not himself find peace."

"Happiness? That's nothing more than good health and a bad memory."

"There are two means of refuge from the miseries of life: music and cats."

Today

is Humanitarian Day on which people wear white to honor all humanitarians.

- One such humanitarian was civil rights leader and reverend, Dr. Martin Luther King, Jr. who was born on this day in 1929. This is also Martin Luther King, Jr. Day.

- Dr. Martin Luther King, Jr. was the best known leader of the civil rights movement. He made many speeches and led many marches and peaceful demonstrations. He preached change through nonviolence.

- He won the Nobel Peace Prize in 1964 for his efforts in bringing equality to African Americans in the U.S.

- Dr. Martin Luther King, Jr. was shot and killed while helping to organize a march in Memphis, Tennessee.

Word of the day

humanitarian A person devote to promoting the welfare of humanity; a philanthropist.

Imagine...

Write about what you could do to help people live together in peace or, draw a picture of people of different races living together in peace.

Quote of the day

"I have a dream. I have a dream that . . . little children will one day live in a nation where they will not be judged by the color of their skin but by the content of their character. I have a dream . . ."

Dr. Martin Luther King

Activity of the day

King's Heroes

These are some of the people who inspired Dr. Martin Luther King to be a promotor of peace. Can you match their names with their accomplishments?

1. Frederick Douglass (1817–1895)

2. Harriet Tubman (1821–1913)

3. Booker T. Washington (1856–1915)

4. George Washington Carver (1861–1943)

5. Jesse Owens (1913–1980)

A. Black leader and educator; founder and head of Tuskegee Institute, a vocational school for Alabama

B. Track and field athlete; high school coach urged him to run for his weak lungs "Ambassador of Sports" by President Eisenhower in 1955.

C. Was born into slavery and escaped; encouraged Lincoln to make Emancipation an issue in the civil war

D. Was born a slave and escaped; led the "Underground Railroad" and, helped more than 200 slaves escape to freedom

E. Born into slavery, raised by his owners; invented 300 uses for peanuts and 100 uses for sweet potatoes.

Answer: 1. C, 2. D, 3. A, 4. E, 5. B

Today in 1932

Dian Fossey, mountain gorilla advocate, was born in San Francisco, CA.

- She began her study of gorilla in 1966 in the forest of Rwanda in South Central Africa.
- Through many years of living and working among gorilla in their natural habitat, she gained their trust and "became" a part of their family.
- She was killed in 1985, most likely, by poachers who saw her gorilla conservation efforts as a threat.
- A movie, starring Sigourney Weaver, chronicled her life.

Word of the day

conservation Protection for the loss of the endangered.

Quote of the day

"We have all been kind of surprised (at the increase). It may have just been a stroke of luck, or it may be that the gorillas have learned to avoid humans. They have learned to spring snare traps . . . learned to keep away from refuge and military camps."

Dr. H Dieter Steklis, chief scientist of the Dian Fossey Gorilla Fund International and professor of anthropology at Rutger's University

Imagine...

Write about an animal you'd like to study. Tell why you think it is important to protect this animal from extinction.

Activity of the day

Endangered Animal Word Search

Find these endangered animals, as well as the person who was a major influence in animal conservation and in what country she did her research.

Africa, Bald Eagle, Blue Whale, Brown Bear, Dian Fossey, Elephant, Giant River Otter, Manatee, Mountain Gorilla, North American Bison, Panda Bear, Rhinoceros, Sea Turtle, Tiger

```
B M O U N T A I N G O R I L L A W
X A E C F I R Q C X A F R I C A F
Y N E S A G D W S E A T U R T L E
E A L D G E A P B R O W N B E A R
S T E I E R V A I N O R T H K Y Z
S E P A N A D U B A M E R I C A N
O E H N E N G M J B I S O N E L X
F H A O A K E L A H W E U L B D M
A T N P L S O R E C O N I H R B Y
R E T T O R E V I R T N A I G Z I
```

Today in 1706

Benjamin Franklin was born in Boston, Massachussetts.

- An American patriot, he had many jobs including printer, statesman, inventor, publisher, scientist, diplomat, and philanthropist.
- In 1732, he published *Poor Richard's Almanac* which was full of tips on weather, gardening, and contained witty sayings about friendship, money, and life.
- He was one of the writers of the Declaration of Independence.
- As an inventor, he proved that lightning was a form of electricity.

Word of the day

almanac a calendar with astronomical data, weather forecasts; a book published annually containing information, usually statistical, on many subjects; from the Latin *alminichiaka* (calendar).

Imagine...

Benjamin Franklin was known as a man of many talents. What other talent do you have or would you like to have?

Quote of the day

"A word to the wise is enough and many words won't fill a bushel."

Bejamin Franklin

Activity of the day

Lightning Rod

Benjamin Franklin was one of the first scientists to conclusively prove that lightning was a form of electricity. He achieved this by flying a kite (that was attached to a wire and key) in a thunderstorm. It gave him an electric shock.

Later he tried it again, but with four kites. Unfortunately, he's only holding onto one of them. Two of the other kites are attached to each other and the fourth is flying free. So,

Answer: B is attached to D, A is flying free, and Ben is holding onto C

Today

is Pooh Day.

- Children's author, Alan Alexander Milne, best known for his "Winnie-the-Pooh" stories, was born on this day.
- "Winnipeg" or "Winnie" for short, was a black bear cub, a favorite London Zoo animal of Christopher Robin's (Milne's son).
- Christopher Robin called his own teddy bear, Winnie, and Milne added "Pooh" to the name from a swan that was in a poem in his book *When We Were Very Young.*
- Other characters such as Eeyore, Piglet, Tigger, Kanga, and Roo were based on stuffed animals that belonged to Christopher Robin. The 100-Aker-wood was based on Milne's country home in Ashdown Forest, Sussex.
- Walt Disney brought Pooh to film in 1966. The feature-length, animated film The Many Adventures of Winnie the Pooh was released in 1977.

Word of the day

wonder To marvel at; to have curiosity; from the Old English *wundor*.

Quote of the day

"No where can I think so happily as in a train . . . . I see a cow and wonder what it is like to be a cow, and I wonder whether the cow wonders what it is like to be me."
A. A. Milne

Imagine...

Read the Quote of the Day. Make a list of what you think a cow's life must be like. Using all of your senses, think about what a cow sees, hears, smells, tastes, and feels. Would a cow on a dairy farm have a different life than a cow in the pasture?

Do some early spring-cleaning. Clean out your closet or toy chest. Did you make any exciting discoveries?

Activity of the day

Spring Cleaning Discovery
Milne thought it was okay to be messy sometimes and that when he looked through his papers, he would find things he hadn't seen in a while.

"One of the advantages of being disorderly is that one is constantly making exciting discoveries," he once said.

Today

is Tin Can Day. On this day in 1825, the tin canning process for food was patented.

- This month is also National Soup Month.
- In 1897, the company owned by Joseph A. Campbell sold a 10 1/2 oz. can of condensed soup for a dime, compared to more than 30¢ for a typical 32 oz. can of soup that was not condensed.
- Dr. John T. Dorrance, Campbell's nephew, invented condensed soup.
- In 1904, the cherubic Campbell kids were introduced.
- In 1922, Joseph A. Campbell adopted the name Campbell Soup for his company.

Word of the day

can A container made of metal in which foods or other perishable products are sealed for preservation;. from the Old English *canne* (a cup)

Imagine...

It's time for a change . . . in soup brands, that is. Invent your own brand of soup. Design your own label and include a list of ingredients. Develop new flavors and give the soup names that will appeal to kids. For example, "Cream of Bubble Gum" and "Chicken Lickin' Noodle" sound good.

Quote of the day

"M'm! M'm! Good"

Campbell's Soup radio ad jingle which began in the 1930s

Activity of the day

Soup Scramble
Unscramble these popular kinds of soup.

1. kincheck doolen
   _____
2. blagtevee feeb
   _____
3. merac fo cobcrilo
   _____
4. topato eschece
   _____
5. mootat
   _____
6. thabelpa
   _____
7. slipt ape
   _____
8. mensomoc
   _____
9. yarble efeb
   _____
10. macl dowcher
    _____

Answer: 1. Chicken Noodle; 2. Vegetable Beef; 3. Cream of Broccoli; 4. Potato Cheese; 5. Tomato; 6. Alphabet; 7. Split Pea; 8. Consomme; 9. Barley Beef; 10. Clam Chowder

Today

is Presidential Inauguration Day in the United States.

- Since 1937, this day has been designated for the new president of the United States to communicate his message.
- Some notable phrases from these speeches include:

  Franklin D. Roosevelt saw "one third of a nation ill-housed, ill-clad, ill-nourished."

  Harry S. Truman observed that "the supreme need of our time is for men to learn to live together in peace and harmony."

  Dwight D. Eisenhower said that "whatever America hopes to bring to pass in the world must first come to pass in the heart of America."

Word of the day

inaugurate To induct into office in a formal ceremony; from the Latin *inaugurare* (to practice augury).

Quote of the day

"Ask not what your country can do for you; ask what you can do for your country."
John F. Kennedy

Imagine...

You have just been elected president of the United States! Write an inaugural speech. Be bold. Be positive. Inspire the nation! State what you want for this country.

Activity of the day

Presidential Coin

After you have given your inauguration speech, you will want to mint a new presidential coin with your likeness on it. How much will your coin be worth? What will it be called? Use gray construction paper and a pencil to sketch an enlarged version of your new coin. You can look at real coins to give you ideas for the front and back of your coin.

My Coin

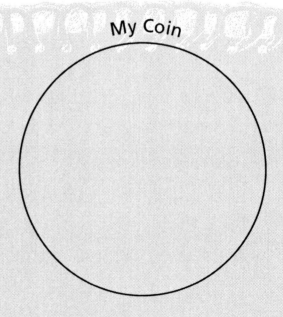

Answer: Answers will vary

Today

is a day for speed and power.

- On this day in 1954, the *U.S.S. Nautilus,* the first atomic submarine, was launched in Groton, Connecticut.

- On this day in 1967, the microwave oven was invented.

- On this day in 1970, Pan Am's Boeing 747 was the first wide body jet to take flight.

- And in 1976, the supersonic Concorde was put into service in England and France.

Word of the day

power The physical force of energy.

Imagine...

What's more powerful than an atomic sub, more luxurious than a Boeing 747, and faster than the Concorde? You know, . . . you invented it. As chief transportation engineer, tell the world about your new mode of travel. What is it called? Does it move by air, land, sea, or all three? How powerful is it? How luxurious? How fast? Maybe you'd like to draw the blueprints for your design, too.

Quote of the day

"Faster than a speeding bullet! More powerful than a locomotive! Able to leap tall buildings in a single bound!"
From the Superman television series

Activity of the day

Paper Airplane

Make three paper airplanes. Use different kinds of paper—construction paper, copy paper, and newsprint. Fly your airplanes. Which is faster? Which flies farther? What conclusions can you draw from your observations?

Here is one idea:

Basic Flyer: Use an 8½ x 11'' sheet of paper. Fold along dotted lines as shown.

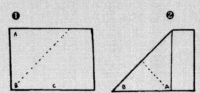

Fold to middle of page.

❼ Turn plane over.

Fold up on dotted line.

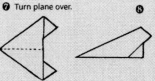

Open up wings for finished airplane.

JANUARY 22

Today

is National Popcorn Day.

- Popcorn is the world's number one snack food.
- Though popcorn probably originated in Mexico, it was grown in China, Sumatra, and India years before Columbus visited America.
- The oldest ears of popcorn ever found were discovered in a bat cave in New Mexico in 1948. They are estimated to be about 5,600 years old.
- In tombs in Peru researchers have found grains of popcorn that were 1,000 years old and so well-preserved that they can still be popped.
- America alone consumes 18 billion quarts of popcorn a year. That's about 73 quarts per person.

Word of the day

popcorn A variety of Indian corn with small ears and hard grains which pop open in a white, puffy mass when heated.

Quote of the day

"He's been one of the greatest forces for promoting popcorn. Many people thought he was a media creation, but what people saw on television, that was him."

William E. Smith (executive director of the Popcorn Institute in Chicago, referring to Orville Redenbacher)

Imagine...

Well, it was your first time making popcorn. So how did you know that one pound of unpopped popcorn was too much per person? Write about the day you were having a movie party and threw twenty pounds of popcorn into the kettle to pop. Tell what happened.

Activity of the day

Popcorn Flowers
You will need:

- popped popcorn
- glue
- brown and green paint
- paint brush
- construction paper

Directions:

1. Paint a tree trunk with the brown paint.

2. Paint the branches of the tree next.

3. Paint some leaves on the branches and let the picture dry.

4. Glue "popcorn" blossoms along the branches.

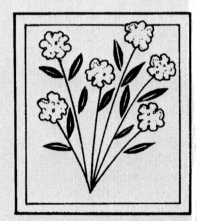

Answer: Answers will vary

Today

is National Handwriting Day.

- On this day in 1737, John Hancock, President of the Second Continental Congress from 1775–1777, and the first signer of the Declaration of Independence, was born in Braintree, Massachussetts.

- On this day, people are encouraged to write neatly so that other people can read their writing.

- It is also known as Practice Your Penmanship Day.

- The term "John Hancock" refers to a person's signature.

Word of the day

penmanship Handwriting as an art or skill.

Imagine...

It's time for a little self-evaluation, a little handwriting analysis. Write about your own handwriting or find a friend and write about each other's handwriting. Is it neat? Messy? Big? Small? Do you like it? Why or why not?

Quote of the day

"The expectations of life depend upon diligence; the mechanic that would perfect his work must first sharpen his tools."
Confucious

Activity of the day

Changing Your "John Hancock"
How many ways can you sign your name? Write it small. Write it large. Create fancy swirls and loops. Decorate it with flowers. Make it reflect your personality at the moment. Write your name as if you were calm, wild, crazy, happy, ...

Answer: Answers will vary

Today

is Go For the Gold Day.

- On this day in 1848, gold was discovered by John Sutter in California's Sacramento Valley in the United States.

- The lure of gold brought thousands of people out west to seek their fortunes in what was dubbed the '49er Gold Rush.

- The California Gold Rush set the groundwork for the growth of civilization in the American west.

Word of the day

gold Heavy, yellow, metallic chemical element that is highly ductile and maleable; it is a precious metal that is used in coins and jewelry.

Quote of the day

"The best way to tell gold is to pass a nugget around a crowded room, and ask them if it's gold. If it comes back, it's not gold."
Lennie Lower

Imagine...

You are a gold prospector and have just made a huge gold strike. Write a letter to a friend telling of your discovery. Where did it happen? How did it happen? What will you do with your newfound wealth?

Activity of the day

Pan for Gold

Have some fun here by re-living the California Gold Rush.

To prepare the "gold," purchase gold or yellow aquarium gravel and gold glitter, or have an adult help you paint the pebbles with gold spray paint (let dry, of course). Then mix the gold gravel, pebbles, and/or glitter with dirt and enough water to make a muddy mixture.

To pan for the "gold," pick up a clump of the muddy mixture and place it in a pie tin with some water. Swish the tin gently in a back and forth motion. Sift or separate out the "gold" by picking out the "nuggets" and pouring off the water.

Congratulations! You're a prospector now!

Today in 1924

the first Winter Olympics games were held in Chamonix, France.

- Winter Olympics sports include ski jumping, skating (speed and figure), luge (speed tobogganing), and ice hockey.
- Bobsledding has been around for a long time; one Finnish bobsleigh was dated as being 8,500 years old.
- Ski jumpers have been known to reach distances of nearly 200 meters.

Imagine...

The Mojave Desert "luge" team has been practicing for the next Winter Olympics for the past year. They've carved a course from the sandstone rock and greased it with suntan lotion. They've become pretty good too. Bruce certainly cuts a fine figure tobogganing along in his tank top and shorts. Of course, no one ever thought they'd actually qualify. Write about what happens when they do.

Word of the day

winter The coldest season of the year; From the Old English *wæter* (water).

Quote of the day

In skating over thin ice, our safety is in our speed.
Ralph Emerson

Activity of the day

Olympic Crossword

What city hosted the 2002 Winter Olympics? Use the clues to solve the puzzle.

Strongbox

Molten rock

Narrow road

Electrical measurement

Solid surface

second letter in the Greek Alphabet

Male ruler of a county

Color

Small restaurant

Grocery and eatery

Small nail

Group of soldiers

Answers: Safe, lava, lane, volt, land, beta, king, blue, café, deli, tack, army
SALT LAKE CITY

Today in 1919

millionaire publisher William Randolph Hearst hired Julia Morgan to design his new home.

- He wanted his San Simeon, California mansion to have 100 rooms, 31 bathrooms, 2 libraries, and a garage large enough to house 25 limousines.
- It took 28 years to build and when completed, consisted of 165 rooms filled with art and antiques.
- On a hill above the California coast, Hearst Castle sits on 127 acres of gardens, terraces, pools, and walkways.
- Today the mansion and grounds are split into five different tours (four daytime tours and one nighttime tour) and is a very popular tourist destination.

Word of the day

home The place where a person (or family) lives; one's dwelling place; from the Old English *ham*.

Quote of the day

" . . . something that would be more comfortable than the platform tents . . ."

William Randolph Hearst in his instructions to Julia Morgan

Imagine...

Write about your dream house. Will it be a large mansion or will it be a small cottage? How will the grounds look? Give plenty of details and then draw up blue prints (a floor plan) to go with it.

Activity of the day

There's No Place Like Home Word Search

Find and circle the following

apartment	house
brownstone	igloo
cabin	mansion
castle	teepee
cottage	condominium
townhouse	"Home Sweet Home"
flat	

Bonus: Where do Pluto, Lassie, Snoopy, and Rin Tin Tin live?

```
A C O T T A G E D Q E W B
B R O W N S T O N E X R L
T O W N H O U S E P G A E
E O O B D M A N S I O N D
E L C L N O Y M C H C F Z
P G Z T N E M T R A P A C
E I A Z Q A M I S S B T I
E L H O U S E T N A M I J
F D O G W Z L P K I K U N
H O U S E E L U R V U O V
H O M E S W E E T H O M E
```

Today in 1970

the movie rating system changed: "M" ratings became "PG."

- The first film censorship board was set up in 1909 in the United States.
- Early British movies were classified as either "A" for adults or "U" for general audience.
- Today, several ratings are used to decide who should be allowed to view movies: G, PG, PG-13, NC-17, R, and X.

Word of the day

censor An official who examines publications or films for objectionable material. Latin, from *censere* (to give one's opinion).

Imagine...

Film classification systems only tell you what age the film is suitable for. Try creating a system that tells us more about the film. How about SRFA (soppy romance for adults), or GSGE (great story, great effects)?

What might SE mean? Or CTI? Or LOK?

Quote of the day

"Why should people go out and pay to see bad movies when they can stay at home and see bad television for nothing?"

Sam Goldwyn

Activity of the day

Find the Movie Titles

The titles of eight movies are hidden in this story. Some titles are separated into parts. One word is used in two different movie titles. Can you find them all?

I'll never forget it as long as I live, Anne, not if I live to be 101. I know I can trust you to keep my secret. It will be as safe with you as it is in my diary. The other day when the king and I were in the garden, walking the dalmatians, I thought he was going to give me a ring. Instead, he was very angry and as fierce as the lion. He called me a babe, told me I wasn't very bright, and said I had not been frank with him. Just because I told him I didn't want him to go deer hunting because I think of all of them as Bambi, too. He doesn't think I should be afraid to go in the water. I guess he no longer thinks of me as his little lassie.

Answers: 101 Dalmatians, The King and I, Bambi, The Lion King, Ring of Bright Water, Babe, Lassie, The Diary of Anne Frank

Today in 1547

King Henry VIII of England died.

- King Henry married six times and is said to have written the song "Greensleeves."

- During his reign he had the *Bible* translated into English (from Latin) for the first time.

- His daughter from his marriage to Anne Boleyn was crowned Queen Elizabeth I when he died.

Word of the day

royal Of kingly ancestry. From the Latin *regere* (to rule).

Quote of the day

"Greensleeves was all my joy, Greensleeves was my delight, Greensleeves was my heart of gold, and who but my Lady Greensleeves?"
Attributed to King Henry VIII

Imagine...

There's a letter in the mail for you today, a rather mysterious looking one, with your name in calligraphy and what appears to be a royal seal in red sealing wax on the back. It appears that a very very distant relative has died and made you king/queen of a country you've never heard of. Your duties start tomorrow! Tell the story of the kingdom you've inherited, where it is, what it looks like, and what you will do as the new ruler.

Activity of the day

Henry's six wives

Henry's six wives are lost in the spiral! Can you find them all? **Hint:** He married three Catherines, two Annes, and a Jane.

Answers:
Catherine of Aragon
Anne Boleyn
Jane Seymour
Anne of Cleves
Catherine Howard
Catherine Parr

E	S	C	A	T	H	E	R	R
V	E	Y	N	J	A	N	I	
R	E	L	E	O	F	A	E	N
R	L	O	N	C	A	R	S	E
A	C	B	I	■	T	A	E	H
P	F	E	R	E	H	G	Y	O
E	O	N	N	A	N	O	M	W
N	E	N	N	A	R	U	O	A
I	R	E	H	T	A	C	D	R

Today in 1929

Seeing Eye, Incorporated, was founded.

- This company trains dogs to help people who are visually impaired.
- When fully trained, the guide dogs help their owners by leading them through busy streets and crowded areas.
- Trainers teach dogs to obey commands and recognize unsafe obstacles.
- January is National Eye Care Month which encourages people to seek medical care at the earliest signs of eye trouble, to prevent blindness.

Word of the day

guide To point out the way for, conduct, lead; from the Old French *guider*.

Imagine...

Pretend that you can no longer see and need a guide dog to help you through your day. Now, write from your dog's perspective. How would you help your master through the day? What things would you watch for? (You will have to think about what your life is like right now—for example, what do you do on a typical school day, from the time you wake up in the morning to the time you go to sleep at night?)

Quote of the day

"Every person takes the limits for their own field of vision for the limits of the world."
Arthur Schopenhauer

Activity of the day

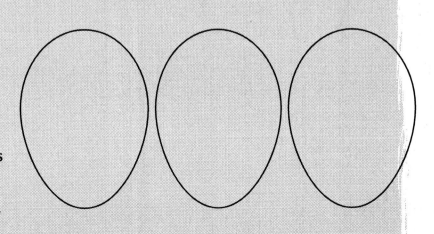

Designer Glasses

Eyeglasses (and sunglasses) are fashion statements these days. For people who wear them, it is a part of their daily wardrobe. Design some eyewear. On the faces provided, draw on some glasses to reflect these people's personality (or rather, how you'd like their personality to be). You can make the eyewear plain, fancy, or crazy. You are the creative genius here.

Today in 1956

Elvis Presley recorded his version of "Blue Suede Shoes."

- The song was written by Carl Perkins. He was hospitalised after crashing his car on his way to promote the song on a TV show. Elvis recorded the song instead.

- Elvis had 51 gold records and 149 hit singles between 1958 and 1986.

- Other performers to record the song include the Beatles, John Lennon, Jimi Hendrix.

Word of the day

suede Leather with a napped (softly brushed) surface; from the French *gants de Suéde* (Swedish gloves).

Quote of the day

"Good mashed potato is one of the great luxuries of life and I don't blame Elvis for eating it every night for the last year of his life."

Lyndsey Bareham

Imagine...

They arrived today. The shoes. The ones you bid for on that Internet auction site. They were claimed to be Elvis Presley's original blue suede shoes. Of course, who'd believe that? Still, for $10, they're pretty cool. Go on, put them on. Hmm, nice fit. Although, . . . all of a sudden you feel like, well, as though you want to . . . .

Activity of the day

Elvis song word search

Find all the hidden Elvis songs. The letters left over spell out another great Elvis hit!

Blue Moon
Blue Suede Shoes
Don't Be Cruel
Heartbreak Hotel
Hound Dog
In the Ghetto
Jailhouse Rock
Kentucky Rain
Love Me Tender
My Way
Promised Land
Suspicious Minds

```
    H O U N D D O G A R E Y O U N
    B L U E S U E D E S H O E S O
  L R E D N E T E M E V O L O N O
  D O N T B E C R U E L Y A W Y M
  S U S P I C I O U S M I N D S E
  E O T T E H G E H T N I S O M U
  P R O M I S E D L A N D E T O L
  L E T O H K A E R B T R A E H B
  N I G N I A R Y K C U T N E K
  J A I L H O U S E R O C K H T
```

Answer: Are You Lonesome Tonight?

Today in 1912

Jack Judge (with Harry Williams) wrote the song "It's a Long Way to Tipperary" after a friend bet him five shillings (50¢) that he couldn't write a popular song in one day.

- The song's popularity prompted the publisher to give him a pension of five pounds a week. Since then, royalties have been awarded to his nieces.
- The song is reported to have been originally called "It's a Long Way to Connemara."
- He wrote many other songs including "Paddy Maloney's Aeroplane" and "The Place Where I was Born."

Word of the day

Tipperary A county in Southern Ireland.

Imagine...

Bet you can't write a complete story in ten minutes. You can? How about one that includes: Tipperary, two guys named Jack and Harry, has three nieces in it, and is about a bet? Still think it's easy? Well, it might be easier than writing a song.

Quote of the day

"Good-bye Piccadilly, Farewell Leicester Square; It's a long, long way to Tipperary, but my heart's right there. "
Jack Judge

Activity of the day

What can you find in Tipperary?

How many words of at least four letters can you make from "Tipperary"? Oh, and they have to start with a T.

T	I	P
P	E	R
A	R	Y

Answers: Here are 19—how many did you find? tape, tarp, tear, tier, tire, trap, tray, trip, type, tyre, taper, tapir, teary, trier, tripe, tapper, tipper, trapper, tripper

Today in 1708

Alexander Selkirk was rescued from a desert island. The book *Robinson Crusoe* by author Daniel Defoe, was based on his experiences.

- Selkirk was marooned on the island Más a Tierra (now Robinson Crusoe Island) in the Juan Fernandez group off the the coast of Chile.

- Defoe, aside from being a novelist, was also a hosiery merchant, a journalist, the owner of a tile and brick factory, and a secret agent.

Word of the day

maroon To abandon on a desert island; from the American Spanish *cimarrón* (savage).

Imagine...

You're going to be marooned on a desert island for one month. Make a list of what you'd want to take packed into your one and only suitcase. Music to listen to? A good book to read? A box of matches? A laptop computer with Internet access?

Quote of the day

"I takes my man Friday with me. "
Daniel Defoe

Activity of the day

Poem Puzzle

Robinson Crusoe would never have survived without help—from whom?

My first's in maroon but not in lagoon
My second's in palm but not helm.
My third is in land and also in sand
My fourth is in fir but not elm.
My fifth is in rifle but nowhere in gun.
My sixth is in sink but not sunk.
My seventh's in danger and hazard, not axe!
My eighth is in water and wax.
My last is in years, and every and why—
My all's a beloved friend.
I'm named for the day that we met on the beach
And the day that the working week ends.

Answer: Man Friday

Today in 1932

wooden money was issued in Tenino, Washington, U.S.

- The wooden coins included 25¢, 50¢, and $1 pieces and were printed on spruce and cedar wood.
- Canada at one time used playing cards signed by the governor as money.
- Early forms of money included shells, circular stones, and even people.

Imagine...

The federal government has decided to change what we use for money. Instead of coins and bills, pencils and pens will be our legal tender. If one no. 2 pencil is equal to the old dollar, then what are the other kinds of pencils and pens worth? Will a no. 3 pencil be worth more or less than a no. 2 pencil? How much will a colored pencil be worth? a ballpoint pen? a felt-tip pen? a fountain pen? Will anyone ever use a pencil sharpener again? Will erasers affect the values of the pencils? You decide. Making it as inclusive as you can, draw up a chart that indicates the worth of each different kind of pencil and pen.

Word
of the day

numismatist A collector of coins; from the Greek *nomisma* (coin).

Quote
of the day

"Money speaks sense in a language all nations understand."
Aphra Behn

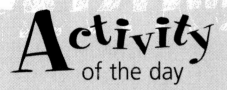

Activity
of the day

Money Pictures
Indicate on which bill or banknote each picture is found.

A
Andrew Jackson

B
George Washington

_____

_____

C
Alexander Hamilton

D
Abraham Lincoln

_____

_____

Answers: a. $20, b. $1, c. $10, d. $5

Today in 1815

the world's first commercial cheese factory was established in Switzerland.

- Cheese is made by separating the solid part of milk (the curds) from the liquid part (the whey).
- Cheese can be made from the milk of many different mammals including goats, camels, and reindeers.
- There are more than 2,000 different types of cheese.

Word of the day

cheese A solid food made from the curd of milk. From the Latin 'caseus' (cheese).

Quote of the day

"Cheese: milk's leap toward immortality. "
Clifton Fadiman

Imagine...

You had to leave that last house in a hurry. That cat the owners got in to rid the house of its mice was a real monster! So you've moved in here. A cheese factory! Cheese everywhere you look, everywhere you sniff. Any other mouse would think they're in heaven! Tell the story of what makes your stay in the cheese factory an unexpected nightmare.

Activity of the day

Cheese Word Search

So many kinds of cheese, so little time to try them all! Find and circle the following types of cheese in the puzzle.

Blue Stilton
Brie
Camembert
Cheddar
Cottage
Cream
Crottin
Edam
Fromage
Kikorangi
Mozzarella
Munster
Parmesan
Ricotta
Swiss

Cheese

```
        N G I N I C
        O A G A E A
  P A B T L N S G M M P N
  R T R L L A E A E U M I
  A T I I E R M M M N A T
  D O E T R O R O B S E T
  D C M S A K A R E T R O
  E I A E Z I P F R E C R
  H R D U Z K S L T R A C
  C N E L O E G A T T O C
    B M D B L U
    S S I W S E
```

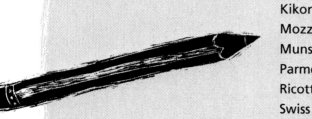

Today in 1974

a chimpanzee called Nim Chimsky signed his first 'word' at the age of two months.

- The chimp was named after Noam Chomsky, the linguist.
- Another chimp, Kanzi, has a vocabulary of 200–500 words.
- Baby chimps are capable of making over 30 different sounds.

Word of the day

chimpanzee Intelligent, tree-dwelling ape of Africa, From the Kongo word *chimpenzi*.

Imagine...

You've had weird assignments before, but interviewing a chimp has to be one of the strangest ever! But your boss insists that Lexi is extremely intelligent and the story will be great for the readers. Write the interview. What would you ask a chimp? And what does Lexi reply?

Quote of the day

"How like us is the ape, most horrible of beasts."
Quintus Ennius

Activity of the day

Sign me up

Lexi sure was talkative—in a signing sort of way! Here are six more "signs." What do they all mean?

1.
STANDU
I

2. speak

3. stay   me

4.
slip
banana

5. treesswingtrees

6. go sleepsleep

Answers: 1. I understand you. 2. Speak up! 3. Stay away from me. 4. Slip on a banana. 5. Swing in the trees. 6. Go to sleep.

Today in 1953

Walt Disney's movie *Peter Pan* was released .

- *Peter Pan*, the story of the little boy who never grows up, was originally a stage play written by dramatist Sir James Matthew Barrie in 1904.

- He wrote two story versions of the play and was never quite happy with the way it ended.

- "Wendy" houses (small playhouses for children) are named after the character of Wendy in the play.

Word
of the day

Pan The Greek god of pastures, flocks, and shepherds.

Imagine...

The doctors can find nothing wrong with you. The specialists can't find anything wrong with you. You feel normal. You look normal. Well, kind of normal. How many thirty-year-olds look twelve? Write about what it would be like to never grow old. Would you like to stay your age forever?

Quote
of the day

"To die will be an awfully big adventure. "
Sir J. M. Barrie

Activity
of the day

Alliteration Challenge
Peter Pan's name is alliterative; it has the same consonant (P) at the beginning of each word. Can you match up these other alliterative characters?

Black	Tucker
Blinky	Duck
Donald	Doolittle
Doctor	Bill
Goosey	Beauty
Maid	Mouse
Mickey	Rabbit
Miss	Marian
Mister	Gander
Peter	McGregor
Roger	Pan
Tommy	Muffet

Answers: Peter Pan, Roger Rabbit, Doctor Doolittle, Blinky Bill, Donald Duck, Mickey Mouse, Black Beauty, Miss Muffett, Goosey Gander, Mister McGregor, Tommy Tucker, Maid Marian

Today

is New Zealand's Independence Day.

- The first Maori settlers arrived in New Zealand in AD 600 after its discovery by Kupe, a Polynesian explorer.
- The first Europeans reached New Zealand a thousand years later in 1642.
- New Zealand was named after the Dutch province of Zeeland.

Imagine...

Kupe, with his friends, had been traveling by canoe outrigger for many weeks. The winds had been favorable and the fish plentiful, but water was running out. Ahead of them clouds were gathering—long, white clouds. But was there land where they could go ashore? Tell the story of the discovery of what became New Zealand, as you imagine it happened.

Word of the day

Aotearoa Maori name for New Zealand (Land of the Long White Cloud).

Quote of the day

"Sing all things sweet or harsh upon these islands in the Pacific sun,
The mountains whitened endlessly and the white horses of the winter sea. "
Denis Glover

Activity of the day

Spot the flag!

Here are nine flags. All have either a union jack and/or a southern cross. But which flag belongs to which country? An encyclopedia might help!

1.

2.

3.

4.

5.

6.

Solomon Islands, Samoa, Australia, New Zealand, Micronesia, Cook Islands

Answers: 1. Australia 2. Solomon Islands 3. New Zealand 4. Cook Islands 5. Micronesia 6. Samoa

Today in 1875

New York tattooist Sam O'Reilly introduced the world's first tattooing machine.

- Records show that the ancient Egyptians had tattoos, while the Maori people were the first to introduce pigments to create colored tattoos.
- Only a laser beam will safely remove tattoos.

Word of the day

tattoo A design made by pricking and staining the skin; from the Dutch *tap toe* (taps shut).

Quote of the day

"Thou cunning'st pattern of excelling nature . . ."
Shakespeare (Othello)

Imagine...

You bought a packet of those stick-on tattoos on the weekend. Stuck 'em all over your arms, your shoulders, even one on your forehead! Cool, eh? Monday morning—better wash them off to get ready for school. Problem. They won't come off. Sponge, face-cloth, scouring pad—nothing will budge them! They seem to have soaked into the skin. Uh oh. What do you do?

Activity of the day

Tammy's Tattoos
Tammy the Tattooist will only do tattoos of objects that have the word *tattoo* in them. Her range, to say the least, is limited. What can she draw?

T A T T O O	+ HOP	A cooked spud	
	+ CILN	Small rabbit	
	+ EHPS	Paste for cleaning teeth	
	+ EEPSW	Type of yam	
	+ HPS	Photocopy	
	+ DDEPS	Amphibian with spots	
	+ EEMR	South American plant that looks like a tomato	

Answers: hot potato, cottontail, toothpaste, sweet potato, photostat, spotted toad, tree-tomato

Today in 1828

Jules Verne was born.

- Jules Verne is considered to be the first true Science Fiction writer.
- In his books he wrote about trips to the moon, submarines, helicopters, air-conditioning, and movies, all before they actually happened.
- His books include *Journey to the Center of the Earth*, *20,000 Leagues Under the Sea*, and *Around the World in Eighty Days*.

Imagine...

What will life be like fifty years from now? Make five predictions about school, home, work, travel, and entertainment. What will you write about before it actually happens?

Word of the day

Sci-Fi Abbreviation of Science Fiction

Quote of the day

"Science fiction is no more written for scientists than ghost stories are written for ghosts. "
Brian Aldiss

Activity of the day

Jules Verne Acrostic

The missing words come from titles of Jules Verne's novels, or predictions he made about the future.

J
U
L
E
S
V
E
R
N
E

_____ to the Center of the Earth

Clipper of the _____

Flying machine with rotating wings

Around the World in _____ Days

The Mysterious _____

Animated photographs

20,000 _____ Under the Sea

A submersible boat

Round the ____

From the _____ to the Moon

Answers: Journey, Clouds, helicopter, eighty, island, movies, leagues, submarine, moon, Earth

Today in 1894

Adolphe Sax invented the saxophone.

- He also invented the saxtromba and the saxhorn.
- The saxophone family of instruments includes the baritone, tenor, alto, and soprano.
- The alto saxophone has a similar fingering pattern to the descant recorder.

Word of the day

-phone Used as a suffix in names of musical instruments and sound-transmitting devices (e.g., telephone, microphone).

Imagine...

Be the new Mr./Ms. Sax! Invent a new instrument—wind, string, percussion, or electronic. Draw a diagram showing its shape and how it works. Now name it, making sure you use your name and the suffix "phone." If the name doesn't sound quite right, use your surname or middle name.

Quote of the day

"Small wonder we have so much trouble with air pollution in the world when so much of it has passed through saxophones."

Anonymous

Activity of the day

Hidden words
How many words of four or more letters beginning with "S" can you make from the word saxophone?

S	A	X
O	P	H
O	N	E

_____   _____

_____   _____

_____   _____

_____   _____

_____   _____

Answers: Here are 14 we found: sane, Saxon, saxophone, shape, shoe, shone, shoo, shop, snap, snoop, soap, soon, span, spoon.

Today in 1973

the Postal Telegram Company in New York delivered its first singing telegram.

- George P. Oslin, public relations director for Western Union, is credited with the invention of the singing telegram when he had operator Lucille Lips sing "Happy Birthday" over the phone to vocalist Rudy Vallee on July 28, 1933.
- The unusual birthday greeting was mentioned in a local newspaper and suddenly the singing telegram was in high demand.
- Since then, the singing telegram business has boomed with costumed performers coming to the home or business of the recipient.
- Western Union now only sings over the telephone and only to the tune of "Happy Birthday" with the customer providing the lyrics.

Word of the day

casino A public gambling building; from the Italian *casa* (house).

Imagine...

The paper says your lucky numbers today are 3, 8 and 11. You drive to work at 8 A.M. and get 11 straight green lights! So you buy a lotto ticket at 3 P.M. and it's number 883113! After working all evening you sit down to watch the TV and the Lotto results come on at 11P.M. What happens?

Quote of the day

"Life is a gamble, at terrible odds. If it was a bet, you wouldn't take it."
Tom Stoppard

Activity of the day

four the same (e.g., 4H or 4T)	three and one (e.g., 3H + 1T or 3T + 1H)	two and two (e.g., 2H + 2T)

Casinos rely on probability to make a profit. Probability is the measure of how likely something is to happen, and our "common sense" ideas aren't always right. (Which is why casinos make a profit!)

Try this simple game. You'll need four coins, a pencil and some paper. If you were to toss the coins, which combination of heads (H) and tails (T) do you think would come up most? Number the boxes above from 1 (most likely) to 3 (least likely).

If this was a betting game, how would you work out which to bet on? One way is to actually try it—throw the coins and see which combination comes up most often. The other way is to write down all the combinations the four coins can land in and see which one happens most, like this:

HHHH HHHT HHTH THHH, etc.

Try either or both ways. Was your original choice the best one?

Answers: There are 16 different ways to toss the four coins.
"Four the same" comes up 2/16 times.
"Three and one" comes up 8/16 times—the 'best bet'.
"Two and two" comes up 6/16 times.

Today in 1878

the first weekly weather report began.

- Contrary to popular belief, weather forecasting has improved in accuracy. Three-day forecasts are now as accurate as one-day forecasts 40 years ago.
- Forecasts now use, "Numerical Weather Prediction" (NWP). NWP was invented in 1922 but because of a lack of computers, a one-day forecast in 1950 took 24 hours to compute.
- A one-day forecast now takes five minutes and involves over a trillion calculations!

Word
of the day

report A detailed account or statement; from the Latin *reportare* (to carry).

Quote
of the day

"Advice from your friends is like the weather, some of it good, some of it bad."
Anonymous

Imagine...

Write your own long-range weather forecast for the coming week. Include the general forecast (hot/warm/cool/cold), the maximum and minimum temperatures, and the amount of cloud cover (overcast, storms, etc). Check your forecast each day. How accurate is it?

Activity
of the day

Weather report

The weather forecast is in. But the words (which should be in the middle row of each grid) are missing. Find them by completing each of the three letter words going down the grid.

C	S	B	A
Y	D	D	Y

S	P	W	A
E	T	T	E

A	I	P	S	O
E	L	T	M	D

O	H	A
F	G	E

Answers: Rain, hail, cloud, & fog.

Today in 1851

baseball pioneer Al Spalding opened the first sporting goods store, along with his brother and an $800 loan from his mother.

- He was also instrumental in the formation of the National League.
- He worked as a pitcher, manager, and president of the Chicago White Stockings.
- He formed A. C. Spalding and Bros., which became the world's largest sporting goods company, manufacturing the official baseballs used exclusively by the major leagues until 1976.
- Later, he turned to the manufacturing of tennis equipment when players blamed their poor performances on the rackets. Manufacturing golf clubs soon followed. Then the company started to manufacture inflated balls.
- Today Spalding makes the official basketballs used exclusively in the National Basketball Association.

Word of the day

sporting goods Any products used for the enjoyment of recreational activities.

Imagine...

Wow! You just got struck by lightning and now you can fire off your pitches at 300 miles perhour! Now all of the baseball teams in the nation want you to be on their team. What team would you want to play for and why? What products would you like to endorse and why?

Quote of the day

"Baseball gives a growing boy self poise and self reliance."
Al Spalding

Activity of the day

Baseball Hang-man

Here's a new twist to an old game. Play baseball hangman by using terms only used in the game of baseball. Use words like runs, hits, errors, batting average, player positions, and more. You can also use the names of famous baseball players, baseball stadiums, and so on.

To play Hang-man:

1. Draw a scaffold like the one shown.
2. Make blanks for the word you are thinking of. _ _ _ _ _ _ _
3. Have others guess one letter at a time.
4. For each missed letter, draw a body part on the scaffold (head, torso, arm, arm, leg, leg).
5. If the body is done before the word is guessed, you win.
6. If the word is guessed the guesser gets to be the next Hang man.

Today in 1981

the *New York Times* published its longest ever sentence: 1,286 words.

- The New York Times Sunday edition is also the heaviest newspaper printed: it has reached over 7 kg!
- The shortest sentence in the Bible is John 11:35; "Jesus wept."
- The longest word in the Oxford dictionary is *floccipaucinihilipilification* (the action of estimating as worthless).

Word of the day

sentence A string of words that contains a complete thought. From the Latin "sententia" (opinion).

Quote of the day

"If you can't sell an idea in a sentence, don't waste your time writing it."
Lionel Bart

Imagine...

What's the longest sentence you can write? Just one rule: You can only use joining words (such as *and*, *then*, or *after*) once each.

Activity of the day

Punctuation puzzle

Help! Editor needed!

This long sentence (from an old nursery rhyme) needs some punctuation. It certainly doesn't make much sense at the moment! Perhaps a sprinkling of commas or periods (and capitals!) might do the trick.

I saw a fish-pond all on fire I saw a house bow to a squire I saw a parson ten feet high I saw a cottage near the sky I saw a balloon made of lead I saw a coffin drop down dead I saw two magpies run a race I saw two horses making lace I saw a girl just like a cat I saw a kitten wear a hat I saw a man who saw these too and said though strange they all were true.

Answers: I saw a fish-pond. All on fire, I saw a house. Bow to a squire, I saw a parson. Ten feet high, I saw a cottage. Near the sky, I saw a balloon. Made of lead, I saw a coffin. Drop down dead, I saw two magpies. Run a race, I saw two horses. Making lace, I saw a girl. Just like a cat, I saw a kitten. Wearing a hat, I saw a man who saw these too and said though strange, they all were true.

Today

is Valentine's Day.

- St. Valentine's Day was originally celebrated for two Christian martyrs of the same name—Valentine. One was a physician and the other a priest. Both lived in Rome and were beheaded on this day.
- According to legend, birds choose their mates on this day.
- Today Valentine's Day is the most widely observed unofficial holiday and is celebrated with gifts (usually flowers and candy) and cards that show love and affection.

Imagine...

Your heart beats every second of every minute of every day. Sometimes you can feel it beating when you are playing hard or when you are scared. Write about a time when you last felt your heart thump, thump, thumping away.

Word
of the day

Valentine A sweetheart chosen or complimented on St. Valentine's Day.

Quote
of the day

"And now here is my secret, a very simple secret; it is only with the heart that one can see rightly, what is essential is invisible to the eye."

Antoine de Saint-Exupery, author

Activity
of the day

Valentine Puzzle

Make a heart-shaped puzzle for someone special.

You will need:

- pink or red paper
- pen or pencil
- scissors
- envelope

Directions:

1. Cut out a heart, large enough to write a valentine's message on.
2. Write a message or a short letter on the heart.
3. Cut the heart into puzzle pieces. The more pieces you cut, the harder the puzzle will be.
4. Place the pieces in an envelope and send it to a friend!

Today in 1978

Muhammad Ali lost his heavyweight boxing title to U.S. Olympic champion Leon Spinks in a 15-round decision at Las Vegas, Nevada.

- On March 18, the World Boxing Council withdrew its recognition of Spinks and awarded the title to Ken Norton.
- Norton lost the title to Larry Holmes on June 9 in a 15-round decision at Las Vegas.
- Ali regained the World Boxing Association title on September 15 by winning an easy 15-round decision over Spinks in the Superdome in New Orleans.

Word of the day

humble pie A pie formerly made from the edible organs of a deer or hog.
idiom: **eat humble pie**. To be forced to admit one's faults in humiliating circumstances;
from the Latin *lumbulus* (loin) + pie

Quote of the day

"At home I am a nice guy: but I don't want the world to know. Humble people, I've found, don't get very far."
Muhammad Ali

Imagine...

You are getting ready for your weigh-in before a big boxing match. The TV cameras will be there, and you want to come up with some lines like those of Muhammad Ali: "float like a butterfly, sting like a bee." You want to let your opponent know that he/she should be prepared to "eat humble pie"—and that it will not be sweet. Prepare about six lines that you can use to make your opponent fearful of your expertise.

Activity of the day

A sweet puzzle
Here are 14 words. Just place them correctly in the squares, and you will have nine sweets.

AND, BUT, CHEW, CORN, GUM, IN, MALL, MAR, MARS, OFF, PAN, POP, RICE, SCOT

M			T					
C			Y					
T			E	E				
			Z	I				
L	I	Q	U	O				
				I	N	G		
				H			O	W
			T	E	R		C	H

Today in 1937

nylon was patented.

- Nylon is used in making products as diverse as parachutes, toothbrush bristles, and fishing lines.
- It was invented by the DuPont company, which also invented Teflon (non-stick surfaces), Lycra (expanding fiber), Stainmaster (for carpets), and Kevlar (used in bullet-proof vests).
- The U.S. army is considering replacing its soldiers' metal dog tags with new nylon ones. They would contain the soldiers' complete medical history.

Word of the day

nylon A trade name from "NY" for New York and "LON" for London.

Imagine...

Look around the classroom. Write a list of ten objects that you can see that are made of plastic. What would they be made of if plastic hadn't been invented? Wood? Paper? Metal? Glass? What objects would be impossible to make without plastic?

Quote of the day

"Beth, like, your car is so disgustingly grody and gnarly. Like, I almost snagged my nylons on your seat."

Trish, from *The Vals*

Activity of the day

Plastic Memory Game

Look carefully at the picture. It shows 12 different objects. Each object is either made completely out of plastic or plastic parts. Looked long enough? Turn this sheet over and see how many you can remember.

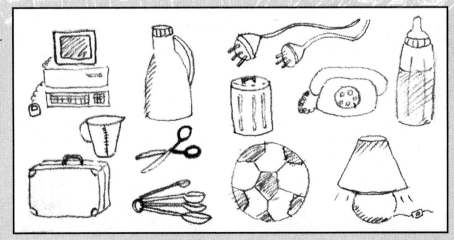

Extra: Make the test harder. Have friends look, then ask them to not only name the objects but answer questions about them, such as "How many spoons were there?'

Today in 1972

the last original, classic Volkswagen Beetle came off the assembly line.

- The last "Beetle" was number 15,007,034.
- The first vehicles were called *Kraft durch Freude* [strength through joy] *Wagen*.
- The Beetle was designed by Porsche founder Ferdinand Porsche.

Word
of the day

Volkswagen A German car manufacturer. German for *people's car*.

Quote
of the day

"Without a real car, I'm only half a man."

Jim Douglas in *The Love Bug*

Imagine...

The Love Bug movie was about a Volkswagen Beetle with a mind of its own. Give your family car, or a neighbor's car, a name. What sort of personality does it have? Where is it happiest? When does it get grumpy? Does it enjoy being washed? How do you know?

Activity
of the day

Assembly line blues.

Unlike the car in the circle, the other five Beetles below have defects. The assembly line quality control supervisor spotted them. Can you?

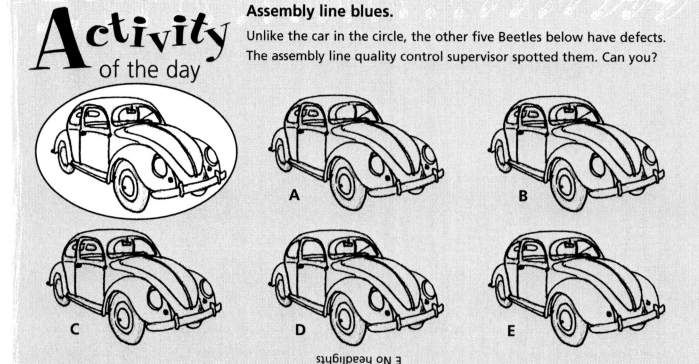

A   B

C   D   E

Answers: A Missing rear-vision mirror B Missing indicators C Missing windscreen wiper D No back window E No headlights

Today in 1802

the Canadian lumberjacks union was formed.

- Paul Bunyan, a giant legendary lumberjack in the U.S., was reputed to have created the Grand Canyon.
- The first wood-cutting competitions were held in Tasmania in 1874.
- One tree in California is believed to be over 12,000 years old. It is called "Eternal God."

Imagine...

The sun's up, the birds are singing, and it's a beautiful day. But this part of the forest is dark and eerily silent. That doesn't matter. You've been told to clear the trees from this section, and clear you will. But you feel as though something's watching, . . . and waiting. The feeling's strongest near the huge, gnarled pine by the dried-up creek bed. You shrug and start up the chainsaw. Write about what happens next.

Word of the day

lumber Wood cut and prepared for use as building material; possibly from *lumbard* (a pawnbroker's shop used to store unused property).

Quote of the day

"I'm a lumberjack and I'm O.K. I sleep all night and I work all day."
Monty Python

Activity of the day

Toppling tree conundrum

Leonard the lumberjack has to cut down the tall tree on the left. Unfortunately, it's surrounded by smaller trees on each side—which he can't drop the big tree onto. How can he work out the tall tree's height to see if he has enough room?

He knows that:
There's 18 m between the trees.
He's 1.8 m tall.
The small trees' shadows are 1 m long.
The drawing is NOT to scale!
The small trees are 1.6 m wide.
The small trees are all about 4 m tall.
The tall tree's shadow is 5 m long
His axe is 1.2 m long.

Answers: Here's one way: The small trees' shadows (1 m) are 1/4 of their height (4 m). The tall tree's shadow (5 m) must also be 1/4 of its height, which must then be 5 x 4 m = 20 m. Not quite enough room to drop it!

Today in 1901

the Mercedes car was first named.

- It was named after Mercedes Jellinick, the 10-year-old daughter of a director of the Daimler Company.
- The company is now known as Mercedes-Benz.
- Carl Benz patented the "tricycle" in 1886—a 9 mph (15 km/h) three-wheeled car.
- Mercedes-Benz is the oldest car manufacturer in the world.

Word of the day

Mercedes A prestige motor car; from a Spanish dialect word for *grace*.

Quote of the day

"You see, Sammy, in California everybody needs a car. I got a friend who bought a Mercedes just to get to the bathroom."

Audrey Paris (*All That Jazz*)

Imagine...

What would you like to have named after you? A car? A boat? A country? A type of food? Choose one and write the story of how it happened.

Activity of the day

Here's a Mercedes wheel. How many words can you make by traveling from one letter to the next along the straight lines? You can't use a letter twice unless it's on the wheel twice. PS: Extra points for harder words!

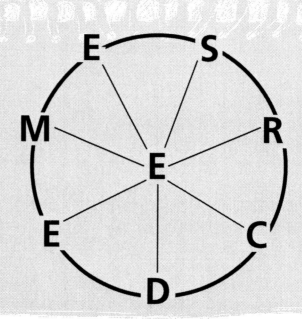

Answers: Here are the ones we found:
1 point each: deer, me, red, reed, seed, seem, seemed
2 points each: cede, creed, deem, seer

Today in 1944

the Batman & Robin comic strip first appeared in newspapers.

- Robin was the first boy "sidekick."
- Comic books were originally given away free as an advertising gimmick.
- The first Batman TV show aired in 1966 with Adam West as the "caped crusader" and Burt Ward as Robin.

Imagine...

Fighting bad guys, foiling evil plots, and escaping from certain death once an episode is tiring work. Write about what superheroes do for relaxation. Where do they go for their holidays? What are their hobbies? What do they do for fun?

Word
of the day

crusader A person fighting for a cause. From the Latin "crux" (cross—carried by the Christian Crusaders).

Quote
of the day

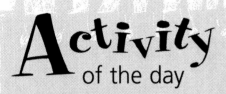

"If one is going to steal, it is considered somewhat sporting to inform the victims beforehand; for examples see any episodes of the Batman TV series."

Robert J. Woodhead

Activity
of the day

The curious case of the missing cartoonist.

Oh no! The illustrator for the Batman comic has been kidnapped! Quick—complete the comic strip before it's too late!

Holy smoke, Batman! What on earth is that?!

I don't know, Robin—let's investigate.

Here come the two bat-fools. They'll never know what's hit them!

Run, Robin, run!

Too late, Batman—far too late!

Not so fast! We have our Bat-bats!

Curses, foiled again!

Today in 1851

Mary Shelley, the author of *Frankenstein*, died.

- The book's full title is *Frankenstein, or the Modern Prometheus.*
- *Frankenstein* is the name of the scientist, rather than the monster (who is known as the "creature").
- The book was based on a nightmare Shelley remembered.

Word of the day

monster A large and frightening imaginary creature. From the Latin *monere* (to warn).

Imagine...

Choose a nightmare (or if you prefer, a good dream) that you remember. Write it as a story. Change the ending if you like—after all, it is your dream!

Quote of the day

"Teach him to think for himself? Oh, my God, teach him rather to think like other people!"
Mary Shelley

Activity of the day

Monster Puzzle

Arrghh! Monsters everywhere! But we can't blame Dr. Frankenstein for all of them...

F
R
A
N
K
E
N
S
T
E
I
N

A cruel, wicked and inhuman person
A grotesquely carved figure of a person
A particular vampire
A monster with live snakes for hair
Giant ape
Alien hunter
Giant snake
A serpent able to kill with its breath or glance
The scariest dinosaur
Creature from another planet
Mutated giant lizard
Scottish sea monster

Answers: fiend, gargoyle, Dracula, gorgon, King Kong, predator, anaconda, basilisk, T rex, alien, Godzilla, Loch Ness

Today in 1797

the Baron von Münchhausen, teller of tall tales extraordinaire, died.

- The Baron was a German cavalry officer whose exaggerated stories were published by a friend.
- His many deeds include "herding bees" and visiting the moon—twice.
- His visit to the moon was probably inspired by an old Serbian story called "The biggest liar in the world".

Word of the day

exaggerate To enlarge a story beyond the bounds of truth. from the Latin *exaggeratus* (heap up).

Imagine...

Other people might exaggerate a story they're telling, to make it more interesting. Not you though. Your stories are always truthful, aren't they. Aren't they? Like the one about the day you saved your house from being flattened by an out of control steamroller or . . . What are some of the taller tales you could tell?

Quote of the day

"Your reality is lies and balderdash, and I'm glad to say that I have no grasp of it."
Baron von Münchhausen

Activity of the day

M	U	N	C
	H	H	A
U	S	E	N

Making Words

How many words of three letters or more (beginning with M) can you make from the Baron von Münchhausen's surname?

Answers: Here are 18 we found: mace, maces, mach, man, mane, manes, mash, mean, means, men, menu, menus, mesh, much, munch, munches, muse, mush

Today in 1911

the wife of inventor John Hammond flew with him in a box-kite over Melbourne—she was the first ever aircraft passenger!

- Kites were used in World War I to lift observers above the battlefields.
- In 1919, a height of over 9,850 yards (9,000 m) was achieved by a string of eight kites flying over Germany.
- Over 7,000 kites were flown on one line in Japan in 1987.

Word of the day

passenger A person traveling in a vehicle who is not operating it from the Middle French *passager* (passing).

Imagine...

It's not easy being a kite, you know. It's certainly not easy when you hate being tied up with string. Or if you don't like birds. Or trees. And especially when you're scared of heights. A kite? Scared of heights? Now how did that happen? Imagine you are that kite— tell the story of the day you were taken out to fly on a very windy day . . .

Quote of the day

"Food poisoning ... probably poses a greater threat to passenger safety than hijacking. "
Professor Stanley Mohler

Activity of the day

Kite Safety Rule Crossword

With both himself and his wife flying in the kite, John Hammond is bound to have followed all the important rules about flying kites!

ACROSS
2 Never fly a kite in the rain or a _____. (5)
6 A ____ is a good target for lightning! (4)
7 Keep away from cars and _____. (5)
9 A kite's ____ keeps it balanced. (4)
10 You should follow ___ the safe-flying rules. (3)
11 Keep away from buildings and tall _____. (5)

DOWN
1 _____/_____ will give you a shock if your kite hits them. (5,5)
3 The kite's string is attached to this: _____. (6)
4 Always fly kites in a wide ____/____. (4,4)
5 A ____ is a good place for kite flying. (4)
8 Keep the kite _____ rules and keep safe! (6)

Today in 1986

the space probe *Voyager 2* made the first Uranus flyby.

- Uranus is the seventh planet in our solar system. It was discovered by astronomer William Herschel in 1781.
- Uranus was originally called "Georgium Sidus" (Star of George) after the king.
- Uranus was the Greek god of the sky. The name is sometimes spelled "Ouranos".
- Herschel lived for 81 years—the exact length of a year on Uranus.

Imagine...

Now whose fool idea was it to send a manned probe out to look for the solar system's tenth planet? More to the point, why send two of you, when all you do is argue? Because you've found the planet and now you have to name it and you can't even agree on who saw it first! So, what does it look like (moons, rings, color, etc.)? Why are you arguing? And what will you name it?

Word of the day

astronomy The study of stars. from the Greek *astronomeîn* (observe the stars).

Quote of the day

"If the Lord Almighty had consulted me before embarking upon Creation, I should have recommended something simpler."

Alfonso X

Activity of the day

Solar System Word Search

The solar system is a busy place, what with planets, sun, space probes, and all. But it's a big place, and sometimes even a planet can be hard to find. Start with a search for these words. The leftover letters will spell out the name of what some scientists believe will be our tenth planet. If we ever find it!

```
U E M A R S Y A P E R
R A S E S R S T S U D
A R P U U T T I B R O
N T N C E N R U T A S
U H R R J U P I T E R
S E O M E T E O R O V
M I T E K C O R H T A
D V E N U S O N E U C
S A T E L L I T E L U
C O M E T N O O M P U
G A S E N U T P E N M
```

asteroid	Jupiter	Neptune	Saturn
comet	Mars	orbit	Sun
dust	Mercury	Pluto	Uranus
Earth	meteor	rocket	vacuum
gas	moon	satellite	Venus

Today in 1841

"Oh! Susanna!" by Pittsburgh songwriter Stephen Collins Foster is sung by G. N. Christy of the Christy Minstrels.

- The song became a staple in every minstrel show.
- It was sung by gold-seekers on their way to the gold fields in California.
- Some other popular Foster songs were "Jeanie with the Light Brown Hair," "My Old Kentucky Home," and "Camptown Races."
- Foster wrote 285 songs, hymns, arrangements, and instrumental works.

Word of the day

lyric Any short poem expressing personal emotion; from the Greek *lura* (lyre).

Quote of the day

"Nothing separates the generations more than music. By the time a child is eight or nine, he has developed a passion for his own music that is even stronger than his passions for procrastination and weird clothes."

Bill Cosby, from *Fatherhood*

Imagine...

Every time you look at certain people in your family and at certain friends, you hear music. You have a different tune for each one of them. Match members of your family and some of your friends with the songs that you associate with them, and explain why you have chosen a particular song for each person. (You may use song titles or lyrics or both.)

Activity of the day

Theme Songs
Choose songs you think would make good theme songs for the following people:

1. Michael Jordan, basketball player
2. Mel Gibson, actor
3. Julia Roberts, actor
4. Lindsey Davenport, tennis player
5. Pope John Paul II
6. Helen Keller, author and lecturer
7. Geronimo, Apache leader
8. H. Norman Schwarzkopf, American general
9. Napoleon
10. Barbara Bush, former U.S. First Lady

Today in 1846

Buffalo Bill was born.

- His original name was William Frederick Cody.

- He gained his nickname after killing more than 4,000 bison (buffaloes) in 18 months. They were used to feed railroad workers.

- As a youth he rode for the Pony Express, covering over 62 miles (100 km) per day on horseback.

Word of the day

buffalo Large, shaggy-haired bison; From the Greek *boubalos* (African gazelle).

Imagine...

The buffaloes seemed easy prey to the cowboys with their rifles and horses. The railroad workers were fed, the buffalo hunters paid and everyone—except the buffaloes—was happy. Then one day the buffaloes got organized. The buffaloes got smart. Write about what the buffaloes did ...

Quote of the day

"Failure to recognize the "no free lunch" law causes the buffalo-hunter mentality syndrome–the unthinking assumption that there will always be plenty because there always has been plenty."

Dr. Robert W. Prehoda

Activity of the day

Answers: Amazon parrot, cheetah, condor, crocodile, dugong, elephant, gazelle, rhinoceros, turtle, whale, woodpecker

Scrambled (and Endangered) Creatures

Look at the list of animals below Do the names seem unfamiliar? If they're not saved from extinction, then people 100 years from now may find the real names unfamiliar, too. So unscramble them and find the names of eleven endangered mammals, reptiles, and birds.

zonama raptor, hateech, conrod, roo-diccle, gun dog, pheelnat, leg laze, orchesrion, lutter, halwe, poorweekcd

Today in 837

was the 15th recorded perihelion passage of Halley's Comet.

- That year the comet came within 3.7 million miles (six million km) of the Earth.

- The comet is named after Edmund Halley, who discovered it had an orbit that brought it back to Earth approximately every 76 years.

- In 1986, several space probes got within 37 miles (60 km) of the comet.

Word
of the day

perihelion The point in the orbit of a comet where it is nearest to the sun; from the Latin *peri* (around) and the Greek *helios* (sun).

Quote
of the day

"Old men and comets have been reverenced for the same reason; their long beards, and pretences to foretell events."
Jonathan Swift

Imagine...

Halley's comet makes the epic journey from out beyond Pluto to the center of our solar system approximately every 76 years. Imagine you were riding the comet's tail. Describe your journey as you pass each of the planets, the approaching sun, the fly by, and the long, lonely journey back out again.

Activity
of the day

Halley's Comet Computations

1. Halley's comet last visited in 1986. The next visit is in 2061. How many years are there between the two visits?

2. Halley found the comet had been seen in 1456, 1531, 1607, and then in 1682. How many years were there between each sighting?

3. Halley lived from 1656-1742. Did he ever see the comet?

4. He predicted it would return in a further 76 years. Halley was correct, and it was seen on Christmas Eve of which year?

5. Did Halley live to see it return?

6. The comet was seen 11 years before Christ was born and again 77 years after it had last appeared. What was the year?

7. One sighting is woven into the Bayeaux Tapestry, which recorded the famous Battle of Hastings. The comet had been seen 79 years earlier in 987. When was the battle?

Answers: 1) 75 years; **2)** 75, 76, and 75 years; **3)** Yes, in 1682; **4)** 1758; **5)** no; **6)** AD66; **7)** 1066

Today in 1956

a patent was issued for computer core memory.

- Early computers used a system of drums to store information. Modern day electronic memory systems are over a million times faster!

- There is no one location for memories in the human brain.

- Alcoholism can prevent new memories being formed in the human brain.

Word of the day

memory The processes through which past experiences are remembered; from the Latin *memoria* (mindful).

Imagine...

Is it possible to remember too much? Imagine if you could remember every exact thing your friends said and did. Write about the problems this might cause. What advantages would there be? Would your brain ever get cluttered up?

Quote of the day

" 'It's a poor sort of memory that only works backwards,' the Queen remarked."
Lewis Carroll

Activity of the day

On—Off—On—Off—

Computers don't work with decimal numbers (0, 1, 2, 3, 4, 5, 6, 7, 8, 9). Instead they use "ons" and "offs"; binary numbers (0, 1).

In decimal numbers

11101= 1 ten-thousand + 1 thousand + 1 hundred + 0 tens +1 unit.

In binary numbers

11101= 1 sixteen + 1 eight + 1 four + 0 twos + 1 unit.

Which is the number 29 in decimal.

Can you change these binary numbers into decimal?

1. 100 = (1 four + 0 twos + 0 units) = _____
2. 110 = _____
3. 1001 = _____
4. 10101 = _____
5. 11111 = _____

Now change these decimal numbers into binary:

6. 19 _____
7. 7 _____
8. 25 _____
9. 10 _____
10. 5 _____

Answers: 1) 4, 2) 6, 3) 9, 4) 21, 5) 31, 6) 10011, 7) 111, 8) 11001, 9) 1010, 10) 101

Today

is Leap Day!

- Leap days are added to keep the calendar "in line." The Assyrians used to add a month every now and then when they thought it was needed!

- Every second year, the Roman calendar included an extra month called "Mercedonius" to keep up with the solar year.

- In the U.S., radio station WWV broadcasts official time signals. Every three years they add in a "leap second".

Word
of the day

intercalary A day added to make the calendar year line up to the solar year. From the Latin "inter-calatus" "inter" (between) and "calare" (to proclaim).

Imagine...

Watch out boys! February 29th is traditionally the day when the girl asks the guy to get married! Of course, you don't need a special day for that now, so write down what else could happen on February 29th, remembering that it only comes around every four years.

Quote
of the day

"Thirty days hath September,
April, June and November.
All the rest have thirty-one,
excepting February alone,
Which has twenty-eight days clear,
and twenty-nine in each leap year."

Anonymous

Activity
of the day

Leaping Leap Years!

A leap year is a year that is exactly divisible by four. But, if the year is exactly divisible by 100, it isn't a leap year. And, years that are exactly divisible by 400 are leap years.

Got all that? Good! So, which of these years would've been/were/are/will be leap years?

1. 1400*
2. 1504*
3. 1600*
4. 1664*
5. 1800
6. 1808
7. 1900
8. 1996
9. 2000
10. 2100

* If leap years had been in use.

Answers: 1) no 2) yes 3) yes 4) yes 5) no 6) yes 7) no 8) yes 9) yes 10) no

Today in 1975

the TV series *Ripley's Believe It or Not*, featuring strange and unusual phenomena, began broadcasting and ran until September.

- The show was revived in 1982 with film star Jack Palance as host and was on ABC for over three years.
- Color TV was first seen officially in Australia on this day in 1975.

Imagine...

First there was color TV, then 3-D, and now—there is smelly-vision! Yes, folks, coming to a TV near you! Smelly-vision. See the sea and smell the sea! See the flowers and smell the flowers! See the skunk and smell the skunk! Write about what smell-vision would be like. How would sports programs be different? How would the news be different? Which programs would you like to smell? or not like to smell?

Word of the day

color The visible aspect of an object, other than its form or size; from the Latin *celare* (to conceal).

Quote of the day

"I find television very educating. Every time somebody turns on the set, I go into the other room and read a book."
Groucho Marx

Activity of the day

TV Word Quiz

What are these missing TV words? Complete the three-letter words going down to complete the answer going across.

E	W	Z	A	A
B	X	P	C	D

TV pioneer

W	O	U	K	E	O	J
G	E	E	G	D	E	B

Receives television signals

F	N	I	M	I	P
Y	W	P	B	S	T

TV controlling device

I	T	E	O	S
E	R	B	D	E

TV transmitted directly to the customer

Answers: Baird, antenna, remote, cable

Today in 1956

Timothy Dalton was born. He was the fourth actor to play James Bond.

- The Bond film was called *The Living Daylights*. In Germany it was called *The Skin of a Corpse* (yuck!).

- Dalton did most of his own stunts in the film including escaping from a plane by riding a Jeep out the back!

- Ian Fleming was the author of the original series of novels. He worked for Naval Intelligence in World War II.

Word of the day

spy A secret agent hired by a state to obtain information about its enemies; from the Latin *specere* (to look).

Quote of the day

Bond: "Do you expect me to talk?"
Goldfinger: "No, Mr Bond, I expect you to die!"

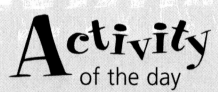

Imagine...

It lies there in your hand. A small, innocent looking yo-yo. But toss the yo-yo just so and all manner of surprising gadgets, devices and equipment appear. List the gadgets contained within the fabulous expanding yo-yo device. . . .

Activity of the day

James Bond Word Search

Hidden in the diamond word search are 15 James Bond movie titles. There are also the surnames of the five actors to have played Bond. Finally, the leftover letters spell out the title of yet another Bond film and the first name of the actor who played him. Phew!

A View To A Kill
Brosnan
Casino Royale
Connery
Dalton
Dr No
For Your Eyes Only
Goldfinger
Lazenby

Licence To Kill
Live and Let Die
Moonraker
Moore
Never Say Never Again
Octopussy
The Living Daylights
Thunderball
Tomorrow Never Dies

```
                              T
                            H E M
                          A O N R D
                        Y B N E Z A L
                      N O T L A D N W I
                    T H U N D E R B A L L
                  A V I E W T O A K I L L T
                F O R Y O U R E Y E S O N L Y
              L L I K O T E C N E C I L H T H E
            N I A G A R E V E N Y A S R E V E N G
          S T H G I L Y A D G N I V I L E H T O L
            D E S E I D R E V E N W O R R O M O T
              C A S I N O R O Y A L E N G U C R
                L I V E A N D L E T D I E O E
                  R E G N I F D L O G N N K
                    Y S S U P O T C O N A
                      N A N S O R B E R
                        E R O O M R N
                          R O G Y O
                            E R O
                              M
```

Today in 1969

the "10 . . . 9 . . . 8 . . ." countdown was heard for the first time from Houston control as they launched *Apollo 9*.

- *Countdown* was the name of a highly successful ABC television pop show, hosted by Ian "Molly" Meldrum.

- *Countdown to Danger*, *Countdown to Freedom*, *The Final Countdown*, *Countdown at Woomera*, *Countdown to War*, and *Countdown to Armageddon* are six of over 40 movies with the word "countdown" in their titles.

Imagine...

Write the numbers from ten down to zero in the center of a page, leaving a line between each. Now think of an event that has a countdown. A rocket launch? The start of a grand finale? An explosion? After each number on your page, write what happens in that particular second. Complete the ten seconds and finish with a description of the event.

Word of the day

countdown To count backwards to indicate the time remaining until an event occurs; count is from the Latin *computare* (to consider), down from the Old English word *dun* (hill).

Quote of the day

"You just start your countdown, and old Bucky'll be back here before you can say 'Blast off!'"
General "Buck" Turgidson (*Dr. Strangelove*)

Activity of the day

Countdown

It's launch time at the Cape launch pad. As it's a European space launch, the countdown is being translated into French and Spanish. Unfortunately, somebody's put the countdown into alphabetical rather than reverse numerical order. Can you use your linguistic skills to translate the numbers and then write them in the correct order again?

French	English	Spanish	English
cinq		cero	
deux		cinco	
dix		cuatro	
huit		diez	
neuf		dos	
quatre		nueve	
sept		ocho	
six		seis	
trois		siete	
un		tres	
zéro		uno	

Answers: dix, neuf, huit, sept, six, cinq, quatre, trois, deux, un, zéro! (French)
diez, nueve, ocho, siete, seises, cinco, cuatro, tres, dos, uno, cero! (Spanish)

Today in 1976

John Pezzin bowls 33 consecutive strikes at Toledo, Ohio.

- Tenpin bowling is related to the games boules, bowls, and skittles.
- The pins (skittles) are placed 12 inches (30 cm) apart. If you can knock them all down with one ball, you have scored a "strike."
- In the French game of *boules*, the ball is thrown through the air, not rolled.

Word of the day

consecutive One after the other; from the Latin *consecutio* (overtake or pursue).

Quote of the day

"There is plenty of time to win this game, and to thrash the Spaniards too."

Sir Francis Drake (after sighting the Spanish Armada during a game of bowls)

Imagine...

Can't see what's so exciting about a game of tenpin bowling. I mean, the pins stand there. You roll the ball down at them. It's not as if the pins can dodge the ball. Or if there were obstacles between the ball and pins. Or if the balls exploded. Or if it was a contact sport . . . . List some possibilities for making tenpin bowling more exciting.

Activity of the day

Ten-pin Puzzle
If a black circle shows a knocked-down pin, how many points does each pattern show? What's the highest score possible?

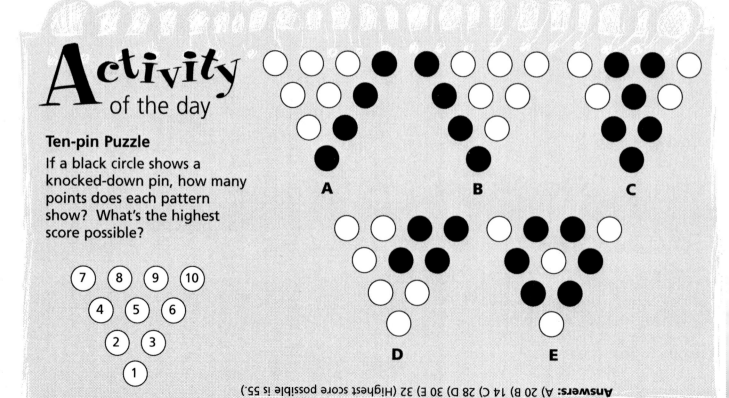

Today in 1868

the first stapler was invented.

- Staplers are an example of a "third-class lever." Third-class levers reduce the force required (to push the staple through) by increasing the distance the lever (handle) travels.

- "SimStapler" is a computer game that allows you to play with a "virtual" stapler. Exciting!

- Some modern photocopiers not only copy but can also collate (sort) a document and staple it at the end.

Word of the day

staple A length of u-shaped wire used to fasten papers together; from the Old English *steppan* (to step).

Imagine...

Staplers join pieces of paper so they keep together. What joins friends so that they stay together? Sharing? Time? Assistance? Presents? Love? Effort? Make an acrostic using the letters in the word *staple*.

Quote of the day

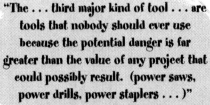

"The . . . third major kind of tool . . . are tools that nobody should ever use because the potential danger is far greater than the value of any project that could possibly result. (power saws, power drills, power staplers . . .)"

Dave Barry

Activity of the day

Joining Devices

Staples are just one way of joining two pieces of paper together. You can also use pins, glue, tape, and so on. If you were creative, imaginative, and just plain inventive, you could probably come up with a dozen different ways. Maybe you can find even more! Make a display showing all of the ways you found.

Answers: button, clothes pin, fold the paper, "glider" clips, glue, masking tape, other paper, paperclips, paper fasteners, pins, staples, tape, string, zippers, etc.

Today in 1918

the U.S. Naval collier, *Cyclops*, disappeared in the Bermuda Triangle.

- The ship was returning from Brazil. It vanished with all hands and no wreckage was ever found.

- The Bermuda Triangle (which isn't really a triangle!) is also known as the "Limbo of the Lost" and the "Devil's Triangle." A similar area in Japan is known as the "Devil's Sea."

- Most of the strange disappearances from the Bermuda Triangle area can be accounted for by bad weather, rough seas, or poor navigation skills.

Word of the day

collier A coal ship. From the Middle English *col* (coal).

Quote of the day

"It has been their [the Coast Guard's] experience that the combined forces of nature and the unpredictability of mankind outdo even the most far-fetched science fiction many times each year."

US Naval report on the Bermuda Triangle

Imagine...

The Bermuda Triangle is mysterious. It might be for some, but not for me. I know what happened to all those lost ships. I know where the planes disappeared to. How do I know? Well, my ship vanished in the Bermuda Triangle. But I escaped to tell my story. And here it is, strange but true . . . .

Activity of the day

The Limbo of the Lost Yachts!

The Bermuda Triangle strikes again, snaring five yachts in its mysterious maze-like currents. Fortunately, four of the yachts can escape. Which is the unlucky one?

Answer: B

Today in 1897

John and Bill Kellogg served the first cornflakes.

- They were served to patients at the Battle Creek Sanatorium, a nursing home.
- John Kellogg was a surgeon before he became a food manufacturer.
- *Cornflakes* is the name of an art performance piece. It involves scattering 250 boxes of cornflakes over a lawn—and watching what happens.

Imagine...

Hah! Just for once you've beaten your kid brother down to breakfast. Even better, you've beaten him to the unopened box of cornflakes in the cupboard. Which means you get the toy inside, not him. You open up the top of the box and reach inside. Your fingers can just touch it. You reach further but then—you're falling! You don't know how it's happening, but you're falling into the box! Tell the story of the day you disappeared into the cornflakes box.

Word
of the day

sanatorium A hospital for rest or for the treatment of diseases; from the Latin *sanare* (to cure).

Quote
of the day

Did you hear about the fatherless Rice Krispie?
He had snap and crackle, but no pop.

Activity
of the day

Cornflake Word Chase

You might find snap, crackle, and pop in some cereals—but what can you find in a corn-flake? How about more than 20 three-letter (or longer) words, all beginning with C!

O	R	N
F	**C**	L
A	K	E

Answers: Here are thirty!

can, car, café, calf, cane, care, clan, clef, coal, coke, cola, core, cork, corn, canoe, carol, clank, clean, clear, clerk, cloak, clone, coral, crane, crank, creak, creak, croak, cornea

Today in 1887

Everett Horton patented a fishing rod with telescoping steel tubes.

- Modern fishing rods are made from carbon-fiber materials developed by NASA.
- A 19-ft. (5.9-m) white pointer shark was caught with a rod in 1982.
- The fishing rod is a third-class lever with the fulcrum (pivot) at the handle and the load (hopefully a fish!) at the other end.

Word of the day

rod A pole with a line and usually a reel attached for fishing; from the Old Norse *rudda* (club).

Imagine...

Just for once, you don't have to tell the story of the one that got away. Because it didn't. No siree! This fish you caught, and even if it needed a semi-trailer to bring it home on, this is one fishing story you're going to love to tell!

Quote of the day

Time is but the stream I go a-fishing in.
Henry Thoreau

Activity of the day

Problem Rods

Here are nine other rods—can you work what they are?

R O D		To poke
		King of Judea who talked to the wise men
		Stepped
		A car modified for speed
		Used with a muzzle-loading rifle
		A rod inside an engine
		A rod for finding water
		A rod that protects a building from lightning
		A rod between 1 cm and 10 cm used in maths

Answers: prod, Herod, trod, hot-rod, ramrod, piston-rod, divining rod, lightning rod, cuisenaire rod

Today in 1882

Jumbo the elephant was exported from the UK to the US after being "sedated" with beer.

- Jumbo was bought from the London Zoo by the Barnum & Bailey Circus in the US.
- He cost $10,000.
- Jumbo was the biggest elephant in captivity and became so famous throughout the world that "Jumbo" became an alternative name for any elephant.

Imagine...

"Hi. The name's Jumbo. I'm the main attraction here at London Zoo. That's fair enough, too.—After all, I am the biggest elephant in captivity. I've been getting some extra attention recently though. Some fancy-dressed guy was here talking to the keepers. He's outside the enclosure with them now. Obviously impressed with my great stature and good-looks! But what are they pouring from those brown bottles into my drinking water?" Write the tale of Jumbo's travels from London Zoo to the circus.

Word of the day

sedate Cause to be calm or quiet; from the Latin *sedatus* (to calm).

Quote of the day

"God is really only another artist. He invented the giraffe, the elephant, and the cat. He has no real style. He just goes on trying other things. "

Pablo Picasso

Activity of the day

A Jumbo Puzzle

Test your Jumbo knowledge here! When you've completed all the horizontal words, the central vertical word spells out an alternative name for an elephant.

1. The largest land animal
2. Smaller of the two types of elephants
3. Larger of the two types of elephants— its ears look like a map of its home!
4. The elephant's ancient hairy ancestor
5. Flesh-eating mammal that preys on elephant calves (baby elephants)
6. An extinct type of elephant
7. To search for food
8. A group of elephants
9. The elephant is this type of animal

Answers: 1. elephant; 2. Asian; 3. African; 4. mammoth, 5. hyena; 6. mastodon; 7. forage; 8. troupe; 9. mammal **Bonus word:** pachyderm.

Today in 1982

all the nine planets were on the same side of the Sun.

- On May 19, 2161, eight of the planets will be lined up on one side of the sun. Be sure to stick around to see it.

- Some researchers claim that big changes in stockmarket shares, big earthquakes, and increased sunspot activity all happen when the planets line up.

- The earth, moon, and sun are all aligned in an eclipse.

Word
of the day

syzygy When the sun and two or more planets become lined up; from the Greek *syzygos* (yoked together).

Quote
of the day

"Observe how system into system runs, what other planets circle other suns."
Alexander Pope

Imagine...

"Ladies, gentlemen, and clones! Welcome to this special Syzygy Day broadcast, live from Earth's moon. Well, it's finally May 19, 2161 and we're about to see if all those doomsday predictions are going to come true as we wait for the last planet to get into line. Here we go, . . . they're lined up now!" Write about what happens when the long-awaited event occurs.

Activity
of the day

Solar System Mystery

Here are the nine planets of the solar system. Look very carefully at their spelling. Can you give three reasons why the name Mars is the odd one out?

Earth
Jupiter
Mars
Mercury
Neptune
Pluto
Saturn
Uranus
Venus

1. _____

_____

2. _____

_____

3. _____

_____

Answers: 1. It's the only four-letter name. **2.** It's the only name with one vowel. **3.** All the other names have a "u". (even Earth—it has you!)

Today in 1302

was Romeo and Juliet's wedding day. (According to Shakespeare!)

- Shakespeare wrote *Romeo and Juliet* in 1595. It is set in the Italian town of Verona.

- An Italian saying says: "If a girl baked a pandoro for me, I'd marry her." A *pandoro* is a cake from Verona that takes over 13 hours to cook.

- At some Italian weddings, the groom's tie is cut into pieces and sold to the guests. The proceeds pay for the band!

Word of the day

love A strong emotion of regard and affection. From the Latin *lubere* (to please).

Imagine...

What a wonderful day for a wedding! Only, . . . the minister has the hiccoughs, the bride is so nervous she's shaking, the groom is half an hour late, the caterers have dropped the wedding cake, a hail storm has erupted, and the best man has a bloody nose. Then things really start going wrong . . . . Write the story of the worst wedding day imaginable.

Quote of the day

"If Shakespeare had had to go on an author tour to promote *Romeo and Juliet*, he never would have written *Macbeth*."

Dr. Joyce Brothers

Activity of the day

Something Old, Something New

Traditionally, a bride wears something old and something new. Can you turn the word "old" into the word "new" in nine letter changes? Use the clues to help you.

O	L	D	
			not even
			increase by several
			help
			a cover
			caused to burn
			idiot
			opposite of is
			a fish trap
N	E	W	

Answers: old, odd, add, aid, lid, lit, nit, not, net, new.

Today in 1832

a ballet tutu was used for the first time.

- The first tutus were calf-length and gave the dancers a dreamy, romantic look.

- Later, the tutu was shortened to just above the knee. This allowed the dancers to show off their footwork.

- "Powder-puff tutus" are modern ballet skirts that extend out from the waist.

Word of the day

tutu A short projecting skirt worn by a ballerina; from the French *tutu* (backside).

Imagine...

"Newsflash! Your state has adopted the tutu as its costume and has passed a new law making all citizens wear a tutu at all times! More news to follow!" Why was the tutu chosen? Would everyone wear one? What would happen if they didn't? Would the army wear them? The police? Your teacher? Would you? Write about what happens when the law takes effect.

Quote of the day

"Ladies and gentlemen, it takes more than one to make a ballet."
Dame Ninette De Valois

Activity of the day

What would we do without tutus? We wouldn't have any of these words or phrases. That's for sure! Add T, U, T, U to the letters below and then unscramble them by using the clues.

T U T U +	OP	things produced	
	MM	tummy	
	RON	attendance for an event	
	HNR	a lie	
	PREB	to flatter	
	ROBS	sudden violent happening	
	BIMK	a city in Africa	
	FLHR	honest	
	ABNOR	rotate through half a circle	
	PRECB	flower	
	EFOON	unmusical	

Answers: output, tum-tum, turn out, untruth, butter up, outburst, Timbuktu, truthful, about turn, buttercup, out of tune

Today in 1462

the *Gutenberg Bible* was printed.

- The *Bible* is famous for being the first book to be printed with movable metal type.
- The Gutenberg bible is also known as the *Mazarin* or "42-line" *Bible*.
- Only two complete copies still exist.

Word of the day

Bible The sacred writings of the Christian religion; from *Byblos* an ancient Phoenician city (from which papyrus [paper] was exported).

Imagine...

Most religions have a set of sacred writings which explain the laws or rules their god expects them to follow. If you had helped write out the list of commands for humans to follow, what might you have included?

Quote of the day

"The number one book of the ages was written by a committee, and it was called *The Bible*."

Louis Mayer (to writers complaining about changes to their work)

Activity of the day

Back-to-front fontfaces

The *Gutenberg Bible* was set in metal type, like a rubber stamp. The type was backwards so when it printed it was the correct way. Printers became very quick at reading back-to-front lettering! Here's some reversed type. It's a quotation from the *Bible*. How quickly can you read it?

To every thing there is a season, and a time to every purpose under the heaven: A time to be born, and a time to die; a time to plant, and a time to reap; A time to weep, and a time to laugh; a time to mourn, and a time to dance...

Answer: To every thing there is a season, and a time to every purpose under the heaven: A time to be born, and a time to die; a time to plant, and a time to reap; A time to weep, and a time to laugh; a time to mourn, and a time to dance...

Today in 1885

Gilbert and Sullivan's comic opera *The Mikado* was performed for the first time at the Savoy Theatre in London.

- It had an initial run of 672 performances.
- The opera is set in the town of Titipu. This town is known as the "cement capital of Japan."
- Other operas by Gilbert and Sullivan include *The Pirates of Penzance* and *The Gondoliers*.

Word of the day

Mikado An emperor of Japan.

Quote of the day

"I'm very good at integral and differential calculus
I know the scientific names of beings animalculous..."

W. S. Gilbert (*The Pirates of Penzance*)

Imagine...

The Mikado has a cast of characters with very unusual names. Write your own story using some of them. Include Nanki-Poo, Yum-Yum, Ko-Ko, Poo-Bah, Pitti-Sing, and Peep-Bo.

Activity of the day

A night at the opera

Design a stage set for an opera, based on the characters and your story from the "Imagine . . ." activity. When designing the set, you'll need to take into account where the audience will be sitting and what they will be able to see from where they are; where the characters will come on and off the stage; the use of color in the set to evoke the mood of your story; the use of lighting and where you'd position the lights for dramatic effect; and what props you'd need and where you'd position them.

Today in 1937

the world's first blood bank opened for business in Chicago, IL.

- About 1 pint (480 ml) of blood is removed in a blood bank donation.
- The first blood transfusion took place in 1667, between a 15-year-old boy and a sheep!
- By 1994, blood donations in United States reached over 1 million a year.

Imagine...

"Hello, ees zees a blood bank? Good! I've come to make a withdrawal. I can't withdraw blood? Eet ees a bank! You put zee blood een, you take zee blood out! You say no to me? You say no to zee great Count Dracula? Vee vill see about that!" Write about the wily way in which you convince the blood bank to let you make a withdrawal.

Word of the day

blood The fluid pumped by the heart; from the Old German *bluot* (blood).

Quote of the day

"Other things are all very well in their way, but give me blood!"
Charles Dickens

Activity of the day

Blood donor logic puzzle

Alan, Chris, and Bronwyn visit the blood bank. They fill out their details and list their professions (not necessarily in order) as scientist, sprinter, and secretary. Their blood types are tested and one is type A, one is type B, and one is type O. If you know the following, can you work out each donor's profession and bloodtype?

1) Bronwyn was ahead of the secretary in the queue and behind Chris.

2) Chris has type B blood but the sprinter

	Alan	Bronwyn	Chris	Secretary	Sprinter	Scientist	A	O	B
Alan									
Bronwyn									
Chris									
Secretary									
Sprinter									
Scientist									
A									
O									
B									

Today in 1881

the Barnum & Bailey Circus made its debut.

- P. T. Barnum invented the phrase "the Greatest Show on Earth" to describe the circus. He also introduced the phrases "rain or shine," "Siamese twin," and "Let's get the show on the road."

- The circus was eventually bought by the Ringling Bros. Circus, which still tours today.

Word of the day

circus An arena covered by a tent and used for shows by travelling entertainers; from the Greek *krikos* (ring).

Imagine...

"Ladies, gentlemen, and children! May I direct your attention to the center ring! Tonight, opening the Greatest Show on Earth is quite simply, the most amazing act that has ever been our pleasure to bring you. Let's give them a huge round of applause as they enter, . . ." Write about what you think would be the most amazing and astounding act ever to be in the Greatest Show on Earth.

Quote of the day

"There's a sucker born every minute."
Phineas T. Barnum

Activity of the day

Big Top Word Search
Come on down to the best show in town. Find all these circus words in the big top. The extra letters spell out a popular circus act.

acrobats
animals
bigtop
clown
fairy floss
high wire
lion tamer
plate spinner
popcorn
ring
ringmaster
ropes
sawdust
trainer
trapeze

Answer: elephants

```
            S           P
        S   P       T L
      H O O S N E R A R
    T I L P E W L A T I L
  A S G F C P O E I   E N I S
  E N U H Y O O L P N S G O T P
  Z I D W R R R C H E P M N A O
  E M W I I N       R I A T B T
  P A A R A           N S A O G
  A L S E F           N T M R I
  R S A N T           E E E C B
  T G N I R           R R R A S
```

Today in 1753

was the first official St. Patrick's Day.

- St. Patrick's original name was Succat. He was born in England but was captured and taken to Ireland.
- He escaped to France then returned to Ireland as a priest.
- His use of the shamrock in sermons led to it being adopted as the Irish national emblem.

Imagine...

The short Irish gentleman wearing the unusual green suit is both friendly and charming. "Aye, that's my lucky charm, to be sure, to be sure," he replies when you inquire about the four-leaf clover hanging from his wrist. "Brought me a pot o' luck that little shamrock has. A very big pot . . ." Imagine that you are that green gentleman, and tell the story of the luck your shamrock brought you.

Word of the day

shamrock A plant with tri-foliate leaves; from the Irish *seamróg* (little clover).

Quote of the day

"Hibernicis ipsis Hibernior.
"(More Irish than the Irish.)
Anonymous

Activity of the day

Lucky Three-leaf Clovers

What a shame! All these leaves and not one of them a lucky four-leaf clover. Ah, but one of them is lucky; three times luckier than all the others!

17 x 8   37 x 9   9 x 15

22 x 6   11 x 21   17 x 18   27 x 5

Answer: All have the lucky number three in them but 37 x 9 = 333 has three threes.

Today in 1850

William Wells and Henry Fargo started their banking and stagecoach business.

- They called the company "American Express" before changing it to "Wells-Fargo."
- The first office was opened in San Franciso with stagecoaches and the Pony Express connecting it to the "wild west" of El Paso.
- The company now has $201 billion in assets, 15 million customers, and 102,000 employees.

Word of the day

express The rapid transport of goods; from the Latin *expressus* (to press).

Quote of the day

"You will hear more good things on the outside of a stagecoach from London to Oxford, than if you were to pass a twelve-month with the undergraduates, or heads of colleges, of that famous city. "
William Hazlitt

Imagine...

The Wells and Fargo stagecoach driver inspects his passengers a little more carefully than usual this morning. He knows there's a chest full of nuggets riding up the top, and the Pinkerton detective riding with him thinks one of the passengers could be in cahoots with the bandits in the area. But which one? The tall, dark stranger? The school ma'am? The portly banker? The cowgirl? The rancher? Or maybe the detective himself. Once the stagecoach is out of sight of San Francisco there's a wild whoop and the sound of galloping hooves . . . . Write about what happens next.

Activity of the day

Roll 'em, roll 'em, roll 'em
The early stagecoach drivers weren't always too accurate when they were drawing their maps. This one certainly isn't to scale! So you'd better add the miles between the towns to work out which of the three routes (A, B, or C) is the shortest.

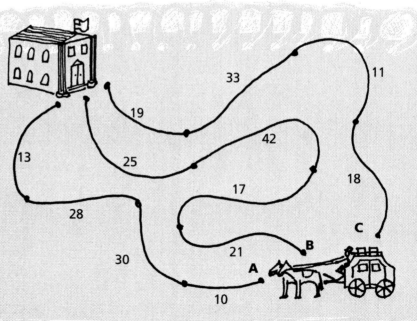

Answer: A (81 miles)

Today in 1932

is the day when hundreds of swallows return to Mission San Juan Capistrano in California from their winter home in Mexico.

- Every year since 1776, when the mission was built, the swallows have faithfully returned to this same town.
- According to legend, the swallows have been late only once-because of a storm out at sea.
- The swallows are a reminder that spring is just around the corner.

Word of the day

swallow Any of various, small, swift-flying birds with long, pointed wings and a forked tail, known for their regular migrations, from the Old English *swealwe*.

Imagine...

You are an orinthologist, a scientist who studies birds. On a bird-watching expedition in South America, you discover a new species of bird. Describe the bird. Tell about the bird's main features: beak, plummage (feathers), wings, and feet. Don't forget to identify the habitat and what you plan to name this bird.

Quote of the day

"We think caged birds sing, when indeed they cry."
John Webster

Activity of the day

Bird Identification

Can you be an amateur birdwatcher by identifying these six birds?

Here are their names: bald eagle, owl, cardinal, hummingbird, woodpecker, duck

1. _____   4. _____

2. _____   5. _____

3. _____   6. _____

Answers: 1-penguin, 2-hawk, 3-parakeet, 4-canary, 5-bald eagle, 6-toucan, 7-cockatoo, 8-sea gull, 9-parrot, 10-vulture

Today

(if it's a Sunday) is the Buzzard Sunday Festival in Hinckley, Ohio, US.

- "Buzzard" is the name given to North American turkey vultures. They are also known as "buteo."
- Buzzards are found everywhere in the world except for Australia and India.
- Buzzards are believed to mate for life.

Word of the day

buzzard A large bird of prey; from the Latin *buteon* (hawk).

Quote of the day

"Cottleston, Cottleston, Cottleston Pie
A fly can't bird, but a bird can fly."
A. A. Milne (from *Winnie-the-Pooh*)

Imagine...

The sun's high overhead and this barren desert offers little shade. You stagger a few more paces, your tongue a bone-dry sponge in your mouth. You shake the water bottle. Empty. A noise makes you look upwards. The buzzards are circling. How did you ever get into this situation . . . ?! Write about just how it happened.

Activity of the day

Birds of a feather

Oh boy! There are bits of birds everywhere! Each bird's name has been split in two—and separated. Join 'em back to see what's in this flock. P.S. One bird (poor thing) got split into three...

AH, ARD, BUZZ, CHICK, CO, CORM, EAG, EN, EON, GAL, KABU, KEET, KOO, LE, LORI, ORANT, OST, OT, PAR, PECKER, PIG, RICH, ROT, ROW, RRA, SPAR, TURE, VUL, WOOD

Answers: buzzard, chicken, coot, cormorant, eagle, galah, kook-aburra, lorikeet, ostrich, parrot, pigeon, sparrow, vulture, wood-pecker

Today

(depending on where you live in the world) is Global Understanding Day, End of the World Day, and even Memory Day!

It's also:

- the birthday of Johann Sebastian Bach in 1685
- Fragrance Day (US)
- Festival of Washerwomen (France)
- National Tree Planting Day (Lesotho), and
- National French Bread Day.

Imagine...

As chairman of the International "What Do We Celebrate Today?" Committee, you've got the final say on just what is officially celebrated on March 21. You can choose one of the established holidays (like those above). Or maybe you'd like to celebrate something else. Your call. Just give five reasons for your selection.

Word of the day

anniversary The date on which an event occurred in a previous year; from the Latin *anniversarius* (returning annually).

Quote of the day

"Most modern calendars mar the sweet simplicity of our lives by reminding us that each day that passes is the anniversary of some perfectly uninteresting event."
Oscar Wilde

Activity of the day

Holiday Puzzle

Here are four more holidays (none on March 21!). To work them out, first complete the three-letter words going vertically. Then write down the center horizontal word. Where are these holidays celebrated?

I	S	E	H	A	A	E	V	U
E	Y	A	T	H	E	U	N	E

E	D	A	P	O	A
B	G	E	E	E	E

T	B	A	I	U	S	A	L	R
G	D	K	S	N	W	P	P	P

I	R	E	F	G	O
L	Y	B	X	M	E

Answers: Christmas, Australia, Boxing & Labour days

Today in 1948

composer Lord Andrew Lloyd Webber was born.

- Weber's musicals include *Cats*, *Jesus Christ Superstar*, and *Phantom of the Opera*.
- He published his first musical composition when he was nine years old.
- *Cats* is the longest-running musical in history.
- Weber was the first composer to have three Broadway shows running at the same time.

Word of the day

Broadway A New York street famous for its theaters.

Quote of the day

" . . . in the great open spaces where cats are cats . . ."

Don Marquis (archy and mehitabel)

Imagine...

The Group for Canine Equality has been complaining for so long that Lord Lloyd Weber has finally consented to write *Dogs*, the follow-up to his highly successful musical *Cats*. Create a cast for the show (Rover, Lassie, Patch . . .) and invent some dog-type songs for them to sing ("I'm Bone Tired," "Barking Up the Wrong Tree," . . .). And don't forget to design the set! (As long as it doesn't get you in the doghouse with your teacher!)

Activity of the day

Musical Word Search

There are nineteen great musicals hidden in this word search—can you find them all? If you do, the leftover letters will spell out the title of Tim Rice and Andrew Lloyd Weber's first successful musical.

```
M Y F A I R L A D Y J O S E P H E A H A N
D T F O O R E H T N O R E L D D I F E M H
L I O N K I N G W R E C K E R S N S L O E
A M A Z C I S U M F O D N U O S N T L H E
A N Y T H I N G G O E S T A R I A A O A S
S H O W B O A T N G T E N C T E H C D L A
M I K A D O N I C O L O E R D I V R O K E
S S E R P X E T H G I L R A T S V I L O R
P I R A T E S O F P E N Z A N C E E L E G
Y R O T S E D I S T S E W A M C O A Y O T
```

Annie	Grease	My Fair Lady	Showboat
Anything Goes	Hello Dolly	Oklahoma	Sound of Music
Cats	Lion King	Oliver	Starlight Express
Evita	Mikado	Pirates of Penzance	West Side Story
Fiddler on the Roof		Rent	Wreckers

Answer: *Joseph and the Technicolor Dreamcoat*

Today

Helen Porter Mitchell (Dame Nellie Melba) had a new kind of toast named after her—Melba toast.

- Melba Toast is very thinly sliced bread toasted to a golden color. It was created by French Chef Auguste Escoffier.
- He also created Melba sauce and peach Melba.
- The name Melba came from her home city, Melbourne.

Word of the day

toast To make bread brown by heat; from the Latin *tostus* (to dry or parch).

Imagine..

Create a new food to name after your teacher. Describe the food and why it would remind people of him/her.

Quote of the day

"The first rule in opera is the first rule in life: see to everything yourself."
Dame Nellie Melba

Activity of the day

Dame Nellie Melba wasn't responsible for all these words, but they do all begin with Mel. Use the list below to help you.

melt, melon, mellow, melody, Melissa, melanoma, Melchior, melodica, Melbourne, melancholy, melodrama, melting-point

a feeling of thoughtful sadness	
type of skin cancer	
Victorian state capital	
one of the Three Wise Men	
girl's name	
unhurried and relaxed	
keyboard instrument played with the breath	
dramatic play	
the tune of a song	
type of fruit	
to change from a solid to a liquid	
the temperature at which a solid starts to melt	

Answers: melancholy, melanoma, Melbourne, Melchior, Melissa, mellow, melodica, melodrama, melody, melon, melt, melting-point

Today in 1974

Ernest Shephard, illustrator of the original *Winnie-the-Pooh* and *Wind in the Willows* books died.

- Shephard's childhood nickname was "giddy kipper".
- Shephard based his drawings of Winnie-the-Pooh on his own son's bear, Growler.
- Winnie-the-Pooh was named after a bear cub that (the real) Christopher Robin saw at the London Zoo. The cub had been found in Winnipeg, Canada.

Word of the day

picture A visual representation created on a surface. From the Latin "pictura" (to paint).

Quote of the day

"I am a Bear of Very Little Brain, and long words Bother me."
A. A. Milne

Imagine...

Write a story based on the toys you had as a small child. Did you have a favorite bear? A doll? An action figure? A special blanket? Include them all. Oh, and don't forget to include yourself!

Activity of the day

Winnie-the-Pooh Downword Puzzle

Solve the clues by using the letters of Winnie-the-Pooh's name as a guide.

Letter	Clue
W	Owl's spelling of his name
I	A bouncy tiger
N	A bouncy kangaroo
N	Winnie-the-Pooh sometimes went under this name
I	The entrance to this character's house seems smaller after eating honey.
E	A grumpy friend
T	Pooh Bear's best friend
H	Pooh Bear's favorite food
E	The characters live in the 100 ___ wood
P	A small pig
O	A wise bird
O	Christopher's other name
H	How Rabbit spells house

Answers: WOL, TIGGER, KANGA, SANDERS, RABBIT, EEYORE, CHRISTOPHER, HONEY, ACRE, PIGLET, OWL, ROBIN, HOWSE

Today in 1769

a Newcastle (UK) man was admitted into the hospital because of his hiccoughs; they could be heard over a half-mile away!

- The Swedes call a hiccough a "hicka," the Spanish, "hipo," and in France, it's "hoquet."
- A pig farmer once had the hiccoughs for over 65 years!
- Men get hiccoughs more often than women.
- Swallowing a spoonful of sugar is reported as being 95% successful in curing the hiccoughs.

Imagine...

Hic. You got them this morning. Hic. And now it's afternoon. Hic. And they're still here. You've tried everything. Hic. Breathing into a paper bag. Holding your breath. Hic. Being scared by friends. Hic. And nothing works. Nothing! Write about what you will—hic!—do.

Word of the day

hiccough A quick inhalation stopped by the closing of the "glottis" producing a peculiar sound. Also spelled hiccup.

Quote of the day

"A hospital is no place to be sick."
Samuel Goldwyn

Activity of the day

Hiccoughs Galore

Let's count hiccoughs! (What could possibly be more exciting?) There's a few hidden in the "H" puzzle. Just find "em all!

```
H H H H H H H H        H H H H H H I H
G I I I I I I I        I I H I I G H I
U C C C C C C C        C C G C C U I C
O C C C C C C C        C C U C C O H C
C O O O O O O O        O O O O O C I O
C U U U U U U U        U U C U U C H U
I G G G G G G G I      C G G C G G I H G
H H H H H H H H C      H H H I H H H G H
H I C C O U G H I      H I C H C I H U I
H I C C O U G H H      G U O C C I H O H
H I C C O U G H H      G U O C C I H C I
H I C C O U G H H      G U O C C I H C C
H I C C O U G H        C I G I O I I G
H I C C O U G H        I C I H I H H I
H I C C O U G H        H G U O C C I H
H I C C O U G H        H I C C O U G H
H I C C O U G H        H G U O C C I H
H I C C O U G H        H G U O C C I H
```

Today in 1937

a statue of Popeye was unveiled in Crystal City, Texas.

- The town's principal crop is spinach.
- Popeye first appeared in the comic strip "Thimble Theatre."
- Robyn Williams played Popeye in his first feature film.

Word of the day

spinach An Asian plant grown for its edible dark green leaves; From the Old Spanish *espinaca* (spinach).

Quote of the day

I yam what I yam.
Popeye

Imagine...

Spinach isn't the only vegetable that'll give you huge muscles and the strength of an ox. See those cans over there? Yep, those ones. They're full of … broccoli. Yes! Broccoli! Guaranteed to put muscles on your muscles! Well, don't believe me then. Try it for yourself!" Write about what happens on the day you open that fateful can of broccoli.

Activity of the day

Spic-and-span Spinach

Spinach the vegetable—full of vitamins and minerals! Spinach the word—full of other words! How many three (or more) letter words can you find in spinach?
P.S. No plurals!

_____

_____

_____

_____

_____

_____

_____

Answers: Here are 34: ash, can, cap, has, hip, nap, nip, pan, sap, sin, spa, cash, chap, chin, chip, hasp, inca, inch, pain, scan, shin, ship, snap, snip, span, spic, spin, aspic, chain, china, panic, Spain

Today in 1939

Cale Yarborough, member of the Motor Sports Hall of Fame, was born in Timmonsville, North Carolina. His main concern about gasoline was probably not its lead content.

- In the early 1970s, low-lead gasolines were introduced because of public concern about air pollution.
- European countries were moving in the same direction, toward low-lead and unleaded gasoline, but more slowly than the U.S.
- Unleaded gasoline first went on sale in 1985 in Australia.
- Another NASCAR champion driver, Richard Petty, also probably did not worry much about lead content in the gasoline in his racecars.

Word of the day

petrol A fuel made from petroleum; from the French *essence de pétrole* (essence of petroleum). Known as gasoline in some countries

Imagine...

Imagine we can run cars on plain old tap water rather than gasoline. Write about what would change. Would every change be for the better? What would we use old petrol stations for? What about tankers? Old drill sites?

Quote of the day

"What a country calls its vital economic interests are not the things which enable its citizens to live, but the things which enable it to make war. Petrol is much more likely than wheat to be a cause of international conflict."
Simone Weil

Activity of the day

Get a Good DEAL on LEAD.

Here are ten sets of clues. The answer to the first clue is an anagram (same letters, different spelling) of the first. For example:

Poisonous metal found in petrol (LEAD); an agreement between two people (DEAL)

Try these!

1. Type of cheese; created
2. Large cup; for chewing
3. A large shopping area; a type of public transport
4. A section; a device for catching things
5. Married; water that has condensed on a cool surface
6. To prohibit; to seize suddenly
7. Part of a boat that keeps it upright in the water; onion-like plant
8. Another name for the Christmas season; boy's name
9. A person who tells untruths; bars of steel that vehicles roll on
10. Perspiration; worthless materials

Answers: 1. Edam made **2.** Mug gum **3.** Mart tram **4.** Part trap **5.** Wed dew **6.** Ban nab **7.** Keel leek **8.** Noel Leon **9.** Liar rail **10.** Sweat waste

Today in 1930

the first washing machine was patented by Nathaniel Briggs of New Hampshire.

- For centuries, sea voyagers would do wash by placing their dirty clothes into a stong cloth bag attached to a long rope, tossing it overboard, and letting the ship drag it.
- Before running water, gas, or electricity, one load-one wash, one boiling, and one rinse used about 50 gallons of water and staggering amounts of time and labor
- The earliest manual washing machines used a lever that when moved, simulated the motion of the human hand on a washboard.
- The first electric washing machines were introduced in the early 1900s.

Word
of the day

launder To wash or wash and iron clothes; from the Latin *lavare* (to wash).

Quote
of the day

"**Laundry increases exponentially with the number of children.**"
Miriam Robbins

Imagine...

You brought a brand new top of the line washing machine. It's extra fancy with lots of buttons and lights that flash when the machine is working. Its super large capacity can hold a week's worth of dirty laundry, with room to spare. The only interesting thing is-there is one button with a label beside it that says, "Warning! Do Not Touch!" You read the owner's manual from cover to cover and can find nothing that mentions this strange button. So one day, you decide to push it. Tell what happens next.

Activity
of the day

Laundry Scramble
The dirty laundry went into the washing machine and came out a mixed-up mess! Can you unscramble these words to spell laundry items?

1. etvs
2. koscs
3. hitsr
4. rsdes
5. oltew
6. hsete

7. alknbte
8. hrstos
9. lubeos
10. rndeuawre
11. acejtk
12. wretsea

Answers: 1. vest, 2. socks, 3. shirt, 4. dress, 5. towels, 6. sheet, 7. blanket, 8. shorts, 9. blouse, 10. underwear, 11. jacket, 12. sweater

Today in 1886

Coca-Cola was invented by John Styth Pemberton.

- Coca-Cola was originally green.
- The original formula contained cocaine!
- Iceland consumes more Coca-Cola per capita than any other nation.
- Only seven people have ever known all the ingredients.

Word of the day

coca A South American shrub; from the Spanish *kuka* (the coca plant).

Imagine...

You're one of the only two people in the entire world who know the Coca-Cola formula. But your memory is failing and you're worried about forgetting it. So you decide to write it down. Every ingredient. On this piece of paper. So tell us (ie write it down!)—what IS in Coke?

Quote of the day

"To be normal, to drink Coca-Cola and eat Kentucky Fried Chicken, is to be in a conspiracy against yourself."

Jerry Fletcher *(Conspiracy Theory)*

Activity of the day

Coke Picture-Words

Here are some soft-drink related picture-words. What do they all mean?

a)
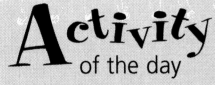

b) BUBBLES   MY NOSE

c) A   COKE   ⊃   N

d) D   R   K   N   I

e) SH OP

Today in 1867

Russia sold Alaska to the United States.

- It was sold for $7.2 million.
- Alaska became the 49th US state in 1959.
- More people walk to work in Alaska than any other US state.
- The Alaskan flag has nine stars, representing the North Star and the "dipper" constellation.

Word of the day

Alaska The 49th state of the United States; from the Aleut word meaning *mainland*.

Quote of the day

"I want him manning a radar tower in Alaska by the end of the day. Just mail him his clothes."

Kittridge (*Mission: Impossible*)

Imagine...

The United States is a bit short of ready cash at the moment, so it's decided to sell one of the states. But which one? Which state could we do without? More to the point, which state would another country like to buy? Choose a state that you think the U.S. should sell and give some good reasons why.

Activity of the day

The Alaskan Trivia Challenge

Here are ten questions about Alaska. How many can you answer without using the word box?

Clues

BEARS, BIRCH, CARIBOU, FORGET-ME-NOT, INUIT, JUNEAU, LARGEST, TRANS-ALASKAN PIPELINE, YUKON, YUKON TERRITORY

1. The Canadian province to the East of Alaska is ____.
2. The capital of Alaska is ____.
3. Alaska is the U.S.'s _____ state.
4. The main river in Alaska is the ____.
5. The state's national flower is the ____.
6. Alaskan Artic deer are called _____.
7. The _____ is almost 1,280 km long.
8. ____ are some of the original inhabitants of Alaska.
9. Alaska's forests have many spruce and _____ trees.
10. Alaska has polar, brown and black _____.

Answers: 1. Yukon Territory 2. Juneau 3. Largest 4. Yukon 5. Forget-me-not 6. Caribou 7. Trans-Alaskan pipeline 8. Inuit 9. Birch 10. Bears

Today in 1889

the Eiffel Tower was completed.

- The tower is 984 ft. (300 m) tall and contains over 6,000 ton of iron.
- 2.5 million rivets were used in its construction.
- 50,000 liters of paint are used to paint the tower every seven years.
- Over 167 million people have visited the tower since it was erected.

Imagine...

The view from the top of the Eiffel Tower is everything you imagined it to be. But your gazing is cut short by a scream. A young child has climbed onto the balcony and stumbled! The child has fallen but become entangled in the girders. Without a thought for your own safety, you leap to the child's aid. Write about what happened on the day you earned a French award for bravery.

Word of the day

Eiffel Surname of the tower's builder, Alexandre Gustave Eiffel. Eiffel also constructed the interior of the Statue of Liberty.

Quote of the day

"The cloud-capped towers, the gorgeous palaces
The solemn temples, the great globe itself . . . "
Shakespeare (*The Tempest*)

Activity of the day

The Eiffel Tower isn't the only tourist landmark in Paris. Here are eight more, all riveted into the Eiffel Tower. So, can you find a park, a cathedral, a museum, a monument, a palace of the president, a church, a fortress, and an art gallery? (Hint: An encyclopedia might be handy!)

Bois de Boulogne

Palais de l'Élysée

Centre Pompidou

Panthéon

Bastille

The Arc de Triomphe

The Louvre

Notre Dame

Answers: Bois de Boulogne (park), Notre Dame (cathedral), The Louvre (museum), The Arc de Triomphe (monument), Palais de l'Élysée (palace of the president), Panthéon (church), Bastille (fortress), Centre Pompidou (art gallery)

APRIL 1

Today

is April Fools' Day (or All Fools' Day).

- Up until 1564, April Fools' Day was celebrated on January 1.
- In France, the April Fool is called an "April fish." In Scotland they're called "gowks."
- In the Middle Ages, people were supposedly let out of lunatic asylums for a few days each year—including April 1.

Word of the day

fool A stupid person; from the Latin *follis* (bellows or bag).

Quote of the day

"The first of April is the day we remember what we are the other 364 days of the year."
Mark Twain

Imagine...

Now, how best to celebrate April Foos' Day? A bucket of water over the classroom door? That'll make a splash... Pin on the chair? The teacher would get the point for sure... Tie shoelaces together? Hmm—that's knot been done before... But all those ideas are old and stale. You can think of something cleverer—can't you? Write a detailed plan...

Activity of the day

Amazing!
Here's an April Fools' maze. Can you find your way from "in" to "out"?

IN

OUT

Happy April Fool's Day!
Answers: Try going around the outside...

Today in 1914

the Jedi Knight "Obi-Wan Kenobi" (Sir Alec Guinness de Cuffe) was born in London.

- He won an Academy Award for best actor in the war movie *Bridge Over the River Kwai*.
- In one movie (*Kind Hearts and Coronets*) he played eight different roles: Ascoyne, Henry, Canon, Admiral, General, Lady Agatha(!), Lord, and Ethelbert d'Ascoyne!
- An anagram of his name is "genuine class."

Imagine...

Lords, ladies! Today's main jousting event is between Sir Harvey Pennyworth and Sir Obi-Wan Kenobi. Sir Harvey will use his weapon of choice, a long stick with a sharp point. Sir Obi is using a—what does this say?—a light saber? I guess that means a saber that isn't too heavy! A fair fight for these two knights? Who will win—and who'll say goodnight? Tell the story of the day medieval met high-tech.

Word of the day

knight A person of noble birth trained for arms and chivalry; from the Old English *cniht* (a man-at-arms).

Quote of the day

"Oh what can ail thee, knight at arms
Alone and palely loitering?
The sedge has withered from the lake
And no birds sing"

John Keats, *La belle dame sans merci*

Activity of the day

Jedi mind power

Put your legendary Jedi powers to the test in this game of bluff and mind control.

You'll need:
- a class
- a Jedi Knight
- a small object (such as a coin)

To play:
1. The class sits on the floor in a circle.
2. The Jedi Knight closes his/her eyes.
3. The coin is given to a random student.
4. The Jedi Knight opens his/her eyes and watches as the coin is passed around the circle, behind the players' backs.
5. After no more than a minute the Jedi Knight shouts "stop!" He/she can now give one of the following three mind-control commands:
   a) Levitate (palms are placed face down and the fingers fluttered).
   b) Brainwash (clenched fists are slowly raised to the forehead and back again).
   c) Surrender (clenched fists are slowly rotated to show the knuckles and then back again).
6. The Jedi Knight then attempts to identify the holder of the coin.

Decide on how players are swapped in and out of the game or if a scoring system is to be used.

Today in 1782

the first pair of commercial jeans were made by Sam Wetherhill of Philadelphia.

- The Levi Strauss Company received a patent in 1873 for riveting denim together.
- Levi is a Biblical name; he was the third son of Jacob.
- The word "jeans" came into common usage for denim "waist overalls" in the early 60s.

Word of the day

denim A cotton fabric woven with colored and white threads; from the French town *Nîmes*.

Quote of the day

"The wise man doesn't give the right answers, he poses the right questions."
Claude Levi-Strauss

Imagine...

Rivets certainly help make jeans stronger. But some kids still seem to be able to wreck any clothing they wear. So how could you make jeans even tougher? Bolts? Nails? Metal threads? Welding? Write about the invention for jeans super-toughness that you intend to patent.

Activity of the day

Mean jeans

Can you turn denim into jeans? In just six moves?

D	E	N	I	M	
					boy's name
					small corner grocery store
					small wooded hollows
					the repeated distribution of cards in a game
					the administrators in charge of a university
J	E	A	N	S	

Answer: DENIM, DENIS, DELIS, DELLS, DEALS, DEANS, JEANS

Today in 1915

acclaimed blues singer Muddy Waters was born.

- Muddy Water's real name was McKinley Morganfield, and he was born at Rolling Fork in Mississippi.
- The Rolling Stones named themselves after one of his songs.
- He was discovered by field collectors recording music for the U.S. Library of Congress's folksong archives.

Imagine...

Here's the first verse in a heartfelt blues song. Write some more verses in a similar style.

"I've opened up my schoolbag, and all my homework's gone.

Without a decent excuse, I think my lunchtime's also gone."

Word of the day

blues An informal term for a state of depression; from the expression *blue devils*.

Quote of the day

"Did you ever see an unhappy horse? Did you ever see bird that had the blues? One reason why birds and horses are not unhappy is because they are not trying to impress other birds and horses."
Dale Carnegie

Activity of the day

Colorful Language
Don't get the blues. Get the reds, greens, yellows, and pinks! Complete each of these sentences with a color.

1. Don't run so fast—you're going _____ in the face!
2. You coward! You're just _____!
3. Wait "til Josh sees my new bike; he"ll be _____ with envy.
4. Oh dear! You've gone _____ as a ghost!
5. We're healthy! We're in the _____!
6. The whole show lost money. The books are way in the _____.
7. Fetch an _____ from the fruit bowl, please.
8. He held his breath until he was _____ in the face.

Answers: Red, yellow, green, white, black, pink, red, orange, blue, indigo (Sorry!)

Today in 1614

Pocahontas married tobacco grower John Rolfe.

- Her real name was Matoaka, and she was born in Werowocomoco. She is thought to have had some 20 brothers and 10 sisters.
- Captain John Smith may have made up the story of how Pocahontas saved him from execution.
- Pocahontas visited England and met King James and Queen Anne. She died there, probably of smallpox.

Word of the day

Pocahontas The name means *playful one.*

Quote of the day

"Civilization says, `Nature belongs to man.' The Indian says, `No-man belongs to nature.'"

Grey Owl

Imagine...

"I thought the colonists' houses back in my homeland were strange with their walls of wood and openings where they look through from inside and see the land, but not be part of it. But here, in London, the sights I have seen! The people I have met! The places I have been! It's so hard to even begin to tell you about it, my brothers and sisters." Write as Pocohontas, and record her first impressions of this strange new place.

Activity of the day

Pocahontas word search

How many of these Pocohontas-related words can you find? When you're finished, the leftover letters spell out the name of John Smith's ship.

Disney
Gravesend
Jamestown
John Rolfe
John Smith
King James
Matoaka
Pocahontas
Powhatan
Queen Anne
Rebecca
Sarah
Tobacco
Virginia
Werowocomoco

```
W E R O W O C O M O C O G A
O N F S U S A C C E B E R I
C N H L A N P O W H A T A N
C A A J O H N S M I T H V I
A N R C O R Y E N S I D E G
B E A N K I N G J A M E S R
O E S A T N O H A C O P E I
T U J A M E S T O W N S N V
T Q M A T O A K A J A N D T
```

Today in 1944

a column titled "Frequently Asked Tax Questions" appeared in the *San Francisco Examiner*. Such columns appear in newspapers and magazines throughout March and the first two years of April every year in the U.S.

- Federal income taxes are filed April 15 in the U.S.
- The earliest instances of a general income tax were those levied in France in 1793, in Great Britain in 1799, in Switzerland in 1840, in Austria in 1849, and in Italy in 1864.
- PAYE is an acronym for "pay as you earn"; GST is "goods and services tax" (both used in the United Kingdom).
- A temporary income tax was first levied in the U.S. in 1862; the system became permanent with the adoption of the 16th amendment (1913) to the Constitution.

Imagine...

Not everybody is happy about paying income taxes. And those are not the only kinds of taxes we pay. Every time we buy something, we pay an additional amount in the form of a sales tax. Some have said that about the only thing left to tax is the air we breathe. Guess what! Tomorrow that tax becomes law. You have to figure out just how you are going to do it. Does everyone pay the same amount? Does someone who holds his breath have to pay? Do you first have to check to see whether a person is breathing? Write about your first week as the Air-We-Breathe Tax Collector.

Word of the day

tax A charge paid to the government, the amount paid often determined by income.

Quote of the day

"Income tax has made more liars out of American people than golf."
Will Rogers

Activity of the day

Taxing sums

When it comes to taxes, your sums have to add up! But can you work out these sums?

a) E = 6

```
  P A Y E
- G S T
---------
  L E S S
```

b) T = 6

```
  T A X
+ T A X
--------
D U T Y
```

c) A = 3

```
  W A G E
- T A X
---------
  T I N Y
```

Answers: a) 9326 - 715 = 8611; b) 634 + 634 = 1268; c) 6349 - 537 = 5812

Today in 1739

is World Health Day.

- On this day in 1948, the World Health Organization (WHO) was founded by the United Nations with the objective of providing for all people in the world the highest possible level of health.
- Every year, a new theme is selected for global awareness such as safe blood, aging, motherhood, infectious diseases, living healthy, etc.
- Past accomplishments of the WHO include the prevention of infectious disease, providing guidelines for healthier cities, and making medicines and vaccinations available to countries in need.

Word of the day

health State of complete physical, mental, and social well being and not merely the absence of disease or infirmity (as defined by who).

Quote of the day

In the case of scandal, as in that of robbery, the receiver is always thought as bad as the thief.
Fourth Earl of Chesterfield

Imagine...

You are in total control of the world's health situation. What are the things you will do to keep the world healthy? What will you do with the world's food supply? How will you go about providing medical care to the world?

Activity of the day

A Day of Health

Make a journal documenting your "health for the day." For a day, write down what you eat for breakfast, lunch, and dinner and snacks. Did you eat a balanced meal from the four basic food groups (cereal, milk, fruit and vegetable, protein)? Did you eat healthy snacks? What did you do for exercise? After reviewing your journal at the end of the day, is there anything you could do to make your future days healthier?

Date _____

Breakfast _____

_____

_____

_____

Dinner _____

_____

_____

_____

Lunch _____

_____

_____

_____

Snacks _____

_____

_____

_____

Today in 1873

oleomargarine (better known as margarine) was first patented.

- Margarine is almost pure white. It is dyed yellow to make it look more like butter.
- Some U.S. states used to require margarine to be colored pink—so people wouldn't be fooled into thinking it was really butter.
- Margarine must contain at least 80% oil and 15,000 IUs of vitamin A.

Imagine...

It's a good thing food advertisements don't have to explain exactly how different foods are made. After all, margarine's made from oil and tons of chemicals. Milk is squeezed out of some poor cow's udder and churned until it's fatty and frothy, and butter—yuck! Write an advertisement for a food that tells in detail how it's made; the messier and yuckier the better!

Word of the day

oleomargarine A butter substitute; from the Greek word *margarites* (pearl) and the Latin *oleum* (oil).

Quote of the day

"The King asked
The Queen, and
The Queen asked
The Dairymaid
'Could we have some butter for
The Royal slice of bread?' "

A. A. Milne (*The King's Breakfast*)

Activity of the day

Butter Gets Better?

Butter certainly crops up in all manner of places, recipes, and words—so read the clues and work out these buttery words!

BUTTER+			
	I		a special TV show honoring a person
	EN		a person with brown hair
	SS		a stone support for a building
	CH		an old-fashioned boy's name
	NO		to button again
	JO	=	a type of engine
	EIQ		a charcoal fuel block
	CPU		a flower
	GIL		someone who litters
	GIJ		a dance from the '50s
	CGSY		a famous battle of the American Civil War

Answers: tribute, brunette, buttress, Cuthbert, rebutton, turbo-jet, briquette, buttercup, litterbug, jitterbug, Gettysburg

Today in 1770

James Cook discovered Stingray Harbour.

- It was renamed Botany Bay after the botanical specimens found there by Cook's naturalist, Sir Joseph Banks.

- The banksia bush is named after Sir Joseph.

- Bare Island, at the entrance to the Bay, was fortified with a gun battery in 1881. It was named after Cook described it as a "small, bare island."

Word of the day

botany The study of plants. from the Greek *botanikos* (of herbs).

Quote of the day

Singing too-ral-aye, ool-ral-aye-addity,
And we're bound for Botany Bay.
Old Australian folk song

Imagine...

Hmmm. So if Captain Cook had been the botanist, we'd have *cooksias* (instead of *banksias*). Look around your class. Name five plants after your friends. Make the names sound really scientific (Eucalyptus Joannasia Smithiensis). Describe the plants, using descriptions of your friends. (Tall and stringy looking, a little crooked.)

Activity of the day

Plant puzzle

Here are a few of the plants that Banks discovered. Complete the three-letter words going DOWN to find the answers going ACROSS.

1.

A	F	A	I	A	F
E	B	E	S	L	E

2.

E	F	A	S	U	A	F
B	X	T	I	E	D	R

3.

F	A	H	I	F	J
T	E	M	E	B	W

4.

F	D	A	L	E	R	S	I	H	A
W	G	T	P	F	E	Y	S	M	K

Answers: 1. wattle 2. banksia 3. acacia 4. eucalyptus

Today in 1849

the safety pin was first patented.

- The inventor, Walter Hunt of New York, took just three hours to come up with the design; he was in a hurry to pay back $15 that he owed.

- He later sold all rights to the pin for $480.

- Hunt also invented a sewing machine but didn't patent it because he thought it would cause unemployment.

Word of the day

pin A small pointed piece of metal used to support, fasten, or attach things; from the Latin *pinna* (a quill or feather).

Imagine...

You look out the window of the skyscraper. From the top floor you can't hear the sirens and noise, but you can see the huge disaster that's overtaken the entire city. You shake your head. All of this could have been averted if only someone had had a safety pin at the right time... Describe the disaster and how a safety pin could have saved the city.

Quote of the day

"Sir, you are like a pin, but without either its head or its point."
Douglas Jerrold

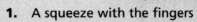

Activity of the day

Pin the Tail on the Words

You'll need to be sharp to work out all these clues—although every answer does begin with a pin.

1. A squeeze with the fingers
2. A colour
3. An apron
4. Old liquid measurement
5. An arcade game
6. Alternative name for table tennis
7. A lofty peak
8. Large sweet tropical fruit
9. To locate exactly
10. A small cushion into which pins are stuck

Answers: pinch, pink, pinny, pint, pinball, ping-pong, pinnacle, pineapple, pinpoint, pin-cushion

Today in 1863

the book *33,530 Ways of Spelling the Word Scissors* was sold.

- The book contained 400 pages but only one word.
- Leonardo Da Vinci invented a type of scissors in the late 1400s.
- Reel lawn mowers (invented in 1830) cut grass in a similar way to scissors, unlike rotary mowers that rip or shatter grass.

Word
of the day

scissor A cutting implement with two crossed blades; from the Latin *cisorium* (cutting instrument).

Imagine...

Item: One pair of scissors, magical. *Scenario*: You fan-fold a long piece of (non-magical) paper and cut out a series of little people all holding hands. *Result*: They come to life. *Question*: What will you cut out now? Write about what you choose to cut out and what happens next.

Quote
of the day

The door flew open; in he ran, the great, long, red-legged scissor-man. Snip! Snap! Snip! they go so fast, that both his thumbs are off at last!

Heinrich Hoffmann

Activity
of the day

Paper, Rock, and Scissors

The paper, rock, and scissors (PRS) game was originally called "mammoth hide, rock, spear" by its stone-age inventors. To play:

1. Face your opponent.
2. Raise your right hands to shoulder height.
3. After a count of three, throw down your hand in one of the following:
   a. Paper (flat palm held vertical)
   b. Rock (clenched fist)
   c. Scissors (index and middle finger held out from fist in scissors shape)

4. The winner is determined by:
   a. Paper COVERS Rock (and wins)
   b. Rock BLUNTS Scissors (and wins)
   c. Scissors CUT Paper (and wins)
5. If both players "throw' the same, a draw is counted.

Play the game a few times then:

1. Draw up a chart showing the different combination of "throws."
2. Invent a fourth shape (one common one is "dynamite," and decide how this new shape wins/loses against the others.
3. Adapt the game for three competitors.

scissors

paper

rock

Today in 1961

Yuri Alekseivich Gagarin became the first human ever to fly in space.

- He orbited Earth once in a flight lasting 89 minutes.

- The rocket, *Vostok 1*, was launched from Kazakhstan and landed 450 miles (720 km) from Moscow.

- The controls on board the space ship were locked—to prevent the cosmonaut from messing it up!

- Two years later Valentina Tereshkova became the first woman in space aboard *Vostok 5*. She orbited the Earth 81 times.

Word of the day

Vostok The first manned Soviet space craft; *Vostok* means "easterly direction."

Imagine...

"Comrade Gagarin! Do you have a few moments to answer some questions for the readers of the Moscow Times? You do? Very good!" What would people want to know about the first flight in space? How would they be answered? Write the interview between the reporter and the cosmonaut.

Quote of the day

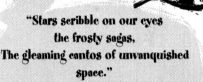

"Stars scribble on our eyes
the frosty sagas,
The gleaming cantos of unvanquished
space."

Hart Crane (*Cape Hatteras*)

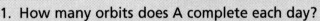

Activity of the day

Orbital Math

Two spacecraft (A and B) are orbiting the earth. They are both traveling at the same speed but A's orbit takes 90 minutes to complete while B's takes 180 minutes.

1. How many orbits does A complete each day?
2. How many orbits does B complete?
3. Which satellite is in the higher orbit?
4. Both pass over New York City together at 9 A.M. When will they pass over next?
5. Spacecraft A is over Australia 45 minutes later. Is it day or night?
6. How often during the day are the two spacecraft over the same spot?
7. A geosynchronous satellite travels at the same speed as the earth rotates. Why is it so special?
8. Name the satellite that orbits the sun once every 365 days.

Answers: 1) 16 2) 8 3) B: the orbit takes longer, must be higher 4) A: 10.30 A.M., B: 12 noon 5) night—it's on the opposite side of the world 6) 8 times a day 7) they stay over the same spot 8) the Earth

Today in 1771

Richard Trevithick, inventor of the steam locomotive, was born in Cornwall, England.

- He was the first person to adapt a steam engine to run on tracks.
- The first locomotive was called a "horseless carriage."
- His first "passenger train" ran on Christmas Eve of 1801.

Word of the day

steam The gas that boiling water becomes; from the Dutch *stoom* (steam).

Imagine...

Imagine that the phrase "horseless carriage" had been retained instead of the word train or railway. Write a report about trains, train stations, train services or railways; just substitute "horseless carriage" every time. (Include some references to real horses—just to confuse things even more.)

Quote of the day

"I see no reason to suppose that these machines will ever force themselves into general use."
The Duke of Wellington (talking about steam engines)

Activity of the day

Train of Thought

Here's a classic—can the black train pass the white?

- The locomotives can uncouple and re-couple their carriages. They can move forward or in reverse.
- Carriages can be coupled to the front or back of each locomotive.
- The siding can hold one locomotive (B1 or W1) and one carriage (B2, B3, W2, or W3)

Suggestion: Use blocks to represent the trains. Draw the tracks on paper.

Answers:

1. W1 backs W2 and W3 to the left.
2. B3 is uncoupled.
3. B1 pulls B2 past the siding then backs in.
4. W1 (pulling W2 and W3) passes the siding.
5. B1 & B2 pulls out of the siding to the far left.
6. W1 (pushing W3 and W2) reverses left past the siding.
7. W3 and W2 are uncoupled. W1 moves right and couples B3.
8. W1 and B3 reverse left then back into the siding.
9. W1 leaves B3 in the siding, reverses left and couples up W3 and W2.
10. W1, W2 and W3 exit right.
11. B1 reverses B2 into the siding, couples up B3, and B1, B2 and B3 exit left.

Today in 1912

Frederick Rodman Law, the first movie stuntman, jumped off the Brooklyn Bridge.

- Other feats included jumping off the arm of the Statue of Liberty, from a skyscraper, and from a moving plane.

- He was killed jumping over a puddle—into a passing car.

- Stuntmen are now paid huge salaries for their escapades. Jumping off a 1,100 foot (335 m) tower earned stuntman Dar Robinson $100,000 in 1979.

Imagine...

Another James Bond movie, another action-packed opening sequence. Write a screenplay for the opening ten minutes, filled with as many stunts as you can cram in. Remember, it's a James Bond movie, so make the stunts far-fetched, unbelievable— and exciting!

Word
of the day

feat An act of skill or endurance; from the Latin *facere* (to make or do).

Quote
of the day

"Do not judge this movement kindly. It is not just another amusing stunt."
Sir Herbert Read (opening a surrealist art exhibition in 1936)

Activity
of the day

Stunt Puzzle

In the latest Jim Band film, the hero is forced to escape from a maze. While escaping, Jim Band (or at least his stuntdouble) must:
- Wrestle a lion
- Escape from ropes
- Jump from a building (it's a big maze)
- Carry a bomb
- Swim shark-infested water
- Swing beneath a bridge
- Jump a double-decker bus (ok, it's a really BIG maze!)

He must enter via the north entrance; and in completing all these stunts, he must cover every path but not travel the same path twice.
So:
1. Where does the stunt double exit?

2. In what order are the stunts done in?

Answers: 1) South entrance; 2) Bridge, ropes, lion, bomb, building, bus, water OR Water, down the right-hand side then up to rope, lion, bridge, building, bomb, bus.

Today in 1747

Dr Samuel Johnson began work on his *Dictionary of the English Language*.

- It took him and his *amanuenses* eight-and-a-half years to write the 40,000 definitions.
- It was the first English dictionary to attempt to standardize spellings.
- The first English dictionary dates back to 1440. It contained Latin words and their English meanings.
- Dictionaries have been found dating back to 700 B.C.

Word of the day

amanuensis A person employed to write from dictation; from the Latin *manu* (slave with writing duties) and *ensis* (to belong to).

Quote of the day

To make dictionaries is dull work.
Samuel Johnson

Imagine...

Writing dictionary entries is tricky even when you know what the words mean. Imagine how much harder it would be if you didn't. Try writing entries for these words (they're all real—just very uncommon!) that all begin with sa: saburration, salification, salutiferous, saponifiable, sacculation.

Activity of the day

Define that word!

People of Samuel Johnson's time would have recognized many of the words underlined in the story below. Use the story to match them to their meanings.

The **malefactor** ran down the street away from the smashed window. His **bluchers** tapped loudly on the cobblestones until he paused at a tavern door. He tossed the still-smoking **flambeau** into an alley and entered. Sitting at the only vacant **gueridon,** he ordered a **jigger** of spirits. At the bar, tea was boiling in a **samovar**; he slipped the stolen parchment behind a painting, the **passe-partout** keeping it from falling. Then the local watch entered, swords drawn and **bucklers** fastened.

1. someone who has been legally convicted of a crime
2. armor carried on the arm to intercept blows
3. a small round table
4. a small glass adequate to hold a single swallow of whiskey
5. high shoe with laces over the tongue
6. a metal urn with a spigot at the base; used in Russia to boil water for tea
7. a flaming torch
8. a mounting for a picture using gummed tape

Answers: 1) malefactor 2) buckler 3) gueridon 4) jigger 5) blucher 6) samovar 7) flambeau 8) passe-partout

Today in 1889

silent movie star Charles Chaplin was born in South London.

- Chaplin's "little tramp" character first appeared on screen in 1914 in the movie *Kid Auto Races in Venice*.

- Chaplin helped establish the United Artists Corporation.

- Chaplin's film *The Great Dictator* attacked the ideas and practices of Adolf Hitler and the Nazis. Although he banned the film, Hitler apparently watched it twice!

Word of the day

tramp A beggar who wanders from place to place; from the Middle Low German *trampen* (to stamp).

Imagine...

Chaplin's character often got the better of a bully. Write a screenplay for Chaplin involving: the clumsy little tramp as a car salesman, a bullying owner, and a doddery old man wanting to trade in his car (which is falling apart).

Quote of the day

"Ignorance is an evil weed, which dictators may cultivate among their dupes, but which no democracy can afford among its citizens."
William Henry Beveridge

Activity of the day

Spot the silhouette

Can you identify these six silhouettes? One of them is Chaplin's "Little Tramp" character.

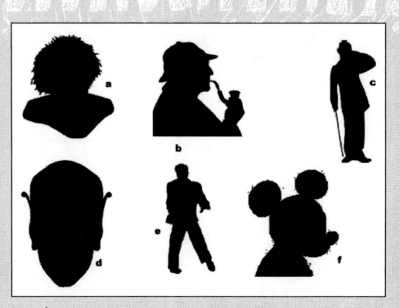

Answers: a) Albert Einstein; b) Sherlock Holmes; c) Charlie Chaplin; d) Mr Spock; e) Elvis; f) Mickey Mouse

Today in 1964

the Ford Mustang was introduced to the public at the New York World's Fair.

- Known as "pony" cars, the car came with a long list of options to personalize it and a sticker price of $2,368.
- The Mustang started a wave of personal cars with sporty characteristics. The Mustang set an all-time first year sales record of 680,992 automobiles.
- Today, the early Mustangs (1964-1973, but especially the 1964 model) are collectors' items.
- The new Mustangs are still popular.

Word
of the day

mustang A small wild horse of the South Western plains of the United States; from the Spanish *mesteno* (belonging to the graziers, wild).

Quote
of the day

"For me, the excitement of the automobile business is to do something different, to pioneer a new concept, and win. . . . It would be a small personal type of car that the average American could afford and enjoy."

Lee Iacocca, (then) chairman, Chrysler Corporation

Imagine...

Wow! You finally got that Mustang you've been eyeing at the auto center. But your parents bought you the "stripped down" version and you have to supply the money for all the personal touches to make it your own. Right now you pretty much have a car body, seats, and engine. You've been working so money is not really a problem. What will you do to jazz up this car to your liking? Make a detailed plan and tell why you want certain features added on to your dream car.

Activity
of the day

License Plate Lingo
Can you read these personalized license plates? Then, try and make up a few of your own.

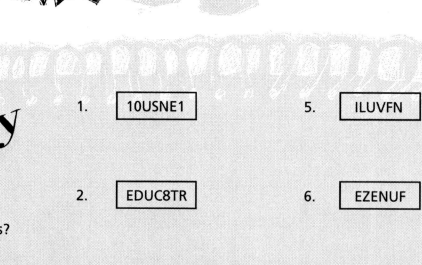

1.	10USNE1	5.	ILUVFN
2.	EDUC8TR	6.	EZENUF
3.	NVRAGN	7.	YY4EVR
4.	BZZDAY	8.	GR8LDY

Today in 1966

the film of the musical of the book *The Sound of Music* won its Oscar.

- The film, based on the musical by Rodgers and Hammerstein, made over $60 million in its first year.
- In the opening film sequence, the birch trees were only planted two days before filming, and the stream was dug by hand and filled with water.
- Julie Andrews played Maria, the governess who eventually married Captain Von Trapp. The real Maria died in 1987 after 30 years as a missionary in New Guinea.

Word of the day

musical A play or film with action, dialogue, singing, and dancing; from the Greek *mousike* (art of the Muses).

Imagine...

Create a poster advertising a new musical about the story of your life. You'll need a title and a selection of hit songs (either original or borrowed), a list of the stars appearing (who will play you?), appearance dates, and ticket prices.

Quote of the day

"Sometimes I'm so sweet even I can't stand it."
Julie Andrews

Activity of the day

Sound of Music Word Search

Find these Sound of Music characters, events, and places in the word search below. The leftover letters spell out the title of a famous song.

```
C A P T A I N V O N T R A P P C L I S
L A V I T S E F G R U B Z L A S M B S
E I V E R N S S E B B A R E H T O M E
B R I G I T T A U S T R I A Y M O L N
U A N P T A I D R O L Y A G E F L O R
N M L S E I L W O H S T E P P U P U E
B A R O N E S S S C H R A E D E R I V
M A X D E T W E I L E R L T E R G S O
K U R T H C I R D E I R F M A R T A G
```

Alpine	Friedrich	Liesl	Mother Abbess
Austria	Gaylord	Louisa	puppet show
Baroness Schraeder	governess	Maria	Rolfe
Brigitta	Gretl	Marta	Salzburg Festival
Captain Von Trapp	Kurt	Max Detweiler	

Today

is Garlic Day!

- Garlic is a member of the lily family.
- Garlic is well-known for its medicinal effects. It is stronger than some antibiotics, can help lower cholesterol, and is thought to lower the incidence of some cancers.
- In Gary, Indiana, it's against the law to eat garlic and go to the movies!
- Legendary Greek hero Odysseus used garlic to keep the sorceress Circe from turning him into a pig.

Word of the day

garlic An aromatic bulb used as seasoning; from the old English *garleac gar* (spear) + *leac* (leek).

Quote of the day

What garlic is to salad, insanity is to art.
Augustus Saint-Gaudens

Imagine...

It said "Super-Garlic" on the box. It said it was "EXTREMELY STRONG." It said "only eat in small amounts." But no, you ignored the warnings. You ate half the packet, and now you've got the most revolting, stinking, malodorous (that's REALLY bad!) breath ever. And it doesn't seem to be fading. Write a story of what happens next.

Activity of the day

Let's Reflect

As everyone knows, garlic is great for keeping vampires away. Everyone also knows that vampires have no reflections in mirrors. But these six vampires all claim to have taken a photograph of themselves holding their name up to a mirror. We're not calling the other vampires liars, but only one photograph is definitely genuine. Which one, and why?

TIVIT

MAHAM

OTTO

TUTTUT

MIYIM

MONIT

Answers: Tinom. All the other vampires' names are symmetrical and don't reverse in a mirror.

Today in 1977

an ancient Anglo-Saxon sword was sold in the Christie's auction house for over $20,000.

- The sword was found in a stream by a 10-year-old boy.
- Over $1.6 million was paid for the Duke of Windsor's sword at an auction in 1987.
- Nearly $400 million worth of silver bars has been recovered from a Spanish treasure ship that sank in 1622 near Florida in the US.

Imagine...

You don't normally take that shortcut behind the abandoned church, but you were in a hurry today. You don't normally open doors to mausoleums in graveyards, but the light glowing under the door was—well, unusual. You don't normally pull swords out of stones—but then you don't normally find swords sitting in stones . . . . Describe the mausoleum, the sword, and the consequences of removing it.

Word of the day

trove Hidden treasure of unknown ownership; from the French *trover* (to find).

Quote of the day

"Whoso pulleth out this sword of this stone and anvil is rightwise King born of all England. "

Sir Thomas Malory

Activity of the day

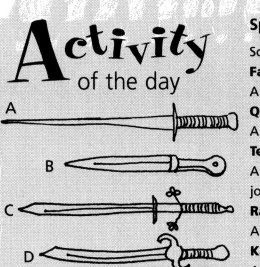

A

B

C

D

E

F

Spot the sword

So, how sharp are you? Match these sword definitions to their pictures:

Falchion:
A short, broad, slightly convex medieval sword with a sharp point.

Qama:
A Russian short sword with no hilt.

Templar Sword:
A big, two-handed sword tapered for thrusting into the seams and joints of plate armor.

Rapier:
A straight sword with a narrow blade and two edges.

Katana:
A curved Oriental sword

Claymore:
A Scottish broadsword with triangular blade guards and downward sloping, brass hand guards.

Answers: a) Templar Sword, b) Qama, c) Claymore, d) Falchion, e) Rapier, f) Katana

Today in 753 BC

(or so tradition says), the city of Rome was founded.

- Rome is the capital city of Italy. It is located on the River Tiber.

- The city was founded, according to legend, by Romulus and Remus, the twin sons of the god of Mars.

- The city was (again, according to legend) first populated by runaway slaves and murderers!

Word of the day

city An incorporated administrative district established by state charter; from the Latin *civis* (citizen).

Quote of the day

If you are in Rome, live in the Roman fashion; if you are elsewhere, live as they do there.
Saint Ambrose

Imagine...

As the saying goes, "All roads lead to Rome." But what if they did? Where would the roads leaving Rome lead? Would walking backwards take you out of Rome? What would we all do in Rome? Chisel, engrave (or just write!) about Roman (or roamin') roads. Write about it!

Activity of the day

All Roads Lead to Rome

Here are eight roads leading to Rome. The names are scrambled but you know that each one contains the letters "R-O-M-E." Use the clues to identify each road.

1. Old-fashioned women's underpants.
2. Examined and noted similarities and differences.
3. A person who creates original music.
4. Someone who pays for goods or services.
5. A person who employs people.
6. Very large.
7. The mathematics of points, lines, curves and surfaces.
8. A tropical plant often found in a swamp.

Answers: 1. Bloomers Rd. 2. Compared Rd. 3. Composer Rd. 4. Customer Rd. 5. Employer Rd. 6. Enormous Rd. 7. Geometry Rd. 8. Mangrove Rd.

Today in 1918

Robert Wadlow was born.

- At a height of 8 ft. 11 in. (272 cm), he was one of the tallest people ever to have lived.
- His shoes were 19 in. (47 cm) long.
- Goliath (of Biblical David and Goliath fame) was reputed to have been 6 cubits and 1 span in height (approximately 9.5 ft. [290 cm]).

Imagine...

Your principal always wanted your class to reach new heights, although she probably meant academic heights, not physical ones. Still, it happened. Those growth spurts spurted and every student in your class is over seven feet tall! What will you do now? Start a basketball team? Hire yourselves out as ceiling painters? Write a newsletter article about it all.

Word of the day

giant An abnormally tall person; from the Latin *gigant* (giant).

Quote of the day

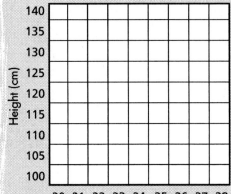

"He was a six-and-a-half-foot-tall scowl."
Igor Stravinsky (referring to pianist Rachmaninov)

Activity of the day

The Long and the Short of It

Robert Wadlow had quite a large shoe; then again he was a quite a large man!

Are people's foot lengths related to their height? If you knew a person's height, could you work out his or her foot length? If you knew a person's foot length, could you work out his or her height?

To find out, you'll need some sample data from your class.

1. Select ten students. They should have a good range of heights, although not necessarily the tallest or shortest.
2. Measure and record each student's height and foot length.
3. Draw up a chart like the one shown. You may need to adjust the units to fit your data.
4. Mark student height against foot length.
5. Examine your graph. Is there a pattern? If so, what?
6. Now see if you can use your chart to predict a person's height from his or her foot length and vice versa.

Height (cm): 140, 135, 130, 125, 120, 115, 110, 105, 100

Foot length (cm): 20 21 22 23 24 25 26 27 28

Today in 1616

the great English dramatist William Shakespeare died.

- He was born in Stratford-upon-Avon in 1564 during the reign of Queen Elizabeth I.
- He wrote over 32 plays and hundreds of sonnets and poems.
- He was named "Briton of the Millennium" in January of 1999.

Word of the day

sonnet A poem with 14 lines and a fixed rhyme pattern; from the Italian *sonetto* (sound).

Quote of the day

"Each change of many-colored life he drew,
Exhausted worlds, and then imagined new."

Samuel Johnson (on Shakespeare)

Imagine...

An old chest in a dusty attic . . . an envelope closed with a wax seal . . . a letter—from Romeo to Juliet—full of thees and thous and other fine sentiments. What does Romeo say? Is the real Romeo like the one in all the stories? Write a letter (on parchment!) using old-fashioned handwriting. Seal it with candle wax.

Activity of the day

The Light Globe Actors Guild was just about to start their new season—nine great Shakespearean plays in a row. Unfortunately, the publicity manager tripped and dropped the box of title words. He's sorted them into alphabetical order. Now, can you sort them into their titles? (Hint: One title is already in order!)

A, About, Ado, and Antony, Cleopatra, Dream, Hamlet, Juliet, King, Lear, Macbeth, Merchant, Midsummer, Much, Night's, Nothing, of (2), Romeo, Shrew, Taming, The Venice

Answers: 1. Antony and Cleopatra; 2. Hamlet; 3. King Lear; 4. Macbeth; 5. The Merchant of Venice; 6. A Midsummer Night's Dream; 7. Much Ado About Nothing; 8. Romeo and Juliet; 9. The Taming of the Shrew

Today in 1815

Anthony Trollope, inventor of the "pillar box" (mailbox), was born.

- Trollope was also a post office inspector and part-time romantic novelist.
- His idea was based on a design dating back to 1690.
- "Pillar-box red" is the original color the boxes were painted.

Imagine...

You're loaded down with what feel like a ton of party invitations that your parents want you to mail. So when the mailbox cries out, "Help! Help! Let me out!" it's not surprising you drop the stack. What is surprising is who's in the box—and why. Write what happens next.

Word of the day

pillar A vertical structure used to support a roof; from the Latin *pila* (pillar).

Quote of the day

"Very sorry can't come. Lie follows by post."
Lord Charles Beresford (telegraphed message to the Prince of Wales, on being asked to dine at the last minute)

Activity of the day

Mail Mix-up

Andre, Ben, Cindy, and Daphne's mail is in the mailbox. There's (not necessarily in order) a parcel, a postcard, a bill, and a letter. They've been sent by (also not necessarily in order) a mom, a dad, a baker, and an aunt. Three items have stamps: flowers, pets, and a building. One item has no stamp. Use the information below to decide who got what from which sender and with what stamp.

1. Andre's mail wasn't a postcard, didn't come from his mom, and had no stamp.
2. Cindy passed on the parcel with the flower stamp to the correct person.
3. One person was jealous because she only got a postcard while her sister got a parcel.
4. The dad put the wrong child's name on his mail.
5. One person's mail, sender, and stamp were alliterative with that person's name!

Answers: Andre, letter, aunt, no stamp; Ben, bill, baker, building; Cindy, postcard, mom, pets; Daphne, parcel, dad, flowers

Today in 1507

the name *America* was first used.

- Cartographer Martin Walseemuller took the name from Amerigo Vespucius, an Italian explorer who had claimed to reach North America in 1497.

- Geradus Mercator called all of the Western Hemisphere "The Americas" in 1538.

- The Americas were also called the "New World."

Word of the day

cartographer A map maker; from the French *carte* (map or card).

Quote of the day

"I called the New World into existence, to redress the balance of the Old."
George Canning

Imagine...

Early maps were often guesses at what lay beyond explored land. Imagine that only the land around your house has been explored. Create a map with your house at the center. Then fill the surrounding area with other points of interest. Would you put in mountains, monsters, caves, rivers, volcanoes?

Activity of the day

Only in America
How many words of three letters or more can you make from the word AMERICA?

Answers: Here are 25 to start you off... ace, aim, air, arc, are, car, ear, era, ice, ram, rim, acme, acre, area, aria, came, care, mare, mice, race, rice, cream, crime, camera

Today in 1977

the Studio 54 disco opened in New York.

- The club was famous for the celebrities and stars who visited, and for whom it did (and didn't) allow in. Two ladies arrived one Halloween riding a horse. The horse was let in but the women weren't!

- The club was investigated by the IRS in 1980 for tax evasion and eventually closed down.

Imagine...

Your new disco, Studio 55, opens tonight. Draw up a guest list of who you'd like to be there. What bands will play at the opening? Describe your club's decor theme and draw a floor plan showing the dance floors, tables, stages, and restaurant area.

Word of the day

discotheque A dance hall for dancing to recorded popular music; from the French *discotheque* (record-library).

Quote of the day

"Darling, it was faaaabulous!"
Lillian Carter (U.S. President Jimmy Carter's mother, after visiting the Studio)

Activity of the day

Dance diagrams

You might not find people waltzing in a disco, but it's certainly danced in lots of other places! Read the instructions while you follow the diagram.

1. Left foot forward
2. Right foot to side
3. Left foot up to right foot
4. Right foot forward
6. Left foot to side
7. Right foot up to left foot

Now you're an expert on the waltz, write the instructions for the tango by following the diagram. Use the dance diagrams and try the steps yourself. Invent a new dance. Cut out black and white "shoes' and construct a life-size diagram of your dance!

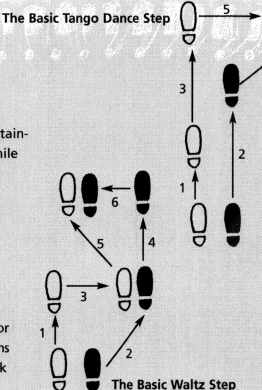

The Basic Tango Dance Step

The Basic Waltz Step

Answers: Here's one way to explain it ...;
1. Left foot forward; 2. Right foot forward;
3. Left foot forward; 4. Right foot swings to side;
5. Left foot closes to right foot

Today in 1965

R. C. Duncan patented the Pampers disposable diaper.

- Pampers disposable diapers were test-marketed successfully in 1966 in Sacramento by Procter & Gamble. The six-cent pad began a revolution in baby diapering.

- The Huggies disposable diaper, introduced by Kimberly-Clark in 1978, had an hourglass shape and elastic fit that challenged Procter & Gamble's Pampers.

- The Dy-Dee-Doll that sucked water from a bottle and wet its diaper was introduced by New York's Effanbee Doll Co. in 1933 after acquiring the patent rights from inventor Marie Wittman.

Word of the day

diaper Folded cloth worn by babies; from the Greek *diaspros*: *dia* (as) + *aspros* (white).

Imagine...

You have decided that you are going to begin to earn money by babysitting. There are several babies in your neighborhood, and their mothers are always looking for someone reliable to stay with them. You're sitting on a gold mine. One way you can convince the mothers of those babies that you are trustworthy and responsible is by preparing for the job. Besides learning how to change a diaper, what are some other things to think about and to be ready for? Make a list and have a copy to show each prospective employer

Quote of the day

"A loud noise at one end and no sense of responsibility at the other."
Ronald Knox (definition of a baby)

Activity of the day

Diaper Puzzle

Gemma and Georgia are twin baby girls. Since they're potty-trained, they wear diapers only at night. Their mother has the diapers professionally washed and ironed at the Golden Stork Diaper Service. The van picks up the soiled diapers early on Thursday morning—before the twins are awake—and delivers the clean ones.

If the girls have clean diapers every night, what is the smallest number of diapers their mother could buy?

Answers: 30 diapers:
Each girl needs 7 diapers for the week
The van must therefore pick up 14 and drop off 14 for the next week. (28)
Since the girls are still asleep there's also the pair of diapers that they're wearing. (total 30)

Today in 1931

Norbet Tossel of Amsterdam started sneezing continuously.

- He stopped on May 2nd, over 3,000 sneezes later.
- Donna Griffiths sneezed for over 900 days, starting on January 13, 1981.
- Sneezes can propel "droplets" at over 99 mph (160 km/h).

Word
of the day

tissue Soft paper used for wiping and cleaning; from the Old French *tissu* (rich material).

Imagine...

Alison Downs, sneezed and sneezed, a dreadful, sneezy sound.

Alison Downs sneezed so much she finally sneezed her head right round.

Then what happened? Finish the poem, draw a picture, or write the rest of the story.

Quote
of the day

There was an old person of Slough,
Who danced at the end of a bough;
But they said, "If you sneeze,
You might damage the trees,
You imprudent old person of Slough.'

Edward Lear

Activity
of the day

1. How many days did Norbet sneeze?
2. What was his SPD (sneezes per day) rate?
3. If Donna's SPD rate was the same as Norbet's, how many times didshe sneeze in her 970 days?
4. Donna's SPD rate was actually much higher. It's claimed she actually sneezed one million times in the first 365 days. What would this make her SPD rate?
5. If this rate was constant, how many times did she sneeze in the 970 days?
6. Assuming Donna slept for 8 hours a day, and didn't sneeze while she was asleep, what would her SPH (sneezes per hour) rate be?
7. And her SPM (sneezes per minute)?
8. Fortunately, these days you can get ESI (excessive sneezing insurance) that pays $0.23 per sneeze. How much would Norbet have made?
9. How much would Donna have made?
10. How many sneezes would she need to make a million dollars?

Answers: 1. 5 days
2. 3,000/5= 600 SPD
3. 900 × 600 = 582,000
4. 1,000,000/365 = 2,739 SPD (rounded down)
5. 970 × 2,739 = 2,656,830
6. 2740/16 = 171 SPH (rounded down)
7. 171/60 = 3 SPM (rounded up)
8. 3,000 × $0.23 = $690
9. 2,656,830 × $0.23 = $611,071.90
10. $1,000,000/$0.23 = 4,347,826 sneezes!

Today in 1842

the zipper (featuring two rows of interlocking hooks) was first patented.

- The first practical zipper was patented in 1893. It was called a "clasp locker."
- A later version had the improved name of "hookless fastener."
- The word "zipper" was first used by the B. F. Goodrich Company in 1923 to describe the fastening system on its rubber boots.
- In 1985, a 690-yard. (630-m) long zip fastener was manufactured. It had nearly 120,000 "teeth."

Word of the day

hook A bent device used to suspend, hold, or pull something; from the Dutch *hoek* (corner).

Quote of the day

"Sweet is every sound,
Sweeter thy voice, but every sound
is sweet . . . "
Alfred, Lord Tennyson

Imagine...

Describe getting dressed and include as many sounds as you can. You might include the sound of pulling a jumper on, tying shoelaces, or the sound of buttons being done up.

Activity of the day

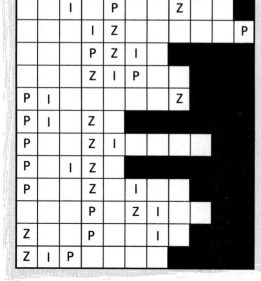

Zip It Up!
Put some zip in your day—and your vocabulary. All the following words have a "zip" in them somewhere. Use the clues to work out the whole word.

1. A type of monkey.
2. Conduct as a citizen.
3. A city in east central Germany.
4. A sweet made with almond paste.
5. Spectacles clipped to the nose by a spring.
6. Italian open pie.
7. Method of playing a stringed instrument by plucking.
8. Award for victory in a contest.
9. A mystery, or bewildering.
10. A quadrilateral with only one pair of opposite sides parallel.
11. A large dirigible balloon.
12. An American postal code.

Answers: 1. chimpanzee 2. citizenship 3. Leipzig 4. marzipan 5. pince-nez 6. pizza 7. pizzicato 8. prize 9. puzzling 10. trapezium 11. zeppelin 12. Zip Code

Today in 1900

John Luther "Casey" Jones died attempting to slow down his speeding locomotive.

- His passenger express collided with a freight train and inspired the popular "Casey Jones" song.
- He forced his fireman to jump from the train while he stayed behind.
- Neither Casey's widow or the original composer received any royalties from the song.

Word of the day

freight Goods carried by a large vehicle; from the Middle English *"fraught"* (to load with cargo).

Imagine...

Casey Jones found himself (and his train) on collision course with a passenger train just around the bend. How might disaster have been averted? Super-heroes? Luck? A long-forgotten, unused stretch of track? Rewrite the story so it ends happily.

Quote of the day

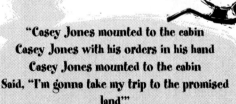

"Casey Jones mounted to the cabin
Casey Jones with his orders in his hand
Casey Jones mounted to the cabin
Said, "I'm gonna take my trip to the promised land'"

Wallace Saunders

Activity of the day

Train of Thought

Arrrgh! Disaster is imminent! Locomotive driver Arnie Watson is walking slowly back to the railroad depot along the Spring Gully railroad track. Deaf as a post, he can't hear the Spring Gully Express roaring up directly behind him. He's wearing dark clothing and isn't carrying a lantern. The express has turned its lights off and there's no moon or stars. There are no lights in this darkly wooded area yet the Express driver still manages to screech to a halt only yards from Arnie's back. How?

Answers: It was daylight and the Express driver could see him.

Today in 1973

Canadian cat Gros Minou fell out a twenty-story apartment building. It survived!

- In 1984, Hamlet the cat was caught after traveling over 60,000 miles (965,000 km) on board a plane.

- Australian tabby-cat, Himmy, is the fattest cat recorded; he weighed nearly 53 lbs. (24 kg) and was carried around in a wheelbarrow!

- One lucky feline, "Blackie," was left $15 million by his owner, Ben Rea.

Word
of the day

feline Of or relating to cats; from the Latin *felinus* (cat).

Quote
of the day

"Alfred de Musset
Used to call his cat Pusset.
His accent was affected.
That was only to be expected. "
Maurice Evan Hare

Imagine...

Gros Minou obviously used up one of his nine catlives falling out that building! Write a poem, news report, or story about how he lost the next seven (or eight, if you want a sad ending.)

Activity
of the day

Cats Word Search

Andrew Lloyd Webber's musical *Cats* is based on fourteen poems in T. S. Eliot's *Old Possum's Book of Practical Cats*. Find all these cats in the word search. The leftover letters tell you where Jellicle cats go.

Alonzo Asparagus	Jellylorum	Rumpleteazer
Bombalurina	Jennanydots	Rumpus Cat
Bustopher Jones	Macavity	Sillabub
Cassandra	Mistoffolees	Skimbleshanks
Coricopat	Mungojerrie	Tantomile
Demeter	Munkustrap	Tumblebrutus
Griddlebone	Old Deuteronomy	Victoria
Grizabella	Pouncival	
Growltiger	Rum Tum Tugger	

```
U P R E Z A E T E L P M U R T J O
A T H E H E L A V I C N U O P E A
S E E L O F F O T S I M V S I L B
P T N Y M O N O R E T U E D D L O
A T O S P A R T S U K N U M I Y M
R U B D D E L A M Y O G E A R L B
A M E E Y P A T S J T O A C B O A
G B L M T N U H R E J J L A U R L
U L D E E G A E L C O E L V B U U
S E D T G L H N A Z I R E I A M R
C B I E L P E S N M O R B T L P I
O R R R O N S O A E N I A Y L U N
D U G T T A L H E R J E Z U I S A
S T S K N A H S E L B M I K S C S
E U L D L H T A P O C I R O C A O
B S R T E G R O W L T I G E R T L
T A N T O M I L E V I C T O R I A
```

Answer: up to the Heaviside Layer past the Jellicle Moon and the Russell Hotel

Today in 1519

Italian inventor and painter Leonardo da Vinci died.

- He was also a gifted sculptor, architect, scientist, and engineer.
- He painted the portrait of the Mona Lisa (with her famous enigmatic smile) when he was 53 years old.
- His inventions included a helicopter, submarine, and tank. Most of the designs were too advanced for the times he lived in.

Word of the day

enigmatic Not clear to the understanding; puzzling; from the Greek *ainigma* (to speak allusively).

Imagine...

Be a modern-day Leonardo—draw up a design for an invention we can't actually make (yet!). How about: a time machine, a matter transporter, a FTL (faster than light) starship, a thought-operated computer, or an anti-gravity car.

Quote of the day

Every man at three years old is half his height.

Leonardo da Vinci

Activity of the day

Leo's Likes and Dislikes

Leonardo Da Vinci liked the shape of an OVAL but not a SQUARE; he invented the ROAD but not the PATH; he liked to LEND money but not BORROW it. So did he:

1. Paint a DANDELION or a ROSE?
2. Predict GLOBAL WARMING or ACID RAIN?
3. Invent the AIRLINE or the TRAIN
4. Invent the THEATER or the DRIVE-IN?
5. Design the RADIO or the TV?
6. Make RADIAL or CROSS-PLY tires?
7. Make a CRADLE or a CRIB?
8. Invent COMPUTER games or ARCADE games?
9. Draw a portrait of an ALIEN or a BIGFOOT?
10. Invent the CASSETTE or the VIDEO?

Answers: DANDELION, ACID RAIN, AIRLINE, DRIVE-IN, RADIO, RADIAL, CRADLE, ARCADE, ALIEN, VIDEO (words whose letters are found in LEONARDO DA VINCI)

Today in 1718

was the first observance of "Sun Day," a solar energy celebration that brings awareness and advancement to alternative energy development.

- Every year, solar events take place across the U.S. People write songs, paint pictures, build exhibits, hold fairs, and arrange tours of solar buildings.
- Ed Passerini unveiled his first solar car, called the Bluebird on this day.
- After the first "Sun Day," U.S. President Jimmy Carter announced a $100 million boost in the federal budget for solar energy research.

Word of the day

solar Of or having to do with the sun; produced by or coming from the sun; from the Latin *solis*.

Quote of the day

"Solar energy . . . can play a lead role in solving our energy problem. . . because it is clean, it is renewable, its supply cannot be affected by foreign countries, and it is free."
Dr. David L. Block, director, Florida Solar Energy Center

Imagine...

It's "Sun Day" and you have decided to participate in the solar energy celebration. What will you do? Paint a picture? Write a song or a poem? Build a solar-powered go-cart? Design a poster? Choose a project and then do it!

Activity of the day

Sun Power
You can use the sun to make solar pictures.

You will need a bright, sunny, day with as little breeze as possible, dark blue or black construction paper, and various flat objects with a definite shape and some weight (i.e., a key, paper clip, a leaf with a small rock to weigh it down, etc.).

To make a picture, place the paper on the ground. Place an object such as a key, on the paper. Leave the paper and object in the sun for a few hours or all day. Check on your picture after a few hours to see if your "print" has appeareed.

Why does this happen?

The bright light from the sun fades the paper that is not covered by the object. The paper underneath of the object is not faded by the sun and retains its color.

Today in 1780

the 6-4 favorite horse Diomed won the very first Derby race in the U.K.

- The horse race (over 1 mile and four furlongs) was called the Derby after its sponsor, Lord Derby.
- Sponsorship of the race had been determined by the toss of a coin; Lord Derby won, and his friend Sir Charles Bunbury lost.
- Derby races are now held throughout the world.

Imagine...

You are a race caller for the Derby. Write down a list of ten horses that will race (check the racing column in the newspaper for ideas). Decide who the winners will be. Think of two or three incidences that can happen in the race (a dog running on the track, a slow horse suddenly galloping into the lead). Now either write or tape-record the race. Make it as exciting as you can!

Word of the day

derby A sporting contest. Also a style of bowler hat, named after Lord Derby.

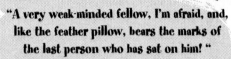

Quote of the day

"A very weak-minded fellow, I'm afraid, and, like the feather pillow, bears the marks of the last person who has sat on him! "

First Earl of Bemersyde (referring to Lord Derby)

Activity of the day

The Decimal Fraction Derby

And they're off! There's No Chance in the outside lane, Fat Chance in the middle lane, and Slim Chance in the inside lane. Who will win the Derby? Add each number each horse crosses—the horse with the lowest total at the end wins!

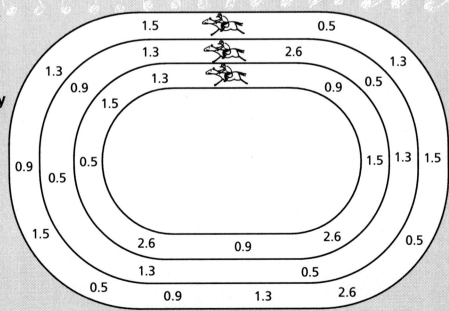

Today in 1867

Nellie Bly, a famous journalist for the New York World, was born.

- Her real name was Elizabeth Cochrane Seaman although she was nicknamed "Pink" after her christening gown.
- She beat the fictional *Round the World in Eighty Days* record by completing the trip in 72 days, 6 hours, and 11 minutes.
- She also missed being a passenger on the *Titanic* when a flat tire on her taxi delayed her arrival by 5 minutes.

Word
of the day

journalist A writer for newspapers and magazines. Also, a person who keeps a daily journal. From the Late Latin "diurnalis" (daily).

Quote
of the day

"To have no thoughts and be able to express them. That's what makes a journalist."
Karl Kraus

Imagine...

Nellie Bly once pretended to be crazy so that she could report on conditions in British mental asylums. Imagine you are an investigative reporter who has gone undercover as a bear to report on conditions in the local zoo. Write a diary of your adventure and a final news report for the paper.

Activity
of the day

Kellie Sly, Investigative Journalist

Kellie Sly (Nellie's rival) has given this story to her editor, who finds a few mistakes—seven to be exact! Can you find them all?

I visited the harbor on Saturday, September 31st. I was after a gang of smugglers operating out of a four-funneled sailing ship moored at pier 3. A quick view of the vessel showed the anchor safely pulled up. I walked up the gangplank onto the deck and looked for somewhere to hide. A barrel full of ropes seemed ideal, so I climbed in and waited. It wasn't long before some men appeared. "We share the loot three ways, like we always do," said one. The others nodded sullenly.

Unfortunately I chose that moment to sneeze. They were onto me immediately, dragging me from the tight funnel. "A spy! Throw her overboard!" cried the one with the black, long-sleeved shirt and the tattoos on his back. "Look behind you!" I screamed, and as they turned I dived into the murky river. Unfortunately the smugglers spotted me and dispatched me with a fatal shot.

Answers: 1. September has only 30 days 2. Sailing ships don't have funnels. 3. They were moored; the anchor would be down. 4. You can't climb into a full barrel. 5. The barrel becomes a funnel. 6. You can't see tattoos through a black shirt. 7. If it was a fatal shot, how was the story written?

Today in 1937

the German dirigible Hindenburg was hit by lightning and exploded.

- The disaster, in which 35 people were killed, was captured "live" on a radio broadcast and film.
- The real cause of the explosion—an outer skin made of a special fabric that burned like dry leaves when ignited—was only discovered in the past few years.
- At the time of its launch, the Hindenburg was the largest aircraft ever built—over 787 ft. (240 m) in length.

Imagine...

If the Hindenburg had been filled with the safer helium gas, we might have fleets of dirigibles flying our skies rather than aircraft. Imagine taking a flight on a huge dirigible flying from Boston to London. Draw a plan of the huge airship (three times bigger than a jumbo jet!), write about the trip and the facilities on board (the swimming pool, the tennis court), or draw a picture of the airship flying above your state's capital.

Word of the day

dirigible A steerable self-propelled airship; from the Latin *dirigere* (to direct).

Quote of the day

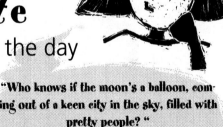

"Who knows if the moon's a balloon, coming out of a keen city in the sky, filled with pretty people? "
e e cummings

Activity of the day

Inside the Hindenberg

How many words of 4 or more letters can you make from the word HINDENBERG?

Answers: Here are 70 we found...
4 letters: been, beer , bend, bind, bird, deer, dine, ding, Eden, edge, gene, grid, grin, heed, herb, herd, here, hide, hind, hire, need, nerd, nine, reed, rein, ride, rind, ring.
5 letters: begin , beige, being, breed, bride, bring, diner, gender, genie, genre, greed, green, grind, hedge, hinge, hired, inner, neigh, ridge, reign.
6 letters: behind, binder, bridge, dinner, ending, engine, grinned, hinder, hinged, rebind, reined, ringed.
7 letters: bending, heeding, herding, needing, neighed, reigned
8 letters: beginner, breeding

Today in 1934

the Pearl of Laotze was found at Palawan in the Philippines.

- At 240 mm x 140 mm (9.5 in. x 55 in.), the pearl is the largest ever found. It has been valued at over $32 million!
- La Régente was a pearl once part of the French crown jewels. It sold in 1988 for over $840,000.
- Pearls are "molluscan concretions" formed when a tiny piece of grit becomes lodged inside the oyster's shell.

Word of the day

mollusk An invertebrate with a soft body enclosed in a shell; from the Latin *mollis* (soft).

Imagine...

"Dear Diary: Today a bit of grit washed into me. It's really scratchy and annoying . . ."

Complete Marmaduke Mollusk's diary as he grows a protective coating around the grit, evades ocean creatures, finally gets opened, and has the pearl removed.

Quote of the day

"She named the infant `Pearl', as being of great price. Purchased with all she had, her mother's only treasure. "
Nathaniel Hawthorne

Activity of the day

Oyster antics

Here's a bunch of oysters all sleeping in a shallow pool.
Eight of them have pearls inside; the rest don't. To help you find the pearls, the oysters have labelled themselves. They've also arranged themselves into a helpful pattern. So find the pearls!
(**Hint:** what are pearls often made into?)

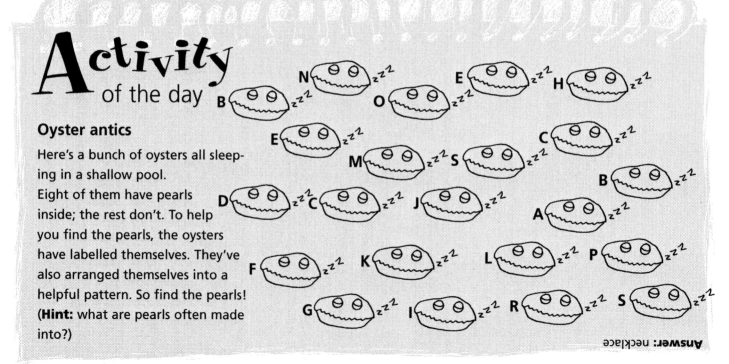

Answer: necklace

Today in 1902

the volcano Mount Pelée exploded on Martinique in the West Indies.

- Nearly every one of the 30,000 inhabitants of the town of Saint-Pierre were killed in the explosion.
- Most deaths were caused by asphyxiation from gas and dust.
- One prisoner survived, having been locked in an underground prison cell.

Imagine...

It's always tricky being a volcano expert; nobody believes you when you tell them the volcano next door is about to explode; then they all blame you for not warning them earlier when it does! Imagine you were the volcano expert warning the people of Saint-Pierre about Mount Pelée. Write a series of reports describing the growing danger (small earth tremors, leaking gases, dust, and finally the explosion). Do you escape from the volcano yourself? If not, what are your final words?

Word of the day

asphyxia A lack of oxygen in the blood that causes death; from the Latin *a* (not) + *sphuxis* (pulse).

Quote of the day

"Never expose yourself unnecessarily to danger; a miracle may not save you . . . and if it does, it will be deducted from your share of luck or merit."
The Talmud

Activity of the day

What goes up and out, and down

Complete these 21 three-letter words to discover five different things that come out of volcanoes.

A	G	I
E	S	Y

H	S	R
M	A	G

E	P	I
U	T	E

G	L	A
M	W	H

S	U	I
Y	E	P

J	S	K
B	Y	G

E	O	A
G	R	K

Answers: 1. lava 2. pumice 3. ash 4. smoke 5. gas

MAY 9

Today in 1800

anti-slavery campaigner John Brown was born in Torrington, Connecticut, U.S.

- He spent most of his life fighting slavery and was a well-known abolitionist.
- In an effort to free slaves by force, he captured Harper's Ferry, a small town in West Virginia.
- Although he was captured and hanged for treason and murder, his name is remembered in the words of the song "John Brown's Body."

Word
of the day

abolitionist A reformer who wishes to abolish (do away with) slavery or capital punishment; from the Latin *abolare* (to destroy).

Imagine...

What would you like to abolish? Something important like racism, hunger, or war? Or would you simply like to rid the world of things like homework, clothes that don't fit, or TV commercials? Write a pamphlet explaining your issue, and listing ways in which it could be abolished.

Quote
of the day

"Am I not a man and a brother?"
Josiah Wedgwood (the motto of the Anti-Slavery Society)

Activity
of the day

John Brown's body

The song "John Brown's Body" (sung originally about a different John Brown) has a simple structure.
Lines 1, 2, and 3 are identical. Line 4 is "His soul goes marching on'

John Brown's body lies a-mouldering in the grave,
John Brown's body lies a-mouldering in the grave,
John Brown's body lies a-mouldering in the grave,
But his soul goes marching on.

Chorus:
Glory, Glory, Hallelujah!
Glory, Glory, Hallelujah!
Glory, Glory, Hallelujah!
His soul goes marching on.

Make up some additional verses using a similar structure and theme. The additional verses could be about the raid on Harper's Ferry, his friendship with the slaves, or his trial.

Answers: Here are four more verses from the original song:
He's gone to be a soldier in the Army of the Lord ...
John Brown's knapsack is strapped upon his back ...
John Brown died that the slaves might be free ...
The stars above in Heaven now are looking kindly down ...

Today in 1874

a giant squid reportedly attacked a 150-ton ship and dragged it to the ocean's depths.

- A giant squid over 55 ft. (17 m) long was washed up in New Zealand in 1887. Its tentacles were each 50 ft. (15 m) long.
- The Kraken is a mythical Norwegian squid, supposedly over 1.2 miles (2 km) long. It was said to disguise itself as an island and then eat unsuspecting sailors who landed there.
- The squid is a mollusk, just like the octopus, nautilus, and cuttlefish.

Word of the day

tentacle A long, flexible appendage that is used for grasping or movement; from the Latin *temptare* (to handle, or try).

Imagine...

The island you've landed your small boat on is rather peculiar. It's grey, smooth, and treeless. Still, your boat does need repairs after last night's storm. You decide to rest first on a large rock, but you don't feel comfortable; it's as though someone or something's watching you. Then the rock—blinks! Complete the story as a cartoon strip.

Quote of the day

Below the thunders of the upper deep;
Far, far beneath in the abysmal sea,
His ancient, dreamless, uninvaded sleep
The Kraken sleepeth.

Lord Tennyson

Activity of the day

Spot the Sea Monster!

If you're going to survive on the seven seas, you'll need to be able to identify and name these creatures (mythical AND real) of the deep.

		Clue
S		common fast-moving, ten-armed mollusk
E		the largest mythical monster
A		a carnivorous marine fish with tough skin
M		giant burrowing marine mollusk
O		home of the mythical Scottish sea serpent
N		large venomous ray with barbed spines
S		a snake-like sea monster
T		eight-legged sea creature
E		huge marine mammal
R		mythical Norwegian seamonster

Answers: squid, leviathan, shark, clam, Loch Ness, stingray, sea-serpent, octopus, whale, kraken

Today in 1811

Siamese twins Chang and Eng were born.

- They were born connected by a small band of flesh in the chest area.
- After 30 years of touring the world, they settled in the U.S. They married two sisters and produced 22 children between them.
- Chang died of a blood clot. Eng died (most likely of shock) three hours later.

Word of the day

Siamese twins Two people born physically joined together; from *Siam* (now Thailand), where Chang and Eng were born.

Quote of the day

"We must learn to live together as brothers or perish together as fools."

Dr. Martin Luther King, Jr.

Imagine...

Imagine if you and your brother or sister were Siamese twins. What would the advantages be? (You'd always have someone to talk to!) The disadvantages? ('But I don't need to go to the toilet!'). Write about your childhood, growing up, and what job(s) you might end up doing.

Activity of the day

Word twins

Some words just seem to fit together like, well, like day and night, or sugar and spice, or bread and butter. Almost like twins! Here are two lists of 19 separated word-twins. Just go back and forth between the two lists and put them back together. Can you find them all?

List 1
aches, again, alive, bacon, bangers, bells, bits, chalk, cut, fair, fish, night, nuts, odds, rock, salt, stars, thick, wrack

List 2
again, bolts, cheese, chips, day, eggs, ends, kicking, mash, pains, paste, pepper, pieces, roll, ruin, square, stripes, thin, whistles

Answers: 1. aches and pains 2. again and again 3. alive and kicking 4. bacon and eggs 5. bangers and mash 6. bells and whistles 7. bits and pieces 8. chalk and cheese 9. cut and paste 10. fair and square 11. fish and chips 12. night and day 13. nuts and bolts 14. odds and ends 15. rock "n" roll 16. salt and pepper 17. stars and stripes 18. thick and thin 19. wrack and ruin

Today in 1820

Florence Nightingale was born.

- She was named after her birthplace—Florence, Italy.
- For her work amongst the casualties of the Crimean War, she was named "The Lady of the Lamp."
- Her insistence on clean working conditions in her hospitals reduced the death rate from 42% to 2% in just five months.

Imagine...

"Being a veterinary nurse sure has its ups and downs. Certainly helping the animals back to full health is rewarding. We get some strange patients too; lizards, rats, and even snakes. But the strangest animal we had also had the strangest complaint. Let me tell you about it." What was the animal? What was wrong with it? Write the story.

Word of the day

nurse A person skilled in caring for the sick; from the Latin *nutrire* (to nourish or feed).

Quote of the day

"To understand God's thoughts we must study statistics, for these are the measure of his purpose. "
Florence Nightingale

Activity of the day

Nurse Quiz

There are many different kinds of nurses. Complete the grid, using the best answer from the list below. Then the letters in the shaded squares will spell out an old name for a nurse that helps deliver babies.

director, district, enrolled, graduate, head, midwife, nurse, registered, scrub, student

Grid	Clue
	someone who has completed the course of study at a nurses' training school
	a nurse who helps a surgeon prepare for surgery
	a nurse who is paid to visit the sick in their homes
	a nurse who has enough training to be enrolled by a state to provide routine care for the sick
	nurse in training who is undergoing a trial period
	the nurse in charge of nursing in a medical institution
	nurse in charge of other nurses
	one skilled in caring for the sick
	a graduate nurse who has passed examinations for registration
	a nurse skilled in aiding the delivery of babies

Answers: graduate, scrub, district, enrolled, student, head, director, nurse, registered, midwife; ACCOUCHEUSE

Today in 1886

tunnel workman George Monroe found "daylight."

- He was working on a subway beneath the Thames when an explosion sucked him into the wall of the tunnel.
- He was then pushed by a bubble of high pressure air through 33 ft. (10 m) of clay into the bed of the River Thames.
- He rose up through another 33 ft. (10 m) of water to be finally propelled 26 ft. (8 m) into the air. He lived!

Word
of the day

tunnel An underground passage; from the Middle English *tun* (a large beer or wine cask).

Quote
of the day

"Sweet Thames, run softly, till I end my song."
Edmund Spenser (*Prothalamion*)

Imagine...

George Monroe was quite a celebrity after his "journey" and was probably asked to speak publicly about his ordeal. Draw a set of four diagrams showing how he went from under the Thames River to floating on top.

Activity
of the day

Tunnel Vision

George is stuck in another tunnel. The best way out is the one where he passes the smallest total, adding up the numbers as he goes.

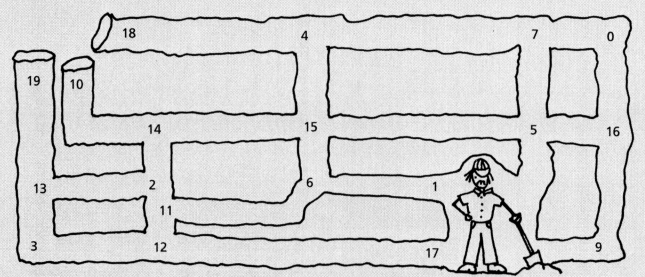

Answer: 5 + 7 + 4 + 18 = 34

Today in 1978

Schweppe and Company (the original makers of Schweppes) was formed.

- The bubbles were put into Schweppes to make it taste like spa water.
- The company was the official refreshments supplier to the Great Exhibition of 1851.
- Schweppes opened a factory in Sydney in 1877.
- The bubbles in "fizzy" drinks are carbon dioxide.

Word of the day

spa A health resort near a spring or at the seaside; named after the Belgium town of *Spa*.

Imagine...

Whoops! The delivery van has accidentally dropped off bottles of laughing gas at the soft-drink factory. Write a story about what happens when people start buying soft drinks that make you laugh—and laugh! (And what happens when the bubbles get up your nose?)

Quote of the day

"Life is mostly froth and bubble,
Two things stand like stone,
Kindness in another's trouble,
Courage in your own. "
Adam Lindsay Gordon

Activity of the day

Bubble Prints

You'll need the following:
Powder paint, dishwashing liquid, a straw, paper

1. Cover the table with newspaper.
2. Mix 2 teaspoons of dishwashing liquid, 3 tablespoons of water, and 3 heaped tablespoons of powdered paint.
3. Gently blow into the mixture to create bubbles (and DON'T suck!)
4. Gently place the paper onto the bubbles to make a bubble print.

Today in 1940

the first nylon stockings went on sale in the United States. Competing producers bought their yarn from E. I. DuPont, whose nylon production would go almost entirely into parachutes the following year.

- Nylon is a synthetic polymide that replaced silk, rayon, and jute in many applications.
- Nylon is characterized by great strength, toughness, and elasticity.
- A popular music album in 1982 was *The Nylon Curtain* by Billy Joel.

Word of the day

fiber A natural or synthetic filament, as of cotton or nylon, capable of being spun into yarn; from the Latin *fibra*.

Quote of the day

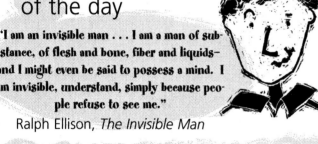

"I am an invisible man . . . I am a man of substance, of flesh and bone, fiber and liquids—and I might even be said to possess a mind. I am invisible, understand, simply because people refuse to see me."

Ralph Ellison, *The Invisible Man*

Imagine...

Nylon is used in the manufacture of fabrics for such things as hosiery, raincoats, and other clothing. Nylon fibers are also used for parachutes, insect screens, medical sutures, strings for tennis rackets, brush bristles, rope, and fishing nets. Molded nylon is used for insulating material, combs, dishware, and machinery parts. Can you figure out what materials were used for all of these items before nylon was developed?

Activity of the day

Fiber Fill-in

Place letters in the blanks to complete the names of the fibers. Then, label each fiber **N** for natural or **S** for synthetic.

c __ __ el hair   l __ n __ n

An __ o __ a   r __ y __ n

s __ __ k   c __ t t __ __

j __ t __   n __ l __ __

w __ __ l   m __ h __ __ r

r __ m __ e   c __ __ hm __ r __

Answers: 1. camel hair, N 2. Angora, N 3. silk, N 4. jute, N 5. wool, N 6. ramie, N 7. linen, N 8. rayon, S 9. cotton, N 10. nylon, S 11. mohair, N 12. cashmere, N

Today in 1975

Japanese mountaineer Junko Tabei climbed Mount Everest via the South-East Ridge.

- She was the first woman to reach the peak and was one of a group of 15 women mountain climbers chosen to make the climb by a Japanese TV company.
- The first woman to reach the summit from both the northern and southern slopes was Cathy O'Dowd of South Africa in 1996 and 1999.

Imagine...

Write journal entries for an expedition to climb Mt. Everest. Describe the base camp (where you start from), the equipment you carry, the easy climb to begin, the cold, camping on the icy slopes, the wind, the danger, the crevasses, and how it might feel to finally stand on the peak of the Earth's highest mountain.

Word of the day

Chomo-Lungma The Tibetan name for Mount Everest (goddess of the universe).

Quote of the day

"I can't understand why men make all this fuss about Everest—it's only a mountain."
Junko Tabei

Activity of the day

Graphing Mt. Everest

Mt. Everest is a very unforgiving mountain; 13 mountaineers died before Sir Edmund Hillary and Tenzing Norgay reached the summit in 1953. The chart shows the number of people who reached the summit and the number of people who died on the mountain for the years 1969 to 1989. Make a column graph of the data. Show both the "summits" and the "deaths" on the same graph, perhaps by coloring in the bottom section of each "summits" column with the number of deaths.

Year	Summits	Deaths	Year	Summits	Deaths
1969	0	1	1980	10	3
1970	4	8	1981	5	1
1971	0	1	1982	18	11
1972	0	1	1983	23	3
1973	10	1	1984	17	8
1974	0	6	1985	30	7
1975	15	2	1986	4	4
1976	4	1	1987	2	4
1977	2	0	1988	50	10
1978	25	2	1989	24	8
1979	18	6			

Today in 1920

KLM, the Netherlands national airline, made its first scheduled flight.

- KLM organized an overseas tour in 1938 for Nancy Bird Walton, one of Australia's aviation pioneers. She used the trip to study passenger transport.

- In 1924, KLM became the first airline to commercially transport animals. Their first "client?" Nico the Bull!

Word of the day

KLM Dutch for *Koninklijke-Luchtvaart-Maatschappij.*

Quote of the day

"The scientific theory I like best is that the rings of Saturn are composed entirely of lost airline luggage."
Mark Russell

Imagine...

One moment you're chewing a nice clump of grass in your paddock, and then it's up, up, and away into the wild blue yonder! Describe Nico the Bull's airplane flight. How did they get him on board? Did he sleep? Did he get airsick? What was the food like? (Airline food is supposed to be terrible!) Where did he fly to? Did he ever fly again?

Activity of the day

Arrivals and Departures

Here is the arrivals and departure board for a busy airport. See if you can answer the questions below. (Remember, all times are in 24-hour format.)

Airline	Destination	Departure	Arrival	Flight time
KLM	Amsterdam	01:15	17:55	
KLM	Paris		15:05	13:10
KLM	Berlin	17:20	05:25	
Qantas	New York	12:50	16:50	4:00
British Airways	London	17:00		12:30
British Airways	Auckland		12:00	4:55
Ansett	Melbourne	09:00	10:20	

1. How long does the trip to Amsterdam take?
2. What time does the Paris plane depart?
3. Why does the Berlin flight seem to arrive before it's left?
4. How long does the Berlin flight take?
5. When does the BA flight to London arrive?
6. When does the Auckland flight leave?
7. How long does the Melbourne flight take?
8. What is the country of this airport?
9. Which city?
10. The BA flight to London got held-up—they forgot the food! Which other flight did this delay?

Answers: 1) 16 hr 40 min 2) 01:55 3) It arrives the next day. 4) 12 hr 5 min 5) 05:30 6) 07:05 7) 1 hr 20 min 8) Australia 9) Sydney 10) The KLM flight to Berlin, which takes off after it.

Today in 1953

Michael Stavvides was run over by a steamroller.

- He was seven years old. He was run over when the machine suddenly reversed.

- He survived the ordeal as he was pushed into a trough beneath the warm asphalt.

- A Los Angeles man stole a steamroller. After a frantic 8 km/h chase, police stepped aboard and arrested him. When asked why he stole it, he said, "I was tired of walking'.

Imagine...

"Wanted: Steamroller with driver for special flattening job. Money's no object. Apply within." Imagine you're the driver. What might the "special flattening job" be? Does it involve roads, gardens, or even food-perhaps a giant pizza? Write about the job interview and what you have to do.

Word of the day

squash To flatten or crumple; a variation on *quash* (to put down by force) from the Latin *cassus* (null or void).

Quote of the day

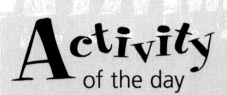

Even if you are on the right track, you'll get run over if you just sit there.
Will Rogers

Activity of the day

Name of steamroller	Height of roller	Stretched-out height
Age of Steam	1.4 m	4.4 m
The Iron Maiden	1.0 m	3.1 m
Ring of Roses	0.8 m	2.5 m
Flat Stanley	1.6 m	5.0 m

Mr. Bouncy

Mr. Bouncy, the amazing stretching rubber man, has a death-defying stunt in which he has himself run over by a steamroller. To start the stunt, he stretches himself until he's exactly the same height as the front roller. Then he lies down and the steamroller runs over him until he's rolled right around the roller and his feet touch his head. His assistant then peels him off the roller to thunderous applause.

Mr. Bouncy uses a range of different-size steamrollers. He's often wondered if there's a way to predict just how far he'll stretch each time, so he decided to keep a chart, but couldn't find any pattern. Next week he's

being flattened by the huge Longreach Leviathan steamroller with its 6.8 ft. roller, and he's a little worried about just how far he'll stretch. Can you help him out?

(**Hints**: Can you see a relationship between the height of the roller and his stretched-out height? Try drawing a diagram. What's another name for the height?)

P.S. Mr. Bouncy only does the stunt once a week as it always leaves him feeling a little flat.

Answers: The stretched out height (the circumference of the roller) is about 3.14 times the height (or diameter). The Longreach Leviathan will stretch him out nearly 6.6 m!

Today in 1935

writer, adventurer, and freedom fighter Lawrence of Arabia was born.

- Originally an archaeologist, Lawrence joined the British Military Intelligence. He worked with the Arabs (in what is now Saudi Arabia) to overthrow the Turkish government.
- He became a hero in England after a journalist composed a "travelogue" of his adventures in the desert.
- He was responsible for convincing the RAF to use high speed rescue launches to reach crashed aircraft. As a consequence, thousands of lives were saved when World War II began.

Word of the day

travelogue An illustrated lecture about travel; travel comes from the word *travail* (hard work or painful effort) and from the Latin *trepalium* (instrument of torture).

Quote of the day

What I have done, what I am doing, what I am going to do, puzzle and bewilder me. Have you ever been a leaf and fallen from your tree in autumn and been really puzzled about it? That's the feeling.

T. E. Lawrence

Imagine...

The towering sand dunes hold many secrets—secrets you will unlock if you can only reach the desert oasis of Ben-Grahmin by sunset. Your camel climbs slowly to the shifting peak and stops. You raise your spy-glass to your eye and peer into the far distance. What secrets will you discover at the oasis? What danger awaits you there? How will you overcome it? Write a travelogue of YOUR adventures!

Activity of the day

Sand dune word puzzle

Can you make sand into a dune and back into sand by changing one letter at a time? Use the clues to help!

S	A	N	D
D	U	N	E

D	U	N	E
S	A	N	D

Answers: SAND, SANK, DANK, DANE, DONE, DUNE, JUNE, JANE, SANE, SAND

Today in 1790

Jeremiah Carlton went to bed—and stayed there for seventy years.

- He was 89 when he died (in bed).
- He had a team of forty servants to look after him.
- A French company constructed a 19.5 foot (6 m) x 14.4 foot (4.4 m) bed in 1986. It weighed 1.5 tons and could sleep 39 people.

Imagine...

Design a bed to live in. It should have an entertainment console, food supplies, library, games, machines, and a built-in bathroom. Draw a diagram of the bed and its many facilities—and of you resting in it.

Word of the day

mattress A large, thick pad incorporating springs, used as part of a bed; from the Arabic *matrah* (place where something is thrown).

Quote of the day

"I haven't been to sleep for over a year. That's why I go to bed early. One needs more rest if one doesn't sleep."
Evelyn Waugh

Activity of the day

End With a Nap!

Can you make a bed? Into a cot? Then end with a nap? Just change one letter at a time to make the next word (use the clues to help).

B	E	D	
			a wager
			a striking implement
			feline
C	O	T	
			policeman
			type of hat
N	A	P	

Answers: BED, bet, bat, cat, COT, cop, cap, NAP

Today in 1846

three Scottish midgets danced a Scottish Reel for Queen Victoria.

- The shortest person ever to live was Gul Mohammed of India. Seven years before his death he had reached a height of 22.5 inches (57 cm).
- The average length of a new-born baby is 19 inches (48 cm).
- The Mbuti pygmies from Zaire are the shortest tribe in the world, averaging 54 inches (137 cm).

Word of the day

pygmy A member of an African tribe of short people; from the Greek *pugmaios* (dwarf).

Quote of the day

"The dwarf sees farther than the giant, when he has the giant's shoulder to mount on."
Samuel Taylor Coleridge

Imagine...

How would your life change if you were only 23.5 inches (60 cm) tall? How would your bedroom, home, travel, school life, and social life change? What if you were 102.4 inches (260 cm) tall? Would that be better or worse? Write about a typical day in your life, either as a very small person or as a giant.

Activity of the day

A Short Word Search

It's not easy being short sometimes. But as the famous saying goes . . . . Well, you'll have to find out the famous saying by circling all of the "short" words and then sorting out the left over letters.

bitty, chunky, dinky, dumpy, elfin, half-length, lilliputian, low-set, miniature, petite, pint-sized, runty, sawed-off, squab, squat, stumpy, teensy, wee

```
R U N T Y H Y P M U T S G D
R E N A I T U P I L L I L E
A T Y T H G I T N I F L E Z
N G T S C N E L B A U Q S I
P E T I T E F F O D E W A S
T O I M N L E Y Y W Y N I T
A I B S N F S M K P S A L N
U L Y P A L W E E N M E C I
Q E R U T A I N I M I U T P
S K A G C H U N K Y E D D S
```

Answer: Great things come in small packages!

Today

is Jumping Frog Jubilee Day in Calaveras County in the U.S. (if it's a Saturday!).

- The special day is based on a story called "The Celebrated Jumping Frog of Calaveras County" written by Mark Twain in 1865.
- The highlight of the festival is frog jumping. Records are kept for the total of three consecutive jumps.
- On May 18, "Rosie the Ribeter" jumped a record 2.6 feet (6.55 m).

Word
of the day

jump To move forward with a leap.

Imagine...

You found Frogger the day she leapt across the road into your open car window. You know she's an amazing frog, and with the training you've given her, an absolute favourite for the annual jumping-frog contest. There's only one problem though… Write about finding Frogger, her training, the big contest—and just what the problem is.

Quote
of the day

"I don't see no p'ints about that frog that's any better'n any other frog."
Mark Twain

Activity
of the day

Frog hop!

Here are the results for the Calaveras County Frog Jumping Competition. The only question is who won.

Remember: the frog's score is the aggregate (total) of their three jumps.

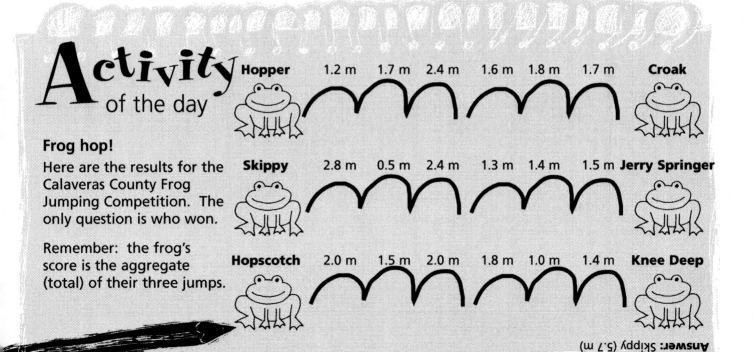

Hopper	1.2 m	1.7 m	2.4 m	1.6 m	1.8 m	1.7 m	Croak
Skippy	2.8 m	0.5 m	2.4 m	1.3 m	1.4 m	1.5 m	Jerry Springer
Hopscotch	2.0 m	1.5 m	2.0 m	1.8 m	1.0 m	1.4 m	Knee Deep

Today in 1707

Swedish botanist Carl Linné was born.

- He devised the grouping system (taxonomy) by which every plant and animal has a Latin group and species name.
- He also devised the names for the flowering parts of plants.
- Linné is better known by the Latin form of his name: Carolus Linnaeus.

Word of the day

taxonomy The practice of classifying plants and animals; from the French *taxonomie*: *taxis* (arrange) + *nomia* (distribution).

Quote of the day

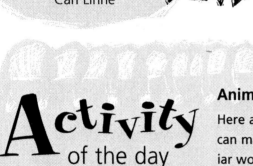

"Natura non facit saltus." (Nature does not make progress by leaps and bounds.)
Carl Linné

Imagine...

You are Noah counting the animals into the ark. There're quite a few you've never seen before, especially those ones from exotic habitats. Choose ten animals and create new names for them. Use a similar system to that of Carl Linné, but be more imaginative. Why not group the animals by friendliness? size? color? If you can make the names "Latin"-sounding, all the better.

Activity of the day

Animalius Quizzicus Trickius

Here are ten Latin names for some quite common animals. See if you can match them up. You'll need to use cunning, guesswork (what familiar word does the Latin remind you of?) and the occasional complete stab in the dark!

1. Cetacea tursiops truncatus	(a) bottle-nosed dolphin
2. Equus caballus	(b) common dolphin
3. Bovidae capri	(c) common horse
4. Panthera pardus	(d) goat
5. Panthera leo	(e) killer whale
6. Nasalis larvatus	(f) leopard
7. Cetacea delphinius delphis	(g) lion
8. Cetacea orcinus orca	(h) proboscis monkey
9. Panthera tigris	(i) tiger
10. Cetacea odontoceti	(j) toothed whale

Answers: 1 (a) truncatus—trunk, nose; 2 (c) equus—equestrian, horse; 3 (d) capri—capricorn, the goat; 4 (f) pardus—leoPARD; 5 (g) leo—lion; 6 (h) NASALis—nasal, nose, proboscis (tricky!); 7 (b) delphinius delphis—dolphin; 8 (e) orca—whale; 9 (i) tigris—tiger; 10 (j) oDONTOceti—orthoDONTIC, teeth

Today in 1934

both the parents of Kim Ung-Yong, a genius with an IQ of over 200, were born.

- IQ is calculated by dividing a person's mental age by his or her actual age then multiplying by 100. An "average" IQ is 100.
- Marilyn vos Savant was measured with an IQ of 228 when she was 10.
- Japan's citizen's are said to have an average IQ of over 111.

Imagine...

You know someone so smart that he/she can answer any question you can think of. Make a list of seven really tricky questions to ask them. How about "Why does your nose run and your feet smell?" or "Does a fish get cramps after eating?" and "How come wrong numbers are never busy?" Now try writing the answers!

Word of the day

genius Someone who has exceptional intellectual ability or originality. In Roman mythology, a genius was a guardian spirit that was believed to give people success or intelligence.

Quote of the day

"If the aborigine drafted an IQ test, all of Western civilization would presumably flunk it."
Stanley Garn

Activity of the day

IQ test

Here are 10 questions that are similar to those found in IQ tests. Complete the pattern with the next letter, number, or shape in the pattern.

1. 1, 2, 4, 7, 11, . . .
2. 23, 21, 19, 17, . . .
3. 1, 4, 9, 16, . . .
4. A, C, D, F, G, I, . . .
5. Z, A, Y, B, X, C, . . .
6. A, E, I, O, . . .
7.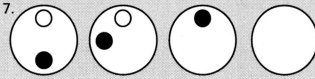
8.
9. I, III, V, VII, . . .
10. What word is least like the other four?
cow, bull, sheep, calf, heifer

Answers: 1) 16 2) 15 3) 25 4) J 5) W 6) U 7) 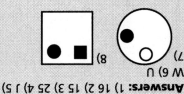 8) 9) IX 10) sheep

Today in 1630

the fork was introduced to dining in the U.S. by Governor Winthrop.

- Forks were first used in Italy in the 1500s. Until then knives and spoons were the only cutlery.
- In the U.S., domestic cutlery is called flatware.
- Chopsticks are the preferred cutlery item for East Asian countries.

Word
of the day

cutlery Implements for cutting and eating food. A *cutler* was a person who made cutlery. *Cutler* came from the word *coulter*, a sharp steel wedge on a plough that cut through the soil.

Quote
of the day

"He was for all the world like a fork'd radish, with a head fantastically carved upon it with a knife."

William Shakespeare

Imagine...

Design new cutlery to make eating special foods easier. Which foods? Peas, corn, boiled eggs, spaghetti, pizzas, or a food of your own choice. Draw the design, describe how it works, then write out your patent application!

Activity
of the day

Dinner time

Whose turn is it to set the table? Yours!

It's a very formal setting tonight (we have guests), so it's out with the silver, the napkins, the funny spoons nobody knows when to use. See how many of the items in the picture you can correctly name.

dinner plate, dinner knife, dinner fork, soup spoon, salad fork, coffee cup and saucer, drinking glass, napkin, dessert spoon, salad plate, bread plate, bread knife

Answers: 1) Salad plate 2) bread knife 3) bread plate 4) dessert spoon 5) coffee cup and saucer 6) drinking glass 7) soup spoon 8) dinner knife 9) napkin 10) dinner plate 11) dinner fork 12) salad fork

Today in 1805

Napoleon Bonaparte was crowned King of Italy.

- Although famous for his exploits as a general, Napoleon also fought for civil reforms, including the right for all people to be treated equally by courts and for freedom of religion.

- He tried to blockade England, calling the country "a nation of shopkeepers."

- He was exiled twice, once to the island of Elba (from which he escaped to raise an army) and then to the island of St. Helena where he eventually died from cancer.

Word of the day

exile To expel a person from his native land; from the Latin word *exilium* (banishment).

Imagine...

Brainstorm time! Make a list of 20 reasons why Napoleon Bonaparte may have kept his hand inside his coat jacket.

Quote of the day

"To his dog, every man is Napoleon; hence the constant popularity of dogs."
Aldous Huxley

Activity of the day

What's in a word?
Napoleon

How many four-(or more) letter words can you make from Napoleon?

N	A	P
O	■	L
E	O	N

Answers: Here are 23 we found: alone, Anne, lane, leap, lean, Leon, loan, lone, neon, Nepal, Noel, none, nope, opal, open, pale, pane, panel, peal, plan, plane, plea, pole

Today in 1937

the Golden Gate Bridge in San Francisco was opened.

- The strait the bridge spans was named the Golden Gate by explorer John Charles Fremont in 1846.

- The bridge is 4,200 feet (1,280 m) long.

- During construction, 19 lives were saved by nets hung below the bridge. These men were known as the "Half-Way-to-Hell Club."

- The bridge was originally planned to be painted black with yellow stripes (so that passing ships could see it more easily). Instead, it was painted "Golden Gate Bridge International Orange."

Word of the day

strait A narrow channel of the sea joining two larger bodies of water; from the Latin word *strictus* (strict or tight).

Imagine...

Where would you like to build a bridge? Over a nearby busy road? Over your school? Your house? As a shortcut to a favorite holiday spot? Either draw a picture of the bridge (is it a steel span, suspension, or a cantilever?) or write about how the bridge was built, the land that was cleared, how people felt about the building, how it was paid for (tolls?), and how it changed your life.

Quote of the day

*"How many po' sinners'll be kotched out late
En find no latch ter de golden gate?"*
Joel Chandler Harris

Activity of the day

Cross a bridge, and ACM and you've got the city of Cambridge. Use the clues to cross these bridges (but only as you come to them).

Answers: 1. bargained 2. big dipper 3. birdcage 4. box girder 5. bridegroom 6. brigade 7. brigadier 8. budgerigar 9. dirigible 10. gingerbread 11. Edinburgh 12. Hindenburg

B R I D G E +	AAN	haggled
	IPP	constellation
	AC	a cage in which a bird is kept
	ORX	a hollow girder used in bridge making
	MOOR	partner of the bride
	A	an army unit
	AIRAN	ARMY OFFICER
	AGRU	a colorful bird
	IIL	an airship
	HNU	cake flavored with ginger
	AEGNR	capital of Scotland
	HNNU	a famous airship

Today in 1977

Anton Christy of Sri Lanka stopped balancing on one foot.

- He'd started some 32 hours before.
- The inner ear is responsible for maintaining your sense of balance (or equilibrium).
- The record time was more than doubled by Amresh Kumar Jah of India in 1995, with a time of almost 72 hours.

Imagine...

An unusual sight greets you this frosty morning as you peer out from your bedroom window. It's the sight of every person in the street hopping on one foot or standing, balancing on one foot. As you rub your disbelieving eyes, you realize it's not just the humans—it's the animals, too (although they're standing on two legs). What's going on? Is it April Fool's Day? A new fad? A medical disorder? Write a story about "The Day of Balancing."

Word of the day

equilibrium A state of balance; from the Latin *equi* (equal) and *libra* (balance).

Quote of the day

"Step with care and with great tact
And remember that Life's a Great Balancing Act
Just never forget to be dexterous and deft
And never mix up your right foot with your left."

Dr. Seuss

Activity of the day

Balancing act

How long can YOU balance on one foot?
The official rules state:
1. The disengaged foot may not be rested on the standing foot.
2. No object can be used for balance or support.

Test the students in your class and record the results.

Can girls balance for longer than boys?

Do short people balance better than tall people?
Do unwell people balance worse than healthy ones?
Do adults balance better than children?

Now try other balancing tests:
- Balance a book on the head. Who can walk the furthest?
- Walk along a low balance beam. Who balances best? Make sure everyone walks at the same speed (no running!).
- Outside, carry a full cup of water. Who can spill the least? (Test your teachers at this—they're usually pretty good at carrying their tea or coffee!)

<table>
<tr><td>

MAY
29

</td></tr>
</table>

Today in 1855

the first lighthouse on the Pacific coast was lit.

- One of the seven wonders of the ancient world was the Pharaohs at Alexandria. It was 400 feet (122 m) tall and shaped like a pyramid. It was destroyed by an earthquake in 1375 A.D.

- The world's tallest lighthouse is in Japan and is over 348 feet (106 m) tall. Its lights are rated at 600,000 candlepower and can be seen from over 20 miles (32 km) away.

Word of the day

candlepower A measurement of light strength; from the Latin *candere* (to shine) and   (be able).

Imagine...

"Ooh arrr, me matey! I can be tellin' you a thing or two 'bout that there lighthouse on Wrecker's Cove! I could be tellin' you 'bout the howling banshee that haunts the light or the ghost ship doomed forever to crash onto the wicked rocks! And that there be the pleasant tales!" Write a story about a haunted lighthouse, its ghosts, and the lighthouse keeper who has to deal with them.

Quote of the day

Anythin" for a quiet life, as the man said wen he took the sitivation at the lighthouse.
Charles Dickens (spoken by Sam Weller in *Pickwick Papers*)

Activity of the day

A Light Humor
Match up the joke and the correct answer for a chuckle. Match up the joke and an incorrect answer for a real laugh.

1. Why was the lighthouse keeper fired?
2. Why did the overweight captain change jobs?
3. How do you know the sea is friendly?
4. Did you hear about the red ship and the blue ship that collided?
5. Why do shipments go in cars—
6. Why did the lighthouse keeper go crazy?
7. How can you tell lighthouses are happy?
8. What lies on the bottom of the ocean and shivers?

A nervous wreck.
and cargoes go in ships?
Both crews were marooned.
He couldn't sleep with the light on.
It's always giving waves.
The spiral staircase drove him round the bend.
They beam all the time.
To become a lighthouse keeper.

Today in 1744

the poet Alexander Pope died.

- He was famous for his satirical poems, sometimes about the famous people of his time.

- Because of a childhood illness, he never grew any taller than 4 feet 5 inches (135 cm) and suffered from headaches and fevers.

- He originated many common sayings such as "A little learning is a dangerous thing" and "For fools rush in where angels fear to tread."

Word of the day

satire Witty language used to insult or show scorn; from the Latin *satura* (medley).

Imagine...

You are a brilliant and clever originator of witty sayings. Write a letter to a friend describing your last week but include lots of proverbs ("many hands make light work," "a rolling stone gathers no moss," "a stitch in time saves nine," etc.), analogies ("as thick as two short planks," "as busy as a beaver," "as black as night," etc.) or well-known sayings. Then make up a few of your own.

Quote of the day

"Blessed is the man who expects nothing, for he shall never be disappointed."
Alexander Pope

Activity of the day

Proverbs (short memorable sayings) are often hundreds of years old. Some still make sense ("You can't teach an old dog new tricks"), but some may be a little harder to understand. Write an explanation for each of these ten proverbs. If in doubt, make an explanation up! After all, "Wise men make proverbs, and fools repeat them."

1. Fine words butter no parsnips.
2. A bad bush is better than an open field.
3. A famine in England begins at the horse manger.
4. A little pot is soon hot.
5. All cats are gray in the dark.
6. A penny saved is a penny earned.
7. Early to bed, early to rise, makes a man healthy, wealthy, and wise.
8. Of soup and love, the first is better.
9. The longest day must have an end.
10. Weeds want no sowing.

Today in 1919

the first wedding was conducted in an aircraft.

- 35,000 couples were married simultaneously in a sports stadium in South Korea in 1995.
- Two cats (Phet and Ploy) were married in a $16,000 wedding ceremony in Thailand in 1996.
- A stadium for 20,000 people was built especially for a royal wedding in Dubai. The wedding lasted seven days and cost some $40 million.

Word of the day

wed To marry; from the Old English *weddian* (to pledge or promise).

Quote of the day

"Let me not to the marriage of true minds
Admit impediments . . ."
William Shakespeare (Sonnet 116)

Imagine...

Weddings in planes. Weddings on trampolines. Weddings underwater. All weird and wonderful, and as a wedding photographer, you've seen them all. But this wedding you're at now—well, it just has to be the weirdest one you've ever seen! Write about the weirdest place a wedding could be held or draw a series of "photographs" that you took at the weirdest wedding of all time.

Activity of the day

Wedding Word Search

A wedding in a plane? It had better be big, to fit the wedding party! Find all of these guests and dignitaries in the word search. The leftover letters are a quote from movie star Mae West.

best man, bridegroom, bridesmaids, father, flower girl, groom, groomsmen, maid of honor, minister, mother, organist, pageboy, photographer, pilot, trainbearer, ushers

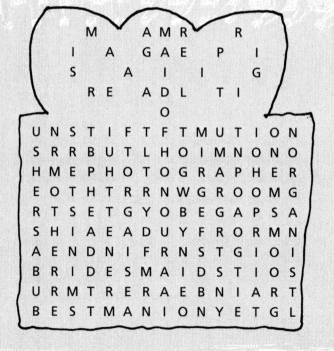

Today in 1968

American author Helen Keller died.

- She had been deaf and blind since the age of 19 months.

- She first learned to communicate when associating "water" with the word tapped into her hand by her tutor Anne Sullivan.

- She wrote three books about her life and spent much of her time lecturing on women's rights, pacifism, and how the deaf and blind might better be helped. She also helped make Braille the standard form of communication for blind people.

Word of the day

deaf Partially or wholly unable to hear; probably from the Greek *typhlos* (blind!).

Imagine...

Imagine you are writing a talking dictionary for a blind person. Try writing definitions for these words: tree, sky, television, book, painting. Naturally, the definitions cannot refer to anything that has to be seen. (Think touching, tasting, hearing, and smelling.)

Quote of the day

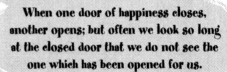

When one door of happiness closes, another opens; but often we look so long at the closed door that we do not see the one which has been opened for us.

Helen Keller

Activity of the day

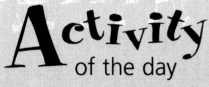

A Sensory Journey Storyboard
Read this short story:

> I set off at dawn* along the path* to the abandoned log cabin. It was cold* and I pulled my gloves* on tighter as I pushed through the closely growing trees*. After an hour, I decided to climb a tree* for a better view. There was no sign of the cabin, but I could smell smoke*. At the bottom of tree I found a scared baby rabbit. I stroked* the rabbit to calm it down and then placed it in my backpack. It started to rain*.

Look at the words with an asterisk. How could you communicate those smells, feelings, and textures without words? Some ideas: cloth, fur, gravel, bark, burnt matches . . . . Write the story out onto paper and glue pieces of material in the appropriate places. Now finish the story (or make up a completely new one of your own). Share the story with a friend.

Today in 1987

world famous Spanish guitarist Andres Segovia died at age 94.

- Segovia made his concert debut at age 14.
- His parents wanted him to study a "proper" instrument like the piano or violin.
- He is considered to be the "father of the modern classical guitar movement" and responsible for introducing its study in music schools throughout the world.
- Australian guitarist John Williams studied with Segovia at a number of guitar summer schools in London.

Word of the day

guitar A six-stringed musical instrument; from the Greek *kithara* (cithara, a type of lyre).

Quote of the day

"Go out in to the world and make my works better known by your marvelous playing."
Manuel Ramirez, guitar maker (to Andres Segovia)

Imagine...

Flam, the six-string acoustic guitar, was made in a small guitar shop in Linares, Spain. Fashioned lovingly from the finest timber, it was bought by a professional performer. When he fell ill, his wife sold it to a small girl who had just started learning. When the girl bought an electric guitar, Flam was left to the dust mites in the attic. Years later the small girl's son found Flam, dusted it off, and learned to play. Then an amazing thing happened . . . . Write Flam's biography.

Activity of the day

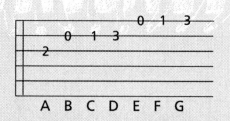

Keeping Tab on Things
Steph is learning guitar by using tablature, a music reading system where numbers are used to represent the notes on the different strings. After playing a few tunes, she discovered she can make words from the different notes. Can you work out what each word is?

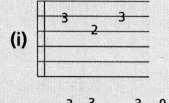

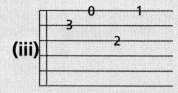

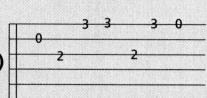

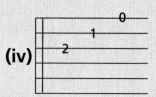

Answers: i) DAD ii) BAGGAGE iii) DEAF iv) ACE; What words can you make up?

Today in 1978

the *Guinness Book of Records* became the most commonly stolen book in British public libraries.

- The *Guinness Book of Records* was first published in 1955.
- Editions are now printed in nearly 80 countries, with half in English.
- Total sales of the book are expected to reach 100 million early in the 21st century.

Imagine...

Your news editor is offering you three choices of assignments today:
- the world record beetle-eating contest
- the world's largest meat-pie baking competition
- an attempt to squash more than 20 people into a bathtub.

Which one will you cover? Write the story (and don't forget to take photos!).

Word of the day

record A best performance; from the Latin *recordari*: *re* + *cord* (heart).

Quote of the day

"Our business in life is not to get ahead of others, but to get ahead of ourselves—to break our own records, to outstrip our yesterday by our today."
Stewart B. Johnson

Activity of the day

Breaking Records

Here are ten world records. Read the descriptions and decide which cannot possibly be true.

1. A set of 1804 U.S. coins was sold for $1,000,000 in 1979.
2. Baseball's most accurate hitter was Joe Trollope, who averaged at least seven strikes a game for his 20-year career.
3. Coby Orr scored a hole-in-one at the age of five on a 308 feet (94 m) hole in Texas in 1975.
4. Dave Spathaky spun 84 plates simultaneously in 1986.
5. Karen Stevenson ate 2,780 cold baked beans with a cocktail pick in 30 minutes.
6. Rowy Thomson completed a marathon charity pole-sit in August of 1988 after spending 300 days perched on the Irish/French border.
7. The largest double-bass ever constructed was 15 feet (4.6 m) tall. It required five people to play it.
8. The oldest coin found was an Egyptian one dated 405 B.C.
9. The record for continuous brass instrument playing was set by Marie Kemp with over 21 days (with a 10-minute break each hour) on a bassoon she later nicknamed "Lips."
10. The world's largest pizza was cooked in Venice, Italy in 1985. It measured 39-in.(12 m) in diameter and was cut into one hundred 19.5 feet x 1.6 feet (6 m x 0.5 m) triangular slices.

Answers: True: 1, 3, 4, 5, and 7 False: 2. You get a strike if you miss the ball; 6. Ireland and France don't share a border; 8. Coins can't be dated anything B.C.; 9. The bassoon isn't a brass instrument; 10. The circumference is too small to cut 100 pieces.

JUNE
4

Today in 1937

the world's first supermarket carts were put into service in Oklahoma City, U.S.

- The first supermarket was called King Cullen, after its owner Michael Cullen, and was started in 1930.
- Soon carts may be fitted with their own scanners, so customers would no longer need to have items scanned one by one.

Word of the day

cart Any small vehicle pushed or pulled by hand.

Imagine...

The local supermarket has just installed the new kind of cart. Equipped with artificial intelligence, they're designed to offer useful suggestions about the location of grocery items, your food choices, and advertised products. Unfortunately, the cart you've chosen seems to be a little . . . strange. What does it look like? What does it say? What does it do? Write the story.

Quote of the day

"Love is like a supermarket cart
Except it 'asn't got any wheels
And when I think about it
It 'asn't got a place to put shoppin' either"

Scroggins

Activity of the day

These are the three finalists' carts in the local supermarket's "Dash for Cash" competition. They had just one minute to fill their carts with cash. But who won? Total each column to find the answer.

	Cart 1	Cart 2	Cart 3	Cart 4
$5	33	5	26	11
$10	10	15	8	12
$20	5	8	8	12
$50	4	5	4	5
$100	4	5	4	5
TOTALS				

Answers: (1) $965, (2) $1085 (3) $970) (4) $1165 (winner)

Today in 1970

the U.S. Department of Labor reported that five percent of the U.S. workforce was unemployed. Among the hardest hit were skilled workers in aircraft, aerospace, and the weapons industries.

- In 1921 a New York Times editorial explained that Robert H. Goddard's rockets could not possibly work because there is nothing in space for their exhausts to push against.
- On March 16, 1926, Goddard launched the first liquid-fuel rocket for a 2.5-second flight from a field on his Aunt Effie's farm near Auburn, Massachusetts.

Imagine...

Whoops! You really should not have pulled shut the door of the new test rocket when you stepped inside to check the guidance computer. Now it is locked. Kicking the computer was not a good idea either because that started the countdown. What are you going to do? Where is the rocket headed for? What do you expect to find when you arrive? How will you get back to Earth? Write about your misadventures.

Word of the day

rocket A vehicle or device propelled by one or more rocket engines, especially such a vehicle designed to travel through space; from the Italian rocca (spindle, distaff)

Quote of the day

"Don't tell me that man doesn't belong out there. Man belongs wherever he wants to go— and he'll do plenty when he gets there [space]."

Wernher von Braun, rocket engineer

Activity of the day

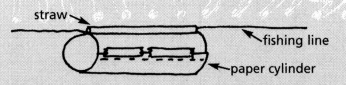

straw

fishing line

paper cylinder

Rocket Launcher
Make your own rocket launcher!
You'll need:
a sheet of card stock or heavy paper
a drinking straw
some tape,
staples
fishing line
a small balloon (preferably long rather than round)

1. Wrap the card into a cylinder and join together. Make the join a strong one by using both staples and tape.
2. Attach the straw along one side.
3. Thread the fishing line through the straw.
4. String the fishing line up across the classroom.
5. Place the balloon in the cylinder and inflate. (Make sure you don't break the cardboard join.)
6. When tight in the cylinder, let go!
   How can you stop the balloon from falling out?
   Can you make it travel faster?
   How else can you improve the design?

Today in 1933

the world's first drive-in opened in New Jersey, U.S.

- The entrance fee was 25¢ per car and 25¢ for each person.
- Over 330 cars could watch the film. They listened to the sound through three large speakers. Individual car speakers were invented later.
- America had over 4,000 drive-in theatres by 1958.

Word of the day

intermission An interval between two films; from the Latin *intermittere*: *inter* (between) and *mittere* (sending).

Quote of the day

"Sit in your car. See and hear movies!"
Sign for the first drive-in movie

Imagine...

Opening the world's first drive-in is one thing; getting people to come along is another! What you need is a flyer—a small advertisement you can push under the windshield wipers of people's cars at a parking lot. Design a flyer, making sure you include the price, time, name of the film, and reasons why people should come.

Activity of the day

Drive-in to This Puzzle!

Cars and film (movies) seem to go together so well, but can you turn cars into a film? Use the clues to help—but you're only allowed to change one letter at a time.

C	A	R	S	
				Rowing implements
				Belonging to us
				Pelts
				Trees
				Combustion
				A steel hand tool
F	I	L	M	

Answers: CARS, OARS, OURS, FURS, FIRS, FIRE, FILE, FILM

Today in 1808

the first four-horse dead heat was recorded at an Irish racecourse.

- The 33rd Olympic Games in Greece (in 648 BC) was the first to feature horse-racing.
- The only dead heat in the famed Cambridge/Oxford race was in 1877.
- Two English men won over $1.6 million in a bet at a racecourse in California, in 1987.
- Distances in horse races are often given in miles and furlongs.

Word
of the day

furlong A unit of length equal to 220 yards (approximately 200 m); from the Old English *furlang*: *furh* (furrow) and *lang* (long)—a furrow long.

Imagine.

Choose an Olympic race (e.g., running, swimming, cycling). Draw a "photo-finish" picture of a four-way dead heat. Each of the finalists should be exactly at the line and should have a very pained expression on his/her face!

Quote
of the day

"Horse sense is the thing a horse has which keeps it from betting on people."
W. C. Fields

Activity
of the day

Who Won What?
There were eight horses in a race. Four ran a dead heat. But which horses and what position did they finish?

- Eclipse won.
- Mayonnaise beat six other horses.
- Fisherman led Orange Cat all the way.
- Inhaler was behind Catherina.
- Loud Racket beat two other horses.
- Penguin Key almost caught Mayonnaise.
- Inhaler trailed Orange Cat the whole race.

Answers: Fisherman, Catherina, Loud Racket, and Penguin Key came in 3rd.

Today in 1964

George the giraffe was discovered eating the telephone cables at Chester Zoo.

- The zoo had been experiencing problems with their telephone system for months.
- George, one of the tallest giraffes in captivity, had found the low-voltage wires rather tasty and had chewed right through them.
- The problem was solved by raising the wires above his head.

Word of the day

giraffe The tallest living mammal; from the Arabic *zirafah*.

Quote of the day

I think the monkeys at the zoo should have to wear sunglasses so they can't hypnotize you.

Jack Handey

Imagine...

George might have caused problems with the telephone system, but he was still a great asset to the zoo. His friendly nature and height came in very handy. He helped the keepers with the eagle-nest problem, rescued the baby chimp, and assisted with the repainting of the sign over the zoo's gate. Write about George's zoo adventures and about the time his height got him into trouble.

Activity of the day

Giraffe Facts
By the time you complete this word puzzle (George has filled in some letters for you), you'll know all about giraffes!

The puzzle's filled-in column reads: G E O R G E G I R A F F E

Giraffes have an excellent sense of _____.
Number of neck vertebrae.
The giraffe's chief predator is _____.
Giraffes live south of this desert.
The giraffe's _____ is long and flexible.
Captive giraffes can live up to 36 _____.
Giraffes do not _____ as their food comes from trees.
The giraffe's favorite tree.
Older giraffes are a darker _____.
The giraffe belongs to this group of animals.
Giraffes bear only one _____ at a time.
Male giraffes use their long necks to _____.
Giraffes live in groups called _____.

Answers: SIGHT, SEVEN, LION, SAHARA, TONGUE, YEARS, MIGRATE, ACACIA, BROWN, MAMMAL, CALF, FIGHT, HERDS

Today in 1904

the London Symphony Orchestra (LSO) gave its first performance.

- The orchestra was formed when 50 or so musicians left the Queen's Hall Orchestra.
- The LSO premiered Benjamin Briton's *The Young Person's Guide to the Orchestra*.
- Most symphony orchestras have around 100 musicians.
- Drums, triangles, and cymbals were added to the orchestra for playing Turkish military music.

Word
of the day

symphony A large orchestra that can perform symphonies; from the Greek *symphonos*: sym (together) and *phone* (voice or sound)

Imagine...

The LSO is having its annual sports day. There are all the usual races (three-legged, wheelbarrow, sprint, baton, etc). The only difference is that the musicians all carry their instruments while taking part. Write about the day, or draw pictures of the more special events.

Quote
of the day

"There are two golden rules for an orchestra: start together and finish together."
Sir Thomas Beecham (conductor)

Activity
of the day

Symphony orchestra word search
Find all these instruments in the word search below. The left over letters tell you what the musician standing in front of the orchestra has to do.

alto clarinet, bass clarinet, bassoon, cello, Cor Anglais, double bass, flute, French horn, gong, piano, piccolo, snare, timpani, triangle, trombone, trumpet, tuba, viola, violin

```
O N A I P G N O G C V T S T
O N I N A P M I T D I U S R
F R E N C H H O R N O B A O
T E N I R A L C O T L A B M
S I A L G N A R O C A U E B
B A S S C L A R I N E T L O
T R I A N G L E T U L F B N
T R U M P E T C E L L O U E
P I C C O L O B A S S O O N
V I O L I N S N A R E C D T
```

Today in 1943

the ballpoint pen was patented (for the second time!).

- The inventor was Laszlo Biró. He first patented the pen in 1938.
- The British Royal Air Force bought the rights. They needed a pen that would work at high altitudes.
- The pen company BIC sells over 14 million ballpoint pens a day!

Word of the day

biro A type of ballpoint pen, named after its inventor.

Quote of the day

"Every drop of ink in my pen ran cold."
Horace Walpole

Imagine...

Pencil cases are dark, crowded, and scary places (especially if you're a small pen). So what happens when you pull the zipper closed? Do the pens talk to the pencils? What do highlighters think? How sharp is a pencil sharpener? Do erasers rub the others the wrong way? Write about the social lives of writing implements.

Activity of the day

How Far Can a Pen Write?

Ballpoint pen manufacturers claim their pens can write up to 3 miles (5 km) of text. How could you find out how far your pen writes? Here's one idea:

1. Remove the inside plastic ink barrel from a brand new pen.
2. Measure the length of ink inside and divide by ten.
3. Measure that distance from the top of the ink down and make a mark. Now you'll need a stack of scrap paper.
4. Draw 8-in. (20-cm) lines across the paper. Every five lines will equal about one yard (one meter). You should be able to fit 50 lines (10 yards) on each page.
5. How many pages can you fill with lines before the ink falls below the marker?

P.S. If the claim is true, your 1/10 of a barrel of ink should make about 50 pages of lines. That's a lot of lines to draw, so you might like to try the experiment over a few days, share the pen around, or think of a completely different way of seeing how far your pen can write.

Today in 1776

famous landscape artist John Constable was born.

- He was one of the first painters to paint landscape pictures outside, rather than in a studio.
- Although he painted landscapes set in France and other countries, he never left England.

Word
of the day

landscape A painting of natural scenery; from the Dutch *landschap*: *land* and *schap* (ship).

Imagine...

Divide a piece of paper into four. In the first box, think about what the landscape around your school would have looked like 200 years ago and draw it. In the second, draw what might it have looked like 50 years ago. In the third box, draw a landscape from today. In the fourth, draw what the landscape might look like in 50 years.

Quote
of the day

"The sound of water escaping from mill dams, willows, old rotten planks, slimy posts and brickwork, I love such things. These scenes made me a painter."

John Constable

Activity
of the day

Spot the Difference.
Two landscape artists drew the same landscape, but on different days and at different times. Can you spot the ten differences?

Answers: 1. different times on clock/tower; 2. sun's position; 3. clear sky/rain; 4. birds/no birds; 5. leaves on tree/no leaves; 6. ducks on pond/no ducks; 7. clean chair/newspaper and leaves on chair; 8. reeds/flowers; 9. differing paths to tower; 10. empty bin with rubbish around/full bin

Today in 1982

zoologist Karl von Frisch died.

- He was the first zoologist to prove that fish can see color and hear sound.

- He also discovered that bees can see all the colors that humans can, except for red.

- His later research showed that bees navigate using the sun, and perform "dances" to communicate to other bees where food is located.

Word of the day

bee A social insect; from the Old English *beo*, the Old High German *bia bee*, the Old Irish *bech*, and the Lithuanian *bitis*.

Quote of the day

If a queen bee were crossed with a Friesian bull, would not the land flow with milk and honey?

Oliver St. John Gogarty

Imagine...

"A tricky human that Karl von Frisch. We didn't realize what he was up to until it was too late. Now he, and the other humans, know that we bees dance. Fortunately, he thinks we dance to tell the other bees where the food is. Hah! Wrong, all wrong! We bees dance because . . . ." Why do bees dance? What do they dance? What music do they dance to? Do they sing, or just hum the words? Write an encyclopedia entry entitled: "Bees: Why They Dance."

Activity of the day

To Bee or Not to Bee
This bee's confused. Its mate has just done a stunning dance to communicate exactly where the pollen is, but it's become confused. Follow the trail and see where the bee ends up.

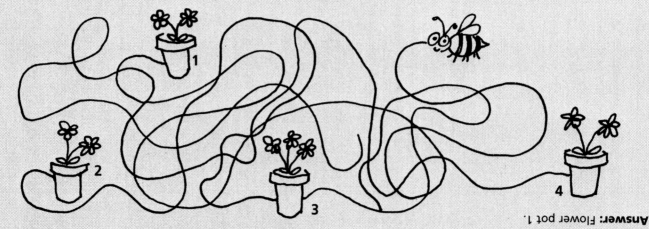

Answer: Flower pot 1.

Today in 1978

Billy White of Massachusetts ended a 134 day holiday—in a coffin.

- The specially designed coffin had a TV and a radio.
- Bill White of Texas, was buried for 141 days between July and December of 1981.
- The Taj Mahal in India is one of the world's largest tombs.

Word of the day

tomb A place for the burial of a corpse; from the Latin *tumere* (to be swollen).

Imagine...

"Being buried in a coffin for 141 days is a record? We vampires sleep in ours for hundreds of years! We've got all the modern conveniences, too—all the things that the progressive vampire needs. You'd like a guided tour? Sure!"

Draw a design for the vampire's, er, "home." Don't forget the garlic-ometer, the holy-waterproofing, and the anti-stake device.

Quote of the day

"It was the cough that carried him off; it was the coffin they carried him off in."
Anonymous

Activity of the day

Start with COFFIN. Add AAELRV. Rearrange the letters. Bingo! Naval officer! Now try these ten (with clues to help you!).

C O F F I N +	H	a sheer fabric of silk or rayon
	GS	laughing at or scorning
	AET	a positive feeling of liking
	AILT	suffering or distress due to ill health
	AELO	an office where loans are repaid (two words)
	AGSTU	struggling for breath

Answers: chiffon, scoffing, affection, affliction, loa-office, suffocating

Today in 1801

former American patriot and traitor Benedict Arnold died.

- Arnold was originally a successful American commander. Needing money to maintain a lavish lifestyle, he sold military secrets to the British during the American War of Independence.

- His treachery was discovered when his letters were found hidden in the socks of an English major!

- He later joined the English army, fighting against the Americans. Despite grants of land and money from the British, he died an unhappy and mistrusted man.

Word of the day

traitor Someone who betrays his country by committing treason; from the Latin *tradere* (to deliver or betray)..

Quote of the day

Start a political upheaval and let yourself be caught, and you will hang as a traitor. But place yourself at the head of a rebellion and gain your point, and all future generations will worship you as the Father of their Country.

Hendrik W. Van Loon

Imagine...

Rivalry between the two top teams in the local sports league has reached fever pitch as the finals approach. Your coach has asked you to carry out a special mission—to spy on the other team. As a patriotic team member you can hardly refuse; so, heavily disguised, you join the other side. What happens? Are you discovered? What do you find out? Write about your life as a spy.

Activity of the day

From Traitor to Patriot

A TRAITOR is only one letter away from a PATRIOT. Use the clues to work out these words. Some will need to be unscrambled.

TRAITOR		R		P	one who loves and defends his or her country	PATRIOT
TRAITOR		T		P	an airfield with control tower and hangers	
TRAITOR	-	I	+	C	a vehicle with large wheels, used in farming	
TRAITOR		O		E	more worn and torn	
TRAITOR		T		C	orange-colored fruit	
TRAITOR		T		Y	trimming shrubs or trees into shapes	

Answers: airport, tractor, rattier, apricot, topiary

Today in 1869

John and Isiah Hyatt discovered celluloid.

- In the 1800s, billiard balls and piano keys were made from ivory. As the supply was becoming scarce, a billiard-ball manufacturer offered a $10,000 prize to anyone inventing a substitute.

- The Hyatts' entry, a newly invented substance called celluloid, didn't win.

- Celluloid was used for making film, brushes, buttons, and combs.

- John Hyatt is regarded as the "father of the U.S. plastics industry."

Word
of the day

billiards A game played on a rectangular cloth-covered table in which cue sticks are used to propel ivory balls; from the French *bille* (log).

Imagine...

Imagine you are an animal lover disgusted with the ivory trade. Design a poster protesting about the killing of elephants to make billiard balls and piano keys. Create a catchy slogan as your rallying cry.

Quote
of the

"My object all sublime I shall achieve in time,
To let the punishment fit the crime
On a cloth untrue with a twisted cue,
and elliptical billiard balls!"

W. S. Gilbert

Activity
of the day

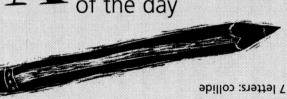

What Can You Make From Celluloid?
Celluloid was used for manufacturing a huge variety of items. Can you manufacture a huge variety of words?

C	E	L
L	U	L
O	I	D

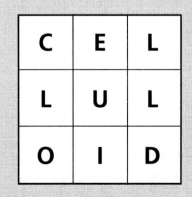

Answers:
Here are 44 we found:
3 letters: cod, cud, cue, die, doe, due, duo, ice, led, Leo, lid, lie, oil, old
4 letters: cell, clue, code, coil, cold, dell, dell, dice, dole, duel, dull, iced, idle, idol, lied, loud, lull
5 letters: cello, cloud, clued, could, lucid, oiled, oldie
6 letters: coiled, collie, docile, loiled, lulled
7 letters: collide

Today in 1885

"Away in a Manger" was first published.

- The famous carol was once thought to have been written by Martin Luther, but now is attributed to an unknown American composer.
- The "Boar's Head Carol" is one of the earliest known carols, and was printed in 1521.
- The words to "Hark the Herald Angels" sing were written as Charles Wesley was walking to church on Christmas morning.

Word of the day

manger An open box from which cattle or horses feed; from the Latin *manducare* (to chew).

Quote of the day

"She brought forth her firstborn child and wrapped him in swaddling clothes, and laid him in a manger; because there was no room for him in the inn."

The Bible, Luke 2:7

Imagine...

Congress is preparing legislation to change Christmas from December 25th to July 31st so that the weather will be better for vacations and school won't be in session. Write ten reasons why you agree or disagree with this move.

Activity of the day

Complete the names of these 10 well-known carols by finding the missing words in the word search below. The leftover letters (minus two) spell out the title of one of the few popular carols by an American writer.

```
G W S T N E I R O F O C L I
T E E L Y R R E M A Y O J F
H A N N L T S G N I K M T I
R D W T C E L N G T S E R R
E O D A L E B A N H A L L S
E O E G Y E S M I F K T O T
G G N W N O M L S U C R F B
E I W O R L D E A L E T A H
J N O E L W L E N S D E H H
E M D L A R E H A N G E L S
```

1. _____ in a _____
2. _____ to the _____
3. _____ the _____
4. _____ _____
5. O _____ All Ye _____
6. _____ _____
   Ye_____, _____
7. The _____ _____
8. _____ the _____
   _____ _____
9. _____ King _____
10. We _____ _____ of
    _____ Are

Today in 1966

Iceland became an independent nation.

- Along with ice and snow, Iceland has some 200 volcanoes.
- Iceland has no reptiles, frogs, or toads.
- The first settler in Iceland was Viking Ingûlfr Arnarson. He and his wife began farming there in AD 874.
- The world's first democratically elected female president was Iceland's Vigdìs Finnbogadûttir.

Word of the day

Viking A member of the Norse people who raided Europe in the 8th-10th centuries; from the Old English *wicing* (camping).

Imagine...

Iceland: land of volcanoes, ice, snow, cold, fog, and very little greenery. Unfortunately, you have the job of promoting Iceland as a tourist destination. Write an informative and alluring tourist brochure titled "Iceland: Your Vaction Dream Come True!"

Quote of the day

Dublin, though a place much worse than London, is not so bad as Iceland.
Samuel Johnson

Activity of the day

Hmm. Ice. Land. Let's call this place Iceland! Are the lands below any more imaginatively named?

What do we call the land of:
1. Colliding?
2. Chocolate eggs and eyes?
3. Fish locomotion organ?
4. Blue plus yellow?
5. Lofty positions?
6. Anger?
7. All women?
8. Long rods?
9. Royalty?

Answers: 1. crash-land 2. Easter Island 3. Finland 4. Greenland 5. highland 6. Ireland 7. no-man's-land 8. Poland 9. Queensland

Today in 1983

astronaut Sally Ride became the first woman to fly aboard the space shuttle.

- She was one of 8,000 applicants. Only 35 were accepted. Six were women.
- On board the shuttle she has worked as a communications officer and a mission specialist, launching satellites.
- She has written three books for children, including *Voyager: An Adventure to the Edge of the Solar System*.
- The first woman in space was Soviet cosmonaut Valentina Tereshkova in 1963.

Word of the day

shuttle To travel back and forwards; from the Old English *sceotan* (to shoot).

Quote of the day

"When I was training to be an astronaut, it wasn't enough to just show up for class. I had to go prepared to learn."
Sally Ride

Imagine...

Elton John's song "Rocket Man" has the lyrics "and all this science, I don't understand, it's just my job five days a week." Write about your 9-to-5 week (both the boring and the exciting parts) as the space shuttle pilot.

Activity of the day

Sally in Space

It took Sally a long time to get into space. How long will it take you to change STARS into SPACE? Use the clues, and only change one letter at a time.

S	T	A	R	S	
					fights
					extra
S	P	A	C	E	

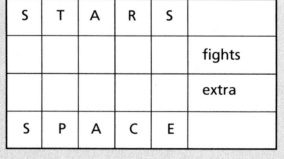
Answers: STARS, SPARS, SPARE, SPACE

Today in 1846

the Knickerbockers played Hoboken in the first official game of baseball.

- Baseball is thought to have developed from the English game of rounders.
- Jackie Robinson became the first black person to play in the major leagues.
- The All-American Girls' Professional Baseball League was formed in 1943.
- Baseball was introduced to Japan in 1872.

Word of the day

baseball A game played with a bat and ball. Two teams take turns at bat, trying to score runs by completing a lap of four bases.

Imagine...

Invent a new game. Start with a playground game (e.g., skipping, Red Rover). Change the game to make it more interesting as a spectator sport. Write the rules, or describe a game in progress.

Quote of the day

"Ninety percent of baseball is half mental."
Yogi Berra

Activity of the day

Complete each of the VERTICAL three-letter words to discover the HORIZONTAL puzzle word. What do each of the puzzle words have in common?

I	E	C	P	O
S	B	B	Y	D

S	S	I	S	S	G
E	N	E	Y	E	M

U	M	O	U	E	R	I	E
E	B	F	E	B	W	L	K

U	M	C	I	A	S	T	A
N	W	B	N	D	W	Y	S

A	W	Z	A	S	S	A
E	Y	P	T	I	T	E

A	V	E	O
E	W	M	F

Answers: T-BALL, HOCKEY, SOFTBALL, ROUNDERS, CRICKET, GOLF. They're all bat and ball games.

JUNE 20

Today in 1977

the Alaska pipeline was opened.

- Over 20 years, over 11 billion barrels of oil have traveled through the line.

- The pipeline took 3 years, 126 shiploads of pipes, and $8 billion to complete.

- The pipeline has 13 bridges, travels over three mountain ranges, and crosses 34 major rivers.

- The 310-mile (500-km)-long Kalgoorlie (WA) water pipeline is one of the world's longest.

Word of the day

pipe A long metal or plastic tube used to carry water, oil, or gas; from the Latin *pipare* (to peep).

Quote of the day

"The society which scorns excellence in plumbing . . . and tolerates shoddiness in philosophy . . . will have neither good plumbing nor good philosophy . . . neither its pipes nor its theories will hold water."
John W. Gardner

Imagine...

"All right people," says the boss. "We need a pipeline to move it from here," she tapped the map, "to here." She tapped it again and peered at us expectantly. We looked at each other. Could it be done? Could we build a pipeline from one side of the U.S. to the other? I raised my hand. "Er, Boss, what will the pipeline carry? Water? Gas? Oil?" The boss smiled. "No.—Something better!" Decide what the pipe will carry, and then draw a map of the route, design the pumping system, or just write about this amazing engineering project.

Activity of the day

Pipeline Puzzle

All those pipes, and so many in need of repair! So, the water goes in at the arrow—and out where?

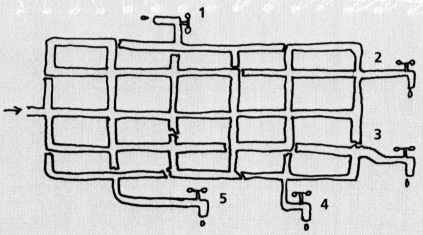

Answer: It comes out at faucet 2.

Today in 1777

the first volume of the *Encyclopedia Britannica* (in its second edition) was published.

- It was published in 100 weekly parts.
- The first encyclopaedia is thought to have been published by Speusippus (a Greek philosopher) in 400 BC.
- The first encyclopaedia available on CD-ROM was *Compton's Multimedia Encyclopedia*.
- Microsoft's Encarta is now the world's best selling encyclopaedia.

Imagine...

Encyclopedia Americana wants an entry from you for their latest edition. Write either a short (but not necessarily true) biography of your life or a short entry about a subject you're an expert on or would like to think you're an expert on.

Word of the day

encyclopedia A reference work containing articles on various topics; from the Greek *enkyklios* (encircling) and *paideia* (education).

Quote of the day

"In everything that relates to science, I am a whole Encyclopedia behind the rest of the world."
Charles Lamb

Activity of the day

Encyclopedias have a language all of their own. How many of these encyclopedia-related words can you identify?

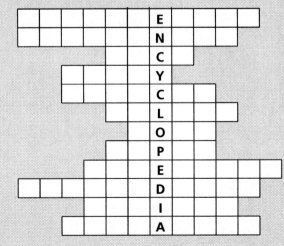

E	arranged in order according to the alphabet
N	a reference book of words and their meanings
C	a piece of true information
Y	an item in a reference work
C	a dictionary
L	a book in a set
O	a written or printed work
P	an entry in an encyclopaedia
E	a book to which you can refer for facts
D	an index of all main words in a book and their context
I	a section of a reference work
A	a book of synonyms

Answers: alphabetical, dictionary, fact, entry, lexicon, volume, book, topic, reference, concordance, article, thesaurus

JUNE 22

Today in 1847

the first doughnut (with a hole) was created.

- The deep-fried batter doughnut originated in the 16th century in Holland. It was known as an olykoek.
- National Doughnut Day in the U.S. is February 15!
- Howard Strick of Spokane, WA closed his doughnut shop after making "at least a million dozen" doughnuts in 42 years. He only ate one a day.

Word of the day

torus A doughnut-shaped surface; Latin word meaning a bulge or cushion.

Imagine...

You're a doughnut shop owner. The judges of the International Decorated Doughnut Competition are visiting today. Draw up six designs for amazingly decorated doughnuts. Remember, if you win, you'll be rolling in dough!

Quote of the day

"Doughnuts. Is there anything they can't do?"
Homer Simpson

Activity of the day

Doughnut Decision
One doughnut.
Eight people.
Three cuts.
Make all the pieces equally tiny!
Can you do it?

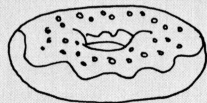

Answers: 1. Slice in half across the hole.; 2. Slice in quarters across the hole.; 3. Slice into eighths by slicing horizontally to the hole!

Today in 1868

the first commercial typewriter was patented.

- It used a QWERTY keyboard and was developed from an idea for automatically numbering the pages of a book.
- The keys pushed the type bar up onto the underside of the paper; this was called "blind-writing" because the typist (originally called a typewriter, too!) couldn't see the typing.
- The machine was manufactured by Remington & Sons, who had previously only made guns and sewing machines.

Imagine...

Oh boy! Your publishing deadline is tomorrow and half the keys of your typewriter are jammed! In fact, every key other than the QWERTY row is useless! Write a short news story using ONLY the letters on that row. (QWERTYUIOP in case you weren't sure!)

Word of the day

type To write using a typewriter; from the Greek *typos* (blow).

Quote of the day

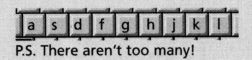

"I'm all in favor of keeping dangerous weapons out of the hands of fools. Let's start with typewriters."
Solomon Short

Activity of the day

How many 5 letter words can you make using the MIDDLE row of the QWERTY keyboard? You can only use each letter once.

`a s d f g h j k l`

P.S. There aren't too many!

```
` 1 2 3 4 5 6 7 8 9 0 [ =
  ' , . p y f g c r l / } \
  a o e u i d h t n s -
  ; q j k x b m w v z
```

The Dvorak keyboard (a special keyboard claimed to be much faster to type on) looks like this: How many 5 letter words can you make using the middle row of letters on this keyboard?

Answers: QWERTY keyboard—flags, flash, flask

DVORAK keyboard—Andes, audio, aunts, dates, deans, death, donut, duets, hands, hated, haunt, hints, hosed, hunts, ideas, noted, saint, shade, shine, shone, shout, sited, sound, stain, stand, stone, those, unite (to name a few!)

JUNE 24

Today in 1867

barbed wire was first invented by Michael Kelly.

- Thirteen different kinds of barbed wire were patented between 1868 and 1874.
- Kelly's design twisted two pieces of wire together, "to form a cable for barbs." It was known as the "thorny fence."
- Barbed wire fences have proved fatal for flying foxes in Queensland, Australia. Flying low to reduce wind resistance, they become caught in the top row of wire.

Word of the day

barb The pointed part of barbed wire; from the Latin *barba* (beard or facial hair).

Quote of the day

"The barbed wire on the fence around the Soviet Union is to keep people inside, in the dark."

Victor Belenko, MiG-25 fighter

Imagine...

Caught. Caught good and proper! There you are, halfway over the fence—the barbed wire fence—and you snagged your jeans in four places. But why are you so frantic? What's following you across the field? Why are you struggling so much? Just why were you there in the first place? Come on, tell us all about it!

Activity of the day

Farmer Kelly has very kindly donated 1/4 of his land to the local school for a new playground. He's also given the school a long roll of barbed wire and some rules.

1. Each of his three prize cows must have her own separate corral.
2. The three corrals and the playground must be the exactly the same size and shape.
3. Each of the cows must be able to lean over her fence and look into the playground.

How did the school do it?

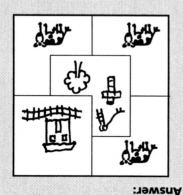

Answer:

Today in 1876

Crazy Horse and his warriors defeated Lieutenant Colonel George Custer at the Battle of the Little Bighorn.

- The battle was also known as Custer's Last Stand.
- Custer was called "yellow hair" (for his long blonde hair) and "Son of the Morning Star" as he often planned attacks early in the morning.
- The battle occurred after prospectors looking for gold trespassed on Native American land.
- Custer led his 264 men against a combined Native American force of over 3,000.

Word of the day

warrior A person experienced in warfare; from the Old North French *werreier* (to make war).

Imagine...

Just up from the school is Gumleaf Drive, a steep hill that ends at a ravine, aptly named Gumdrop Ravine. It's also the site of Bruiser's Last Stand. Bruiser was the school bully—as mean and tough as they come. But he's not a bully anymore. Write about Bruiser's Last Stand. How did he lose? Who did he fight? What happened?

Quote of the day

... they are not running but are coming on.

Note regarding the Native Americans sent from Colonel Custer to his other officers (Reno and Benteen) at the Little Bighorn

Activity of the day

Can you complete this Totem Pole Puzzle?

	Clue
L	existing in fact
I (mad or crazy)	
T	win a victory over
T (wagons in single file)	
L	a book of instructions
E (protection for travelers)	
B	to move upwards
I (old name for Native American)	
G	planning when something happens
H (four-legged mammals used in warfare)	
O	one of Custer's officers
R (a large stream)	
N	a large, flat area of land

Answers: Actual, insane, defeat, train, manual, escort, climb, Indian, timing, horses, Reno, river, plain

Today in 1824

Lord William Thomson Kelvin, inventor of the Kelvin thermometer scale, was born.

- On the Kelvin scale, 0° K (zero degrees Kelvin) is -273.16° C. This temperature is also known as absolute zero.

- Kelvin entered college at the age of ten and had important scientific papers published when he was 16.

- Lord Kelvin also invented a practical way of sending telegraph messages along transatlantic cables, an improved mariner's compass, and better tide prediction charts.

Word of the day

thermometer A device for measuring temperature; from the Greek *therme* (heat) and the French *mètre* (meter).

Quote of the day

" . . . I've been one of those persons who never goes anywhere without a thermometer, a hot water bottle, a raincoat, and a parachute. If I had to do it again, I would travel lighter than I have . . ."

Nadine Stair

Imagine...

You thought you had the flu. Dad took your temperature. As the thermometer touched your lips, it turned white with frost and cracked. He called the doctor. The doctor took your temperature. Add one more frozen, cracked thermometer to the list. "Does my child have a high temperature?" your dad asked worriedly. The doctor looked at the small snow cloud forming around your head. "Well, not a high temperature." Write about your illness, what you do, and whether you get better.

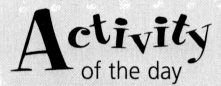

Activity of the day

To convert degrees centigrade to degrees Kelvin, add 273. (rounded off)

To convert degrees Kelvin to degrees centigrade, subtract 273. (rounded off)

Complete this chart of temperatures:

	A	B	C	D	E	F	G	H	I
°C		-173		-50	0		50	100	
°K	0		200			300			400

Answers: (A) -273 (B) 100 (C) -73 (D) 223 (E) 223 (F) 273 (G) 27 (H) 323 (I) 127

Today in 1693

the first woman's magazine, the *Ladies Mercury* was published in London.

- Early magazines were quite "highbrow," such as *Philosophical Transactions*, which appeared in 1665. It is still published today!

- *Le Mercure Galant* (a French publication) was one of the first magazines with broader appeal. It contained poetry, gossip columns (about the royal court), and short stories.

- The September 1987 edition of *Vogue* (U.S.) had 897 pages!

Imagine...

Create a magazine devoted to that most important topic: you! Use your name for the title (like Ralph or Marie Claire), then design the front page. Write several lead articles about the amazingly interesting things happening in your life right now! You can even have a page of contents, photographs, and contests (to win quality time with—guess who?).

Word of the day

magazine A periodic paperback publication; from the Arabic *makhazin* (storehouses).

Quote of the day

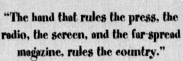

"The hand that rules the press, the radio, the screen, and the far-spread magazine, rules the country."
Learned Hand

Activity of the day

Magazine Word Search

How many of these magazines can you find in the Word Search? When you've found them all, the left over letters spell out the name of an Australian magazine started by Dick Smith.

APC, Cleo, Cosmopolitan, Disney, Dolly, GEO, Girlfriend, New Idea, Noise, Our House, Reader's Digest, Smash Hits, Time, TV Hits, TV Week, Wheels, Women's Weekly, Woman's Day

A	P	C	A	U	S	K	E	E	W	V	T	G	S
C	L	E	O	T	R	A	L	I	G	A	N	I	M
T	S	E	G	I	D	S	R	E	D	A	E	R	A
N	E	W	I	D	E	A	O	W	H	E	E	L	S
C	O	S	M	O	P	O	L	I	T	A	N	F	H
N	O	I	S	E	M	I	T	G	E	O	D	R	H
Y	L	K	E	E	W	S	N	E	M	O	W	I	I
Y	A	D	S	N	A	M	O	W	L	G	R	E	T
O	U	R	H	O	U	S	E	L	A	P	H	N	S
I	S	T	I	H	V	T	Y	E	N	S	I	D	C

Answer: Australian Geographic

JUNE 28

Word
of the day

tomato A mildly acidic red or yellow fruit eaten as a vegetable; from the Mexican *tomatl*.

Quote
of the day

"Tomatoes and oregano make it Italian; wine and tarragon make it French. Sour cream makes it Russian; lemon and cinnamon make it Greek. Soy sauce makes it Chinese; garlic makes it good."

Alice May Brock

Today in 1820

the tomato was proven to be non-poisonous.

- The tomato is a member of the nightshade family of plants.
- The first tomatoes were small, pear-shaped, and yellow. Italian herbalists called them *pomo d'oro* (apples of the sun).
- An Italian study showed that eating seven or more servings of tomatoes a week reduced the risk of developing some cancers by up to 60%.

Imagine...

The local mayor's just returned from abroad after visiting a festival where they send truckloads of tomatoes through the street and throw them at each other. Now he wants to do the same in your area and says it will "add color." Write about the festival, and about what happens on your school's tomato truck.

Activity
of the day

Fruit and Vegtable Circular Puzzle
Here are clues to 8 unusual vegetables and fruits. The first word begins with T. Each answer begins with the last letter of the preceding word. The last word ends in T.

1. mildly acid red fruit eaten as a vegetable
2. small, oval-shaped European fruit important for food and oil
3. berry-like fruit of the elder shrub
4. the edible tuber of a tropical vine
5. large, oval smooth-skinned tropical fruit
6. edible bulb which causes eyes to sting when peeled
7. smooth-skinned variety of the peach
8. egg-shaped vegetable with a shiny, dark purple skin

Answers: 1. TOMATO; 2. OLIVE; 3. ELDERBERRY; 4. YAM; 5. MANGO; 6. ONION; 7. NECTARINE; 8. EGGPLANT TOMATOLIVELDERBERRYAMANGONIONECTARINEGG-PLAN

Today in 1613

Shakespeare's famous Globe Theater burned to the ground.

- The theater was built from the timbers of London's oldest theater (called The Theater) and staged its first play in 1599.
- The front of the theater was carved with the words *totus mundus agit historionem* (all the world's a stage).
- The theater burned down after a cannon (used in a Shakespearean play) set fire to a straw roof.
- The theater was rebuilt and officially reopened on June 12, 1997 by the Queen.

Imagine...

It's the school drama night, and your class is performing next. In an attempt at realism, your teacher has brought in real animals for your class's interpretation of Doctor Doolittle. A recipe for disaster? Sure is, especially when the other class's teacher brings in real fireworks for The Gunpowder Plot. Write about the drama of the drama night.

Word of the day

globe A spherical model (map) of the world; from the Latin *globus*.

Quote of the day

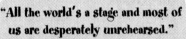

"All the world's a stage and most of us are desperately unrehearsed."
Sean O'Casey

Activity of the day

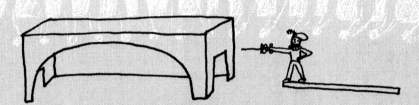

Model Theater
Make a model theater of your own.
You'll need:
- a cardboard box
- a sharp knife
- glue and tape
- straws or thin sticks
- paint
- thin card stock or heavy paper

1. First, cut a proscenium arch from the front. (This is the "window" through which your audience sees the stage. Don't cut right to the sides as a border will add strength.)
2. Now cut rectangular holes in the two sides. These are for sliding your "actors" in and out.
3. Decorate the theater.
4. Cut out a pair of "drama masks" and attach above the theater.
5. Cut out photos of people and glue them onto the thin card.
6. Attach a straw at the bottom (see picture). These are your actors which can be slid in and out through the sides.
7. Now all you need is a play to perform (and some scenery, but choose the play first!).

<table>
<tr><td>

JUNE
30

</td></tr>
</table>

Today in 1908

a giant fireball fell on Tunguska in Russia.

- A 165-ft. (50-m) wide meteorite is thought to have caused the devastation over 13,365 square miles (21,504 square kilometers).

- It left a trail of light 500 miles (800 km) long and the explosion was visible from hundreds of miles (kilometers) away.

- The shaman-chief of the Tungus people closed the region off, calling it "enchanted." Scientists investigated the area 19 years later.

Word of the day

devastate To cause great destruction; from the Latin *devastatus* (to lay waste).

Quote of the day

"Big stone has fallen . . . big as "chyum" (tent), jumped up two or three times, and then sank in a bog."

Nastya Dzhenkoul (eyewitness)

Imagine...

Although most scientists believe a meteorite caused the explosion, some facts just don't fit. Why were there four smaller explosions? Why are some of the trees slightly radioactive? Why have no pieces of meteorite been found? What do you think? Was it a meteorite or something else? Write an account of the explosion as if you were an eyewitness to the event.

Activity of the day

Here are pictographs of words related to the Tunguska incident. See how many you can decode.

Today in 1990

riding a bicycle without a helmet became illegal in Victoria, Australia.

- In the U.S. there are state and local laws requiring the use of helmets for bicycle riders.
- The Child Bicycle Safety Act of 1994 has not gone into effect because Congress has not approved the funding necessary to implement the Act.
- The Tour de France bicycle race was organized in 1903 as a publicity stunt by sport journal editor Henn Desgranges and covered 1,515 miles (2,440 km).
- While wearing a helmet, American bicycle racer Greg LeMond in 1986 became the first American to win the Tour de France, cycling's premier event.

Word of the day

helmet A protective head covering made of hard material; from the Old German *helan* (to conceal).

Imagine...

What features would you like to see incorporated into a bike helmet? Would you like to have a radio so you could head traffic reports? Would you like a display panel on a visor that would tell you your speed, distance traveled, etc.? Perhaps you would prefer certain colors, styles, and artwork. Design, label, and describe your ideal bike helmet.

Quote of the day

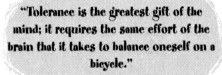

"Tolerance is the greatest gift of the mind; it requires the same effort of the brain that it takes to balance oneself on a bicycle."

Helen Keller, *The Story of My Life*

Activity of the day

Ali's Race

Ali's sponsor, Cheap Stuff for Bikes, has donated a new helmet for the big endurance bicycle race. It's not a very good one, though. Only 15 km into the race, the sponsor's sticker falls off.
For the next one-quarter of the distance, it rains—and Ali discovers the helmet is not waterproof.
The next one-seventh of the distance seems better, but Ali cannot see that the paint on the helmet, also not waterproof, has begun to run down her face. Then the strap breaks, and Ali spends the next one-fifth of the distance holding onto it with one hand. Next, the helmet falls off, and she spends the last three-tenths of the race hoping the race officials and police don't see her. They don't, but she comes in third in the race (she had hoped to take first). She throws the horrible helmet in the trash can. How long is the ride?

Answer: The race is 140 km long.

Today

is the midpoint of the year.

- The midpoint begins at noon, or at midnight in leap years.
- The quarter points of the year are at 6 A.M. on April 2 and at 6 P.M. on October 1.
- The first six months of the year have 181 days; the second six have 184.

Word
of the day

month A measure of time that is roughly 1/12 of a year; from the Old English *mona* (moon).

Quote
of the day

"Write it on your heart that every day is the best day of the year."
Ralph Waldo Emerson

Imagine...

The universe has reached its midpoint. From this time on, everything that has ever happened will happen in reverse. Everything. Write about today as though it were in reverse. Esrever ni erew ti hguoht sa yadot tuoba etirw.

Activity
of the day

Middles

It's the middle of the year, and the temperatures are in the mid-teens. You're feeling fair to middling when you get dropped right in the middle of—all these middles.

M	between youth and old age	
I	the period in history between the Roman Empire and the Renaissance	
D	the note on the first ledger line below the stave in treble clef	
D	not low or high	
L	a cavity essential to hearing	
E	the area from Turkey to North Africa	
+	a person who buys goods and sells them to shops rather than customers	
	views on issues that are not extreme	
	not large or small	
	a wrestler who weighs 172-192 pounds	

Answers: age, ages, c, class, ear, east, man, of the road, sized, weight

Today in 1806

Michael Keens exhibited the first cultivated pineapple strawberry.

- Strawberries are members of the rose family. They are not berries or fruit but the enlarged ends of the plant's stamen (the pollen-producing organ).

- The common (or garden) strawberry is a hybrid (cross) between the scarlet and beach strawberry.

- The berries seem to be strewn among the leaves of the plant. The plant first had the name strewberry, which later was changed to strawberry.

Word of the day

hybrid Offspring produced by breeding plants of different varieties; from the Latin *hybrida* (offspring between a tame sow and a wild boar).

Imagine...

You're a horticultural hybrid specialist and have been asked to produce offspring from some curious mixtures of plants. Choose two pairs from this list and draw and describe just what they'd look and taste like: banana, pear, apple, grape, strawberry, date, plum, pineapple, apricot.

Quote of the day

"Doubtless God could have made a better berry, but doubtless God never did."
William Butler (referring to the strawberry)

Activity of the day

Strawberry Puzzle
Read the clues and complete the words. Each word only contains letters from the word "strawberry."

				clue letter	clue
				S	defeats
ready to cry				T	
				R	declare as true
artistic				A	
				W	scatter
animal				B	
				E	worthless material
try again				R	
				R	liquid ice
dough raiser				Y	

Answers: beats, teary, swear, artsy, strew, beast, waste, retry, water, yeast

Today in 1999

was the last day of the Tom Sawyer Days in Hannibal, Missouri, U.S.

- Hannibal was the childhood home of Samuel Langhorne Clemens.
- *Tom Sawyer*, written by Samuel Clemens (using the name Mark Twain), was published in 1876.
- In the book, Tom is given a huge fence to paint as punishment. He tricks other children into painting it for him and paying for the pleasure.

Word of the day

pseudonym A ficticious name used by a writer; from the Greek *pseudonymos*: *pseud* (false) and *onyma* (name).

Quote of the day

"Horse-high, bull-strong, and pig-tight."
Anonymous (describing a well-built New Zealand fence)

Imagine...

Time: Saturday morning.
Problem: Big trouble with parents.
Punishment: Clean up the backyard.
Task: Con friends into completing job so you can still go to the movies this afternoon.

How would you go about the job? Write about your plan, and whether it succeeds or not.

Activity of the day

To make more money, Tom plans to build a small maze. He draws up four designs but can't decide among them. Which design should he choose if he wants his customers to enter and leave from one side and go through each door only once?

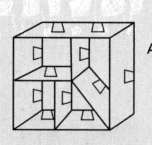
A

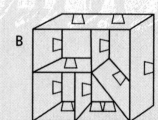
B

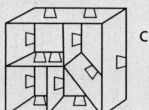
C

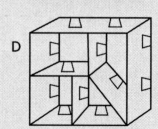
D

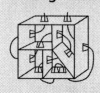

Answers: Here's one solution–using maze B.

Answers: Here's one solution–using maze B.

Today in 1806

the bikini was worn for the first time.

- The bikini was invented by French mechanical engineer Louis Reard.
- Bikini Atoll was the site of the first atomic bomb to be tested after the second world war.
- A big hit song of 1960 was Brian Hyland's "Itsy Bitsy Teenie Weenie Yellow Polka Dot Bikini."

Word of the day

Imagine...

The swimsuit seemed perfectly ordinary when you first tried it on. It wasn't until you wore it at the pool for the first time that you realized it made you swim faster in the water. Much faster. So fast that the local swim coach snapped you up for the state team. And now here you are with the finals in sight-and the swimsuit's missing. Uh, oh . . . . Write about the swimsuit, your discovery, the loss-and what happens next.

Quote of the day

"The unleashed power of the atom has changed everything save our modes of thinking and we thus drift toward unparalleled catastrophe."

Albert Einstein (telegram to prominent Americans)

Activity of the day

CVCVCV

Bikini has an unusual pattern of letters: consonant-vowel, consonant-vowel, consonant-vowel. Even more uncommon is the reverse pattern: vowel-consonant, vowel-consonant, vowel-consonant. Here are some words that are based on that pattern.

	A	A	A	musical instrument
	A	A	A	large desert
	A	A	A	tropical fruit
	A	A	A	a type of hat; a canal
	E	E	E	erase
	E	E	E	calm
	O	O	O	fancy decoration
	O	O	O	part of a pirate chant
A	A	A		mountain peak that Noah's Ark landed on
E	E	E		a cricket team
E	E	E		a metal ring for lining a small hole

Answers: maraca, Sahara, banana, Panama, delete, serene, rococo, yo-ho-ho, Ararat, eleven, eyelet

Today in 1925

rock 'n' roll legend Bill Hayley was born.

- Hayley is credited with releasing one of the first rock "n" roll records "(We're Gonna) Rock Around the Clock."

- The song was number one in the U.S. for eight weeks, sold 22 million copies worldwide, and in Britain has been in the charts seven times (the last time in 1974).

- He claimed it was a mixture of "country and western, Dixieland, and old-style rhythm and blues."

- Hayley and his band sold some 60 million records worldwide.

Word of the day

Dixieland A form of early jazz music. One of the first bands to play this style was the Original Dixieland Jazz Band. "Dixie" was a name given to the 11 states in the Southern U.S.

Quote of the day

"Just give me that old time rock and roll. The kind of music that soothes your soul."
Bob Seger, musician

Imagine...

It was you and not Bill Hayley who had that first hit song. What would it feel like to be the one who makes popular an entire musical style? Write about your first gig (performance), what the teenagers thought, what the parents thought, and what happens to you and your band.

Activity of the day

Music, Music, Music

Rock, jazz, classical, country, gospel, . . . The list of musical styles can seem never ending. Here's a shorter list (only 20 styles). Find them all, and the leftover letters will spell out the names of four other styles that are thought to have come together to create rock and roll.

```
B D N A L E I X I D O S P H O G
R O C K A N D R O L L P O E L E
C O U N T R Y I E W O E P A E G
E G E K E P O H P I H E H V P N
C N V C M O G I E S J D T Y S U
N I A O Y U M P B E L M N R O R
A W R R V U E F R U S E Y O G G
D S S S A R G E U L B T S C S R
D P O B E B O O W B O A P K A H
O N K Y H D I S C O T L O P N K
```

bebop, bluegrass, blues, country, dance, disco, Dixieland, gospel, grunge, heavy metal, heavy rock, hip-hop, rap, rave, rock, rock and roll, speed metal, surf, swing, synth pop

Answers: boogie woogie, jump blues, doo wop, honky tonk

Today in 1883

Pinocchio was printed for the first time.

- The book was *Le Avventure di Pinocchio* and was written by Italian author Carlo Collodi.
- He received the equivalent of 12 weeks' rent for the publishing rights.
- Disney released the animated film *Pinocchio* in 1940.

Imagine...

Recipe for a magical character: Take one piece of magical wood (hopefully shaped a little like a person already). Carve it into a character. Fall asleep as midnight approaches. Wait for a magical creature (elf, fairy, witch, etc.) to bring it to life. Wake up and be amazed. Now it's your turn: describe the wood, your carving (what sort of character?), the magical awakening, and the adventures that come about.

Word of the day

marionette A puppet worked by strings; from the French name *Marion* (Mary).

Quote of the day

"What name shall I give him?" he said to himself; "I think I will call him Pinocchio. It is a name that will bring him luck."

Carlo Collodi

Activity of the day

Words From Pinocchio

Pinocchio was made from a magic piece of wood. How many words of three letters or more can you make from the name Pinocchio?

P	I	N
O	C	C
H	I	O

Today in 1889

the *Wall Street Journal* began publication.

- It was the outgrowth of a daily financial news summary distributed by Dow Jones & Company, a firm organized in 1882 by Charles Henry Dow and Edward D. Jones.

- The Dow Jones Industrial Average became a measure of the stock market's performance. The Journal grew to become one of the major U.S. newspapers.

- On July 8, 1940, the first commercial flight using pressurized cabins, took off from La Guardia Airport, New York, on its way to Burbank, California. Flying time was 14 hours going west and 11 hours, 55 minutes going east.

Word of the day

date Time stated in terms of the day, month, and year; from the Latin *data* (to give).

Quote of the day

"It is all that the young can do for the old, to shock them and keep them up to date."

George Bernard Shaw, Irish-born British playwright

Imagine...

Yesterday was just another ordinary day . . . July 7, 1977. You forgot to notice it, but today when you look at the calendar, you realized it was 7/7/77. All those sevens! All those lucky sevens! But how lucky? And did they mean good luck or bad luck? Write about what you think has been the luckiest day of the 21st century—for the world, for your country, for your family, for you.

Activity of the day

Dates in History

Here are some dates in world history. All you have to do is match them to the correct events. Note that only that last two digits of the years are given—just to make it a bit of a challenge.

1.	7/18/45	a.	atomic bomb test in New Mexico desert a success
2.	6/28/14	b.	invasion of Normandy by the Allied Expeditionary Forces
3.	7/20/69	c.	first concert by the New York Philharmonic-Symphony Orchestra
4.	10/14/66	d.	landing of human beings on the moon for the first time
5.	4/23/16	e.	adoption of the U.S. Declaration of Independence
6.	6/6/14	f.	dedication of the Vietnam Veterans Memorial in Washington, D. C.
7.	11/13/82	g.	assassination of Austrian Archduke Ferdinand followed by WWI
8.	4/7/76	h.	death of playwright and poem William Shakespeare
9.	8/14/35	i.	Battle of Hastings, most decisive victory of the Norman conquest
10.	12/7/42	j.	U.S. Social Security Act signed into law

Answers: 1. a. 2. g. 3. d. 4. i. 5. h. 6. b. 7. f. 8. e. 9. j. 10. c.

Today in 1979

a Ming dynasty wine jar (found in the Earl of Verulam's lavatory) was sold at the Christie's auction house for 95,000 pounds.

- The Ming dynasty ruled China from 1368 A.D. to 1644 A.D.
- Ming means "bright" in Chinese.
- Joseph Bramah patented a flush toilet in 1778.

Word of the day

lavatory a room fitted with equipment for washing the hands and face and usually with flush toilet facilities; from the Latin *lavare* (to wash).

Imagine...

What immensely valuable object is sitting around your house waiting to be auctioned for millions of dollars? A vase? A painting? A ring? Your younger brother or sister? Write a news article, auction poster, or story about it (or them!).

Quote of the day

"France is a country where the money falls apart in your hands and you can't tear the toilet paper."
Billy Wilder

Activity of the day

Off to the Lavatory
Complete this word puzzle.

L			
	A		
		V	
			A
T			
	O		
		R	
			Y

The remainder
Two of a kind
Change position
Molten rock
Melody
Reading material
Caution
Performance

Answers: left, pair, move, lava, tune, book, care, play

Today in 1923

fascist Benito Mussolini became the dictator of Italy. A myth arose that one thing he accomplished for Italy was to cause the trains to run on time. That is refuted by those who lived in Italy during the Mussolini era.

- Rome's first subway, planned by Mussolini, opened in 1955.
- Steam-powered freight and passenger services were first provided by the Stockton and Darlington Railway in England in 1825.
- Many short-run railroads began to appear in the U.S. in the 1840s.
- The Union Pacific and the Central Pacific met at Promontory Point, Utah, on May 10, 1869.

Word of the day

locomotion The act of moving; from the Latin *loco* (place) and *motor* (mover).

Quote of the day

"The only way to be sure of catching a train is to miss the one before it."
K. Chesterton

Imagine...

Read one of the "Thomas the Tank Engine" stories (or any story about one method of transportation) and rewrite them for a different group of vehicles, e. g., construction vehicles, racing cars, boats, spacecraft, etc.

Activity of the day

Beanbag Locomotion
Bring out the beanbags for this activity.

- How many ways are there to "locomote" (move) a beanbag between two partners (hands, feet, head, etc.)?
- How high can you locomote a beanbag and still catch it?
- Locomote two beanbags simultaneously (left/right hands).
- Juggle with beanbags.
- Make up a beanbag locomotion game.

Today in 1955

the first class of 306 cadets in U.S. Air Force Academy was sworn in at Lowry Air Force Base in Denver, Colorado.

- The Air Force Academy was created by an act of Congress and moved into its permanent quarters north of Colorado Springs in 1958.
- Admission of women into the military service academies began in the fall of 1976.
- In 1994, the percentage of women on active duty in the Air Force was 14.7.

Word of the day

tactics The military science that deals with securing objectives set by strategy, especially the technique of deploying and directing troops, ships, and aircraft in efficient maneuvers against an enemy; from the Greek taktikos (to arrange).

Imagine...

You are in the army and have been put in charge of a group of new recruits. Because they may have to face an enemy in wartime, you need to prepare them to be the very best soldiers they can be. What are some of the ways you are going to prepare them—mentally and physically? Prepare a manual which will be your guide.

Quote of the day

"Speak softly and carry a big stick."
Theodore Roosevelt, speech, referring to military preparation

Activity of the day

Academy Sites
Match the service academy with its quarters.

1. U.S. Military Academy	Colorado Springs, Colorado
2. U.S. Naval Academy	New London, Connecticut
3. U.S. Air Force Academy	West Point, New York
4. U.S. Coast Guard Academy	Kings Point, New York
5. U.S. Merchant Marine Academy	Annapolis, Maryland

Answers: 1. West Point, 2. Annapolis, 3. Colorado Springs, 4. New London, 5. Kings Point

Today in 1866

Coca-Cola was invented in Atlanta, Georgia, by John S. Pemperton.

- Coca-Cola sells over 300 million bottles of Coke a day.
- The soft drink market is worth over 30 billion dollars.

Word of the day

cola A soft drink made from cola nuts; from the West African kolo (a type of nut).

Quote of the day

"The bubble winked at me and said, 'You'll miss me brother, when you're dead..'"

Oliver Herford

Imagine...

Coca-Cola is based on a super-secret recipe. What do you think is in it? List the ingredients and describe how to mix your own batch.

Activity of the day

Fill the Bottle

Soft drinks come in a number of different-sized containers, including cans (375 mL), small bottles (600 mL), and larger bottles (1000 mL and 2000 mL).

Question 1: Can you measure out exactly 1 liter (1000 mL) using only cans and small bottles? If not, how close can you get?

Question 2: Can you measure out exactly 1 liter using cans, small bottles, or large (2000 mL) bottles? Hint: It's not always what's in the container that's important!

Answers: Question 1: two cans (750 mL) + two bottles (1200 mL) = 1950 mL. Can you do better? Question 2: Fill five small bottles (3000 mL) to the top. Fill one large bottle (2000 mL) from them. Pour the remainder into two small bottles. You will have one full bottle (600 mL) + one partially-filled bottle (400 mL) which equals a total of 1000 mL.

Today in 1936

a record-setting temperature of 114°F was recorded in Wisconsin.

- On that same day in Mio, Michigan, the temperature was 112°F.
- In the 20th century, the highest temperature recorded under standard conditions was in Azizia, Tripolitania in northern Africa on September 13, 1922—136°F.
- In the 20th century, the record high in the United States was 134°F in Death Valley, California, July 10, 1913.
- In 1907, the Fahrenheit alcohol thermometer was introduced by German physicist Gabriel Daniel Fahrenheit.
- In 1742, the Celsius scale of temperatures was introduced. It was devised by Swedish astronomer Anders Celsius.
- Ray Bradbury's novel Fahrenheit 451 was published in 1953. Fahrenheit 451 is the temperature at which paper burns.

Word of the day

humid Containing or characterized by a high amount of water or water vapor; from the Latin humidus (to be moist).

Imagine...

You are stranded in the desert with no one or nothing in sight. There is no sign of shelter. Most important of all, there is no sign of water. What are some steps that you can take to preserve your energy and try to save yourself until a search party reaches you? Your survival depends on your ingenuity.

Quote of the day

"If you can't stand the heat, get out of the kitchen."
Harry S. Truman, a favorite saying of his

Activity of the day

Converting Temperature

To convert Fahrenheit to Celsius, subtract 32 degrees and divide by 1.8.

To convent Celsius to Fahrenheit, multiply by 1.8 and add 32 degrees.

Celsius	Fahrenheit
-157°	_____°
_____°	-22°
-17.8°	_____°
_____°	104°
32.2°	_____°
_____°	266°

Today

marks Bastille Day, commemorating the beginning of the French Revolution in 1789.

- King Charles V built the Bastille as a fortress. It was later converted to a prison for "enemies" of the king.

- The French National Assembly adopted decrees in 1789, including the right to "liberty, property, security, and resistance to oppression."

Word of the day

Bastille An old fortress in France, destroyed by the revolutionaries in 1789; from the Old French *bastille* (fortress).

Quote of the day

Louis XVI: **"C'est une revolte?"**

Duc de La Rochefoucauld-Liancourt: **"No, Sire, c'est une revolution."**

Imagine...

"Bastille Stormed by Mob for Gunpowder, Young Child a Hero!" screams the headline. What young child? What did he or she do? Write the news story.

Activity of the day

BROTHER JOHN

Frère Jacques

Sing this well-known song in English and French.

- Sing as a round.
- Create new verses.
- Translate the words into a language the class is learning.

Are you sleeping, are you sleeping
Brother John, Brother John?
Morning bells are ringing.
Morning bells are ringing.
Ding ding dong, ding ding dong!

Today in 1938

Howard Hughes set a new round-the-world speed record, flying a twin-engine Lockheed plane from California to California in 3 days, 19 hours, 14 minutes, 28 seconds.

- Hughes" record fell August 10, 1947, when U.S. pilot William P. Odum arrived at Chicago's Douglas Airport after a flight of 73 hours, 5 minutes, 11 seconds—more than 18 hours faster than the 1938 record.
- Jacqueline Cochran (1910-1980) was an American aviator who held many national and international speed records and headed the Women's Air Force Service Pilots during WWII.
- Chuck Yeager was a fighter pilot during WWII and was the first person to fly faster than the speed of sound (1947).
- The Concorde supersonic jet exceeded twice the speed of sound for the first time on November 4, 1970.

Word of the day

sonic Having a speed approaching or being that of sound in air, about 780 miles (1,220 km) per hour at sea level; from the Latin *sonus* (a sound).

Imagine...

You find yourself high above the earth, looking down at it. You are just returning from a two-year stay on Mars. Describe what you see. Tell how you feel about being so far away from the planet. What thoughts come to mind? Do you think of your family? your friends? Do any particular songs or poems that help express your emotions come to mind? What changes do you think may have occurred during the last two years? What is the first thing you want to do upon your return to Earth?

Quote of the day

"Speed, it seems to me, provides the one genuinely modern pleasure."
Aldous Huxley

Activity of the day

Faster! Faster!
Try to match the animals with their speeds and then arrange them in order of fastest to slowest.

Animal	Miles per hour
1. cheetah	a. 32
2. snail	b. 47.5
3. rabbit (domestic)	c. 1.17
4. quarterhorse	d. 27.89
5. three-toed sloth	e. 70
6. human	f. 15
7. hyena	g. 40
8. wild turkey	h. 35
9. spider	i. .15
10. giraffe	j. .03

Answers: 1. e., 2. j., 3. h., 4. b., 5. i., 6. d., 7. g., 8. f., 9. c., 10. a. cheetah, quarterhorse, hyena, rabbit, giraffe, human, wild turkey, spider, three-toed sloth, snail

Today in 1918

Nicholas II (the last Russian czar or tsar and his family were executed by the Cheka (secret police) at Yekaterinburg.

- The film *Anastasia* was based on the belief that not all the members of the family died in the execution and that Grand Duchess Anastasia escaped.

- Anastasia's nickname was "shvibzik," Russian for "imp."

- Boris Godunov, False Dmitri, and Basil Shuisky are all names of Russian Tsars

Word
of the day

Tsar Emperor of Russia; from the Russian *tsar*, from the Gothic *kaisar*, from the Latin *Caesar*.

Quote
of the day

"This will last out a night in Russia. When nights are longest there."
William Shakespeare

Imagine...

Ah, the fame of it all. It's your 40th birthday, and a famous film director wants to make a film of your life! Why are you so famous? What have you achieved? What would you like to be famous for?

Activity
of the day

A Royal Visit

Shuffle a pack of cards.

Turn over the top card.

If it's an ace through 10, you keep the card and turn the next card over.

If it's a royal card (king, queen, or jack), you lose and have to start again.

Question 1: What's your best score?

Question 2: What is the highest score you can get?

Question 3: Can you work out what the chance is that the card will be a royal?

Answers: Question 1 (More than 10 cards is amazing!); Question 2 (Cards in pack-52, royal cards-12 = 40); Question 3 (12 in 52, or 3 in 13, or 0.23)

Today in 1935

"STICKS NIX HICK PIX" headlined *Variety*, the 30-year-old show business newspaper, reporting that rural audiences rejected motion pictures with bucolic stories and characters.

- In 1860, the U. S. had 372 daily newspapers, but newspapers remained generally too expensive for the average man or woman to afford.
- The first newspaper to appear in the American colonies was a newssheet, *Publick Occurrences*, issued in Boston in 1690.
- *The New York Times* was launched in 1851 and achieved worldwide circulation under the supervision of Adolph Ochs.
- Other important American newspapers are the Washington Post, Los Angeles Times, Christian Science Monitor, Atlanta Constitution, Chicago Tribune, USA Today, and Wall Street Journal, which in 1980 became the best-selling daily newspaper in the U.S.

Word of the day

editor The person who edits written material for a newspaper or other publication; from the Latin *edere* (to put forth, publish).

Imagine...

Cut out ten headlines from your daily newspaper. Cut each headline into separate words. See how long you can make a story using only the headline words.

Quote of the day

"I don't care what you say, for me or against me, but for heaven's sake say something about me."
Dame Nellie Melba, to the editor of *Argus*

Activity of the day

Newspaper Crossword

Finish these newspaper headlines to complete the crossword puzzle. The answers are all found in the letters of the word "newspaper."

Across

1. Police Seize Sensitive _____ From Toilet
3. _____ Miss in Darts Accident
5. Deaf Patient All _____ in Surgery Bungle
7. Psychiatrist: It's Crazy Saying the Suspect is _____!
9. Cricket Officials Told to _____ Warne.
10. Septic Tank Explosion a Real Sewer _____.

Down

2. Boxers _____ Sparingly
3. Old ___ is New _____ at _____ Paper
4. _____ Your Old Subscription!
6. I Saw His Sore Leg _____ Off!
8. _____ Caught Monkeying Around!

Today in 64 A.D.

Rome had a fire that began in the night in some wooden booths at one end of the Circus Maximus and spread throughout the city, destroying nearly two-thirds of it.

- The Appian Way is an ancient Roman road between Rome and Capua, begun in 312 A.D. and later extended to Brindisi, with a total length of more than 350 miles (563 km).

- The city of Rome was built upon seven hills: the Palatine, Aventine, Caelian, Capitoline, Esquiline, Quirinal, and Viminal.

Word of the day

mythology A body or collection of myths belonging to a people and addressing their origin, history, deities ancestors, and heroes; from the Greek *muthologia* (storytelling).

Quote of the day

"The bravest sight in the world is to see a great man struggling against adversity."

Seneca, Roman writer, philosopher, statesman

Imagine...

Perhaps you have heard the saying, "When in Rome, do as the Romans do." Pretend that you are going to be the mentor for a visitor from another country, or even another planet—someone who likely leads a very different kind of life from yours and comes from very different customs, manners, and attitudes. What are the things that you will have to teach this person about how to get along in your society so that his speech and behavior help him to blend in? Think of the distances people stand from each other, methods of greeting one another, etc.

Activity of the day

Name the Day
Which day of the week was named after each of the following? (You may need to refer to a dictionary or some books about mythology to figure out some of these.)

1. the sun _____
2. Mars _____
3. Jupiter _____
4. the moon _____
5. Mercury _____
6. Venus _____
7. Saturn _____

Note: The seven-day system we use is based on the ancient astrological notion that the seven celestial bodies (the sun, the moon, Mars, Mercury, Jupiter, Venus, and Saturn) revolving around stationary Earth influenced what happens on it and that each of these celestial bodies controls the first hour of the day named after it.

Answers:
1. Sunday
2. Tuesday
3. Thursday
4. Monday
5. Wednesday
6. Friday
7. Saturday

Today in 1969

John Fairfax completed the first east to west rowing of the Atlantic.

- At its widest, the Atlantic (between Florida and Spain) is 4,150 miles (6,679 km) wide.

- The trip took 180 days to complete.

- His boat (*The Britannia*) was only 22 feet (6.7 m) long.

Word of the day

Atlantic The ocean between North America and Europe; from the Greek *Atlantikos* (the sea of Atlas).

Imagine...

Write selected "excerpts" of the diary of John Fairfax's journey. Include details of wind and weather conditions to make it more authentic. What dangers might he have faced? How tired would he have become? What if the radio broke down? What would he eat? What would he do to pass the time?

Quote of the day

"There are some people who leave impressions not so lasting as the imprint of an oar upon the water."
Kate Chopin

Activity of the day

Row, Row, Row, Your Boat

People have crossed the Atlantic Ocean in many different ways. Use an atlas to locate the start/finish places named below. Draw the three journeys onto a map. If the journeys were in a straight line, who traveled the furthest?

1. John Fairfax started from Las Palmas (Canary Islands) and finished in Fort Lauderdale (Florida), taking 180 days.

2. Tom McLean went from. St. John's (Newfoundland) to Black Sod Bay (Ireland) in the same year but took only 70.7 days.

3. The first solo crossing (sailboat) was in 1786, from Bourdeaux (France) to Surinam (Guinana) and took 35 days.

Challenge: Can you calculate each crossing's average speed?

Answers: 1. Approximately 4,564 miles (25.5 miles/day)–7,350 km (41 km/day); 2. Approximately 2,700 miles (38.5 miles/day)–4,350 km (62 km/day); 3. Approximately 4,700 miles (134 miles/day)–7,575 km (216 km/day). Obviously, a sail helps considerably!

Today in 1976

Viking 1 landed in a desert area near the equator of Mars.

- Mars is 141,525,000 miles (227,900,000 km) from the sun.
- Mars has two moons, Phobos and Delmos
- The Martian year is almost twice as long as that of Earth.

Word
of the day

Mars The fourth planet from the sun in our solar system; from the Roman name *Mars*, the god of war and son of Jupiter.

Quote
of the day

"Have you heard it's in the stars
Next July we collide with Mars
Well, did you evah!
What a swell party this is!"
Cole Porter

Imagine...

What would it be like if Earth had two moons? What if the moons "shone" so brightly there was no night? How would our tides change? What would the night sky look like? How would animals be affected? What other changes might occur? What would we call the other moon?

Activity
of the day

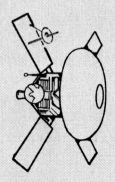

Space Probe

You'll need a large open space with boundaries such as a basketball court or gymnasium. The students are space probes and must respond to your commands (below). Play for fun or have the last student to complete an action declared "out."

- NORTH, SOUTH, EAST, WEST: Run in that direction to the boundary.
- ORBIT: Walk in a small circle around another student.
- CRASH LAND: Sit on the ground—as fast as you can!
- ALIEN ALERT: Stand as still as possible.
- TRANSMIT: Extend an arm upwards and beep.
- EXPLORE: Roll on the ground or floor.

Today in 1848

The clipper ship *Phoenician* docked in Sydney Cove after a 91-day voyage from the U.S., becoming the first clipper ship to arrive in Australia.

- Clipper ships have narrow hulls (deeper at the back) and lots of large sails.
- *The Cutty Sark*, a clipper ship preserved in the UK, was one of the fastest ships on the Australian wool run.
- In 1854, the clipper *Champion of the Seas* traveled over 489 miles (784) km in 24 hours.

Word of the day

clipper A fast-sailing ship, one that "clips" the waves.

Imagine...

Add some more verses to this sea shanty . . .

"Oh our ship she one morning fair,
Pull that rope and tie it down!
A cargo full of wool and tea,
For Sydney Cove we're bound."

Use lines 2 and 4 in each verse. Use lots of sailor words (port, starboard, helm, etc.) and describe the journey. Make up a chorus, too.

Quote of the day

"Resolve to free yourselves from the slavery of the tea and coffee and other slop-kettle."
William Cobbett

Activity of the day

The Clipper Ship Crossword

What is the special name for a mariner who sailed around the tip of South America? Complete the puzzle to find out.

1. A ship's living quarters
2. Where food is cooked
3. Left
4. The back of a ship
5. A ship's body
6. The front of a ship
7. They leave a sinking ship
8. Dropped to keep a ship from moving
9. Replaces sails on modern ships
10. Right

Answers: 1. cabin, 2. galley, 3. port, 4. stern, 5. hull, 6. bow, 7. rats, 8. anchor, 9. engine, 10. starboard; CapeHorner

Today in 1264

the lengendary Pied Piper supposedly appeared in the town of Hamelin and offered to remove the plague of rats.

- Rats, mice, beavers, and squirrels are all rodents.
- There are 120 different types of rats.
- The smallest know rodent is the northern pygmy mouse, which is 7-8 grams when fully gown.

Word of the day

Hamelin A town in Northern Germany on the Weser River; from the English name *Hamelin*.

Quote of the day

"Rats! They fought the dogs and killed the cats, and bit the babies in the cradles . . ."
Robert Browning

Imagine...

We were searching through grandma's attic when we found it. What's that?" asked Prue, the curious one. "I'm not sure," I replied, unwrapping the velvet from what appeared to be a pipe. "It's a flute!" exclaimed Maureen (the excitable one). I raised it to my lips and blew gently across the mouthpiece. Behind me, like an echo to my note was a tiny sound. "Hey!" said Greg (the brave one). "Do you have rats?" Finish the story.

Activity of the day

The Fabulous, All-singing, All-dancing, Straw-o-flute!
Each student will need a drinking straw and a pair of scissors.
Directions:
1. Flatten one end of the straw.
2. Cut two small triangles from the sides (see picture).
3. Place in mouth.
4. Blow.
5. Stop blowing on the command of the teacher.

Extension: Can you change the pitch (high/low) of the flute? Can you make the sound twice as high?

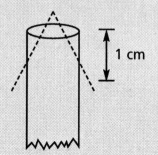

1 cm

Answers: To make the sound twice as high, cut the straw in half. Cutting it in half once more double the pitch. (Each of these notes is an octave higher than the one before.)

Today in 1888

the pneumatic tire was invented by John Boyd Dunlop.

- Dunlop made the first tire as a replacement for the solid wheel on his son's bicycle.
- Tire treads are made of grooves and smaller slits called "spies."
- The world's largest tires are made for dump trucks, are 12 feet (3.65 m) in diameter, weight over 5 tons, and cost $74,000 each. It makes you tired to even think about it!

Word of the day

pneumatic To be filled with air, especially air under pressure; from the Greejk *pneuma*, meaning breath or wind.

Imagine...

Ah, the life of a tire is a hard one. Hot roads, potholes, puddles, skids, and worst of all-the dreaded puncture. Write about a day in the life of a tire. What do tires look forward to? What do they hate? Are some tires special? How does a "mag" wheel talk?

Quote of the day

"The human heart is like Indian rubber: a little swells it, but a great deal will not burst it."

Anne Bronte

Activity of the day

Tire Prints

You will need:
a bike (or two), washable paint, paper, and lots of newspaper (or other protective covering).

Directions:
1. Stand the bike on the newspaper.
2. With permission from its owner, paint the tread of the wheel.
3. Roll the bike gently across the paper to create tracks.
4. While you're being messy, add some handprints, too.
5. Clean up the bike (and hands).

Extension: Do all bike wheels have the same pattern? How are they different? Make a collection of tire tracks from your friends' bikes.

Today in 1857

sixty soldiers were awarded the first Victoria Crosses, Britain's highest military award for conspicuous valor, established by Queen Victoria in 1856.

- The French Legion of Honor was created by Napoleon I in 1802 as a reward for civil and military service.

- In the U.S., the highest decoration for exceptional heroism is the Medal of Honor, followed in importance by the Distinguished Service Cross (Army,), the Navy Cross , and the Air Force Cross. The Purple Heart is awarded for wounds received in action, and the Silver Star and Bronze Star are awarded for, respectively, heroism and outstanding service.

- Albin York of Tennessee, known by all as Sergeant York, received the Medal of Honor and the Legion of Honor for his bravery during the battle for the Argonne in France (1918) in WWI.

Word of the day

hero A person noted for feats of courage, especially one who has risked or sacrificed his or her life; from the Greek heros.

Quote of the day

"Unhappy the land that is in need of heroes."
Bertolt Brecht, German dramatist, from Life of Galileo

Imagine...

What is the bravest thing you have ever done? How did you get into that situation? What was brave about it? Who else was involved? What was going through your mind at the time? How did you feel afterwards? Imagine you are going to get a medal for that act of bravery. What would be written on it? What would you say in your acceptance speech?

Activity of the day

Make a Medal
Everyone deserves a medal for something!

1. Work in pairs.

2. Each student must design and make a medal for his/her partner as a reward for some outstanding achievement (straight As, won a race) or attribute (friendliness, sense of humor).

3. Research the features of medal designs: shapes, sizes, colors, ribbons and bars added, etc.

4. Make the medal. Use silver or gold foil, fabric, chains, ribbons, and other materials.

5. Hold a class medal presentation. Each student will present the medal he/she made to his/her partner, explaining the reason for the medal.

Today in 1909

Louis Bleriot became the first person to fly across the English Channel.

- The crossing took 36.5 minutes.
- Work started on the first channel tunnel in 1875. It began again in 1986 and was completed in 1994.
- Matthew Webb was the first person to swim the channel, also in 1875.

Word of the day

monoplane A single-winged aircraft; from the Greek *monos* (one) and *planum* (smooth surface).

Imagine...

What would you like to be first at? How would you have to train? What obstacles are there to overcome? What would your reward be?

Quote of the day

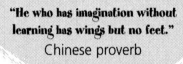

"He who has imagination without learning has wings but no feet."
Chinese proverb

Activity of the day

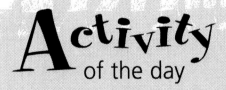

The Great Cross-channel Paper Airplane Competition

Almost everyone has a favorite airplane design. But can it cross the channel to win the Louis Bleriot prize for aviation excellence?

1. Establish class rules: No planes are flown except under the competition guidelines.
2. Construct the planes. Any design is acceptable (are all of them monoplanes?).
3. Decide on the width of the channel: 39 to 50 feet (10 to 15 m) is ideal.
4. Competitors fly their planes in turn. (Ensure spectators are behind the competitors.)
5. Widen the channel until there is a winner.

Today in 1894

Aldous Huxley, English novelist, essayist, and satirist, was born. His works, including *Brave New World*, published in 1932, can be found in libraries throughout the world.

- The world's largest library is the Library of Congress, established in Washington, D.C., in 1800 (mainly by Thomas Jefferson), containing over 100 million items.

- The most famous library of antiquity was in Alexandria, Egypt.

- In 1833, the first U.S. tax-supported library opened in Peterborough, New Hampshire.

- The American Library Association, 1876, spurred improvements in library methods and the training of librarians.

- Libraries in the U.S. and Britain benefited greatly from the philanthropy of Andrew Carnegie.

- Melvil Dewey was the originator of the Dewey decimal classification system for libraries.

Word of the day

library A room or set of rooms where books are kept; from the Latin *liber* (book).

Quote of the day

Over the library door in Alexandria is inscribed: "Medicine for the soul."
Siculus Diodorus

Imagine...

The library books are having a party—but it's not going very well. The encyclopedia is boring everyone, the thesauri have drunk all the punch, and one of the magazines has torn her cover. But then the filing cabinet opens, and . . . . Write about what happens next.

Activity of the day

Library Find-a-Word

Find the words listed below. The unused letters will spell out a place where family or institutional records are kept.

author, book, catalogue, Dewey, dictionary, due, file, index, lend, librarian, library, overdue, Q (found on the spines of the Quarto books), reference, shelf, stacks, tome, volume

F	E	L	I	F	D	E	W	E	Y
L	M	S	K	C	A	T	S	R	R
E	U	G	O	L	A	T	A	C	A
H	L	D	U	E	O	N	A	R	R
S	O	C	H	M	O	K	O	O	B
I	V	V	E	I	X	E	D	N	I
L	A	U	T	H	O	R	Q	E	L
E	E	C	N	E	R	E	F	E	R
N	I	S	O	V	E	R	D	U	E
D	L	I	B	R	A	R	I	A	N

Today in 1866

the Great Eastern steamship finsihed laying the transatlantic telegraph cable.

- Early telegraph systems used Morse code to transmit messages.
- Multiplexing is a way of sending many messages simultaneously along a single wire.
- Radio was originally called "wireless telegraphy.'

Word of the day

telegraph A process for transmitting coded electrical signals along a wire; from the Greek tele (far) and *graphein* (to write).

Imagine...

Suddenly, you can speak only in Morse code. "Dash it all," you think. "Am I going dotty?" What are you to do? How would other people react? Would there be any advantages? What might cure you?

Quote of the day

"What hath God wrought!"
Samuel Morse, quoting from the *Bible* in the first telegraph message

Activity of the day

Morse Code Game
Attention! Attention! Morse code coming through! Use the accompanying chart to decode the message.

— •••• • / —•—• •—• —••• •—•• • / •••• — ••• / —••• • • —• / •—•• •— •• —••!

A	B	C	D	E	H
•—	—•••	—•—•	—••	•	••••

I	L	N	S	T	U
••	•—••	—•	•••	—	••—

Answer: The cable has been laid!

Today in 1866

Author Helen Beatrix Potter was born. She wrote the Peter Rabbit books.

- The Romans reared rabbits for food. They called the stone enclosures "leporaria."
- Myxomatosis was introduced into Australia to kill rabbits.
- Belgian hare, Dutch, Rex, White Flemish Giant are all breeds of rabbits.

Word of the day

rabbit A burrowing mammal related to the hare; from the Flemish *robbe* (rabbit).

Quote of the day

"You may go into the field or down the lane, but don't go into Mr. McGregor's garden: your Father had an accident there; he was put in a pie by Mrs. McGregor."

From the *Tales of Peter Rabbit*

Imagine...

Your vegetable garden is the envy of everyone in the neighborhood. But recently, there have been paw prints in the bean patch and teeth marks in the carrots. Teeth marks—in your vegetables! So you lay a trap and catch—a small rabbit, who tells you her name is Flopsy. Write her story.

Activity of the day

Rabbit Stew
Unscramble the names of these Beatrix Potter characters.

Jam Ben in Nubny
_____

Barbit Preet
_____

Dupled Dime Juckam
_____

Mitt Token
_____

Mr. Klewin Gitgys
_____

Gorger Rmmc
_____

Answers: Benjamin Bunny; Jemima Puddle-Duck; Mrs. Tiggy Winkle; Peter Rabbit; Tom Kitten; Mr. McGregor

Today in 1890

Vincent van Gogh died after spending the last two years of his life in an asylum.

- In the five years before he died, Van Gogh finished over 500 paintings.
- In his lifetime, he sold only one painting.
- His painting *Irises* sold for 53.9 million dollars.
- In, 1888, van Goph cut off his own earlobe.

Word of the day

asylum An institution for the care (or confinement) of people; from the Greek *asulon* (refuge)

Imagine...

Make a list of ten reasons why one of your paintings should be worth 53.9 million dollars. Make the reasons as sensible or as silly as you like!

Quote of the day

"You have Van Gogh's ear for music!"
Billy Wilder

Activity of the day

A Van Gogh Masterpiece
Different artists have particular techniques that make their paintings unique.

Try creating your own Van Gogh masterpiece.

1. Choose a pair of related colors (e.g., yellow and orange) and a complementary color (e.g., blue).
2. Select a person to paint a portrait of.
3. Paint the portrait, using swirling brush strokes.
4. Auction the painting for millions!

Today in 1968

the first woman-to-woman heart transplant was performed.

- The human heart pumps nearly 7,600 liters of blood every day.
- Heart attacks occur when a blood clot blocks a coronary (leading to the heart) artery.
- An artificial heart was placed inside a human for the first time in 1969.

Word of the day

cardiac Relating to the heart; from the Greek *kardia* (heart).

Quote of the day

"Home is where the heart is."
Folk Saying

Imagine...

It was only supposed to be a routine checkup. But when the doctor returned with your x-rays, you knew something was wrong. "What? What is it?" you asked. "Look!" he said, thrusting the x-ray into your hands. And then you saw it—you had two hearts! What happens next? Will you end up a medical curiosity? Do you have extra power from your two hearts?

Activity of the day

Graph Your Pulse

As your heart beats, it pushes blood through your veins. Your pulse is the measurement of this flow. What's your pulse rate? Measure it by resting your fingers (not your thumb, which has a pulse of its own) on the base of your wrist. How does exercise affect your pulse? Try running in place, steadily, for six minutes. Make a graph of your pulse rate before, after, and at two-minute intervals from then on. How long does it take for your pulse to return to normal.

Today in 1971

the Moon Rover made a five-mile (8-km) journey on the moon.

- At its closest, the moon is 221,324 miles (356,399 km) away.
- The time from one full moon to the next is called a synodic month (about 29.5 days).
- Jules Verne wrote the novel *From the Earth to the Moon* in 1865, over 100 years before the moon was actually visited.

Imagine...

Dateline: 2050.
Place: The moon.
Time: 08:30.
You slept in and missed the shuttle to the education center. Everyone else is at their workpods, and the only way you can get to there on time is to fire up the old lunar rover stored in the shed. After donning your spacesuit, you maneuver the rickety old craft down the side of your home's crater. Then your problems really begin. Tell your story.

Word of the day

lunar Relating to the moon; from the Latin *Luna* (the moon, personified by the Romans as a goddess).

Quote of the day

"Slowly, silently, now the moon
Walks the night in her silver shroud."
Walter de la Mare

Activity of the day

Make a Lunar Rover
The lunar surface is very hard and rocky; there are definitely no highways!

Design a model lunar rover with wheels that will adapt to a variety of terrains. One way is to make wheels within a larger wheel. Look at the diagram for ideas. Marshmallows also make great wheels! (If you don't eat them first!)

Once you've made your wheels, you'll need a base to attach them to and axles so they can rotate. Complete your rover with two astronauts for passengers.

Today in 1930

the first photographic flash bulb was invented by Johannes Estermeier of Althegnenberg, Germany.

- Flashbulbs create their bright light when the magnesium wire and the oxygen inside the bulb are ignited.
- The electronic flash is a kind of strobe light (like those in discos).
- Red-eye in photographs is caused by light being reflected off the blood vessels at the back of the eyeball.

Word of the day

photograph An image of an object; from the Greek *phôs* (light) and *graph* (to draw).

Quote of the day

"As far as I knew, he (Tenzing Norgay) had never taken a photograph before, and the summit of Everest was hardly the place to show him how."
Sir Edmund Hillary

Imagine...

What a brilliant idea the flash is! There must be thousands of other inventions that need another invention to make them even more useful. Invent an accessory for the: chair, electric shaver, coffee mug, pencil, wallet, clock.

Activity of the day

Bulb Addition

Add "bulb" to the letter "r." Rearrange into a "promotional statement on a book jacket" and you have a "blurb." Can you complete these ten other "bulb additions"?

bulb + ae = an ornament

bulb + be = a hollow globule of gas

bulb + eh = an orbiting space telescope

bulb + er = the remains of a broken building

bulb + cde = hit someone with a heavy stick

bulb + eiq = to argue over a small item

bulb + adeer = a famous pirate

bulb + begmu = a kind of chewing gum

bulb + ehorstt = a native Australian flowering tree

Answers: bauble, bubble, Hubble, rubble, clubbed, quibble, bluebeard, bubblegum, bottlebrush

Today in 216 B.C.

Hannibal and his elephants defeated the Romans at Cannae.

- Hannibal crossed the Austrian Alps in 15 days, fending off snowstorms, landslides, and attacks by local tribes.
- Indian elephants were used in wars against Alexander the Great as early as 326 B.C.
- The English cricketer Ian Botham re-enacted Hannibal's crossing of the alps in a fund-raising walk for charity.

Word
of the day

pachyderm A thick-skinned animal, especially an elephant; from the Greek *pakhús* (thick) and *derma* (skin).

Imagine...

You wake up to find that all the forms of transport in the world have disappeared—except for the elephant. Will there be elephant freeways? Two-elephant garages? Invent an elephant-powered transport device to get you to school.

Quote
of the day

"One morning I shot an elephant in my pajamas. How he got into my pajamas I'll never know."

Groucho Marx

Activity
of the day

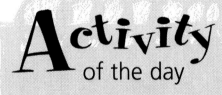

Elephant Jokes

Match these elephant jokes to the funniest answer.

Question:

How do you get an elephant out of the water?

What do you call any elephant who is an expert on skin disorders?

What has two tails, two trunks, and five feet?

What is beautiful, gray, and wears very big glass slippers?

What's gray on the inside and pink and white on the outside?

What's gray, yellow, gray, yellow . . . ?

Why are elephants large, gray, and wrinkled?

Why are elephants wrinkled?

Why do elephants wear sandals?

Answers:

A pachydermatologist.

An elephant rolling down a hill with a daisy in its mouth!

An elephant with spare parts.

An inside out elephant.

Because if they were small, white and smooth they'd be aspirins.

Cinderelephant.

Have you ever tried to iron one?

So that they don't sink in the sand.

Wet.

Answers: There are no correct answers. If the joke's funny, it must be right!

AUGUST 3

Today in 1492

Christopher Columbus set sail from Spain in three Caravels; the *Pinta*, *Nina* and *Santa Maria*. His plan: to find a shorter route to Asia.

- There were 90 crew members in his fleet, including a translator, doctors, servants, a secretary, and an accountant.
- His first landfall was on an island in the Bahamas. He named it San Salvador.
- Columbus believed the island of Cuba was actually Cathay (China).

Word of the day

caravel A Spanish ship, quite small, fast, and light; from the Greek *karabos* (horned beetle).

Quote of the day

"In the United States there is more space where nobody is than where anybody is. That is what makes America what it is."
Gertrude Stein

Imagine...

Now if Columbus had been really serious about a quicker route to Asia, he would have just started digging! Where would a hole dug beneath your school lead to? Japan? China? The center of the Earth?

Activity of the day

Island Math

The navigator on the *Santa Maria* has an unusual way of recording the year in which the expedition lands on each island. Can you work out which were discovered in the same year as Columbus set sail?

373 x 4
213 x 7
165 x 9
746 x 2
1492 x 1
248 x 6
497 x 3
298 x 5
186 x 8

Answers: 1492 x 1; 746 x 2; 373 x 4

Today in 1675

Hans Christian Andersen, Danish author of fairy tales, died.

- Andersen ran away from home at the age of 14.
- Many of his stories have been turned into films, including *The Little Mermaid*, *The Snow Queen*, and *The Ugly Duckling*.
- The Hans Christian Andersen International Medal is awarded to children's authors. Maurice Sendak (*Where the Wild Things Are*) is one winner.

Imagine...

"And then, then I turned him into a frog!" cackled the wizened witch. "Hah!" snorted the wrinkled wizard. "The last time some prince got in my way, I turned him into a . . . ." Into a what? And why was that so bad? Did the prince regain his human form? Did he deserve to become human again? You decide!

Word
of the day

fay A fairy; from the Latin *fata* (the Fates).

Quote
of the day

"Every man's life is a fairy-tale written by God's fingers."
Hans Christian Andersen

Activity
of the day

The Handy Dandy Fairy Tale Writer

Use our (patent applied for) Handy Dandy Fairy Tale Writer to construct your next fairy tale! Just take main characters from columns 1 and 2, throw in a location from column 3, add a problem from column 4 and a solution from 5. Bingo! A brand new fairy tale. Oh, and if you look hard, there are five real fairy tales in there, too.

Main Character 1	Main Character 2	Location	Problem	Solution
A wolf	Large, smelly goat	Bridge	Collecting straw-into-gold-weaving debt	Blow down house
Another wolf	Selfish girl	Castle in the air	Collecting tolls	Dress up as grandmother
Elf with unusual name	Spoilt girl	Dark wood	Fending off starvation	Grind bones to make bread
Giant	Uncooperative pig	Dungeon	Finding pork	Take first born child
Troll	Young lout	House of Bricks	Keeping Englishman out	Wait for bigger brother to come along

Answers: 1. Three Little Pigs; 2. Red Riding Hood; 3. Rumpelstiltskin; 4. Jack and the Beanstalk; 5. The Three Billy Goats Gruff

Today in 1914

the first traffic light was installed in Cleveland.

- The world's first semaphore (flag) traffic lights were erected in 1868 in London. Green and red gas lights were used at night.

- Garrett Morgan invented the first automatic, three-way traffic light.

- The world's largest traffic jam happened in 1980 in France. The jam was 109 miles (176km) long!

Imagine...

They didn't call them sign-nappers for nothing. When the city refused to be blackmailed, that's just what the crooks did; they sign-napped every road sign in the city. And the traffic lights. And the white lines (even the dashed ones!). On the next day when people went to work, what happened?

Quote
of the day

"There are . . . only two classes of pedestrians in these days of reckless motor traffic–the quick, and the dead." Lord Thomas Robert Dewar

Word
of the day

pedestrian A person who travels on foot; from the Latin *pedis* (foot).

Activity
of the day

Traffic Light Chase

Equipment: Three colored balls, one green, and two red.

Set up: Stand in a circle, facing each other.

Aim: Tag whomever is holding the green ball with either of the red balls.

Procedure: The red balls may only be passed around the circle. The green ball may be passed or thrown across the circle. Each player shouts out the color of the ball as it is passed.

(**Note:** Although there are no "sides" in this game, everyone usually ends up on one!)

Today in 1929

Britain's first driving school opened. The school's two cars crashed the following day. They hit each other.

- Mrs. Miriam Hargrave (UK) took 212 lessons and had 39 test failures before finally passing her driving test.
- In Egypt, the driving test consists of driving 20 feet (6 m) forward and then 20 feet (6 m) in reverse.

Word of the day

automobile A car (especially in the U.S.A.); from the *Greek* autós (self) and the Latin *mobilis* (move).

Imagine...

Everything you can do now, you had to learn. Make a list of the five hardest things you've ever learned to do. Then a list of the five easiest things you've ever learned. Then a list of five things you'd like to learn.

Quote of the day

"The real way to travel! Here today–in next week tomorrow! . . . O bliss! O poop-poop! O my! O my!"
Toad (in *Wind in the Willows,* describing the car that smashed his gypsy wagon)

Activity of the day

Prime

Here's a grid of numbers. Color all the primes in black and the rest in yellow and you'll have a very useful item for when you're old enough to drive.

19	9	15	21	25	27	9	15	13
17	15	11	17	25	27	33	35	17
13	21	23	3	15	21	25	27	19
13	25	29	17	27	9	27	39	13
3	25	31	7	15	21	25	27	3
7	27	2	5	27	9	27	39	7
7	33	2	3	11	23	29	9	7
5	35	19	13	7	2	3	15	11
2	9	15	21	25	27	9	15	2
23	29	11	7	1	2	13	1	2

Answer: -A license plate, or in some other places, also know as the plate..

Today in 1888

the revolving door was patented.

- The Phoenicians called the letter D 'daleth' (door) because it looked like the opening of a tent.
- The largest doors in the world are in the Vehicle Assembly Building (Cape Canaveral, Florida). They are over 460 feet (140 m) tall.
- The world's heaviest door is in a laser targeting room (California). It weighs 326.5 tons and is 8 feet (2.43 m) thick.

Word of the day

patent A document granting an inventor sole rights to an invention; from the Latin *patere* (lie open).

Quote of the day

"All things are possible, except skiing through a revolving door."
Unknown

Imagine...

When is a door not a door? When it's ajar! Or a portal into a strange dimension of terror and fear . . . or the entrance to a fantasy world of bizarre of creatures . . . or a wormhole connecting our universe to a parallel one. So, what happened the last time you went through a door?

Activity of the day

Door-to-door

It's a hard life, selling door-to-door. Especially when you're selling doors. Anyhow, here are nine doors. Start with the equation whose answer is one, and end at number nine, drawing a line from one to the next. Just don't go to the wrong door at the wrong time. It could easily unhinge you!

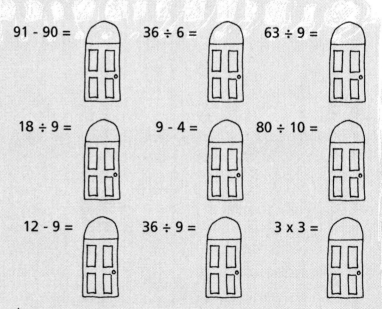

91 - 90 =   36 ÷ 6 =   63 ÷ 9 =

18 ÷ 9 =   9 - 4 =   80 ÷ 10 =

12 - 9 =   36 ÷ 9 =   3 x 3 =

Answers: Down the first column. Up the second. Down the third.

Today in 1972

the first annual Canadian Turtle Derby was held in Boissevain, Canada.

- Turtle fossils have been discovered that are over 245 million years old.
- There are two types of turtles: those that telescope their necks to hide them and those that bend their necks sideways to tuck them in.
- The speed record (on land) for the male giant tortoise is 23 mph (37 km/h).

Word of the day

turtle A reptile with a bony shell and flipper-like limbs for swimming. From the Latin tortuca (tortoise).

Imagine...

The hare, beaten by a mangy, moth-eaten tortoise? The injustice of it all! So naturally, the hare will want to race again and naturally, the hare isn't going to lose this time. In fact, she's taken special precautions to make certain of it. What are they?

Quote of the day

" 'We called him Tortoise because he taught us,' said the Mock Turtle angrily. 'Really you are very dull!' "

Lewis Carroll

Activity of the day

Slow into fast goes-

Can you change SLOW into FAST in five steps, changing only one letter of a word at a time?

S	L	O	W	
				A small slit
				A thin strip
				Level
				Italian car
				Clenched fingers
F	A	S	T	

Answers: slow ... slot ... slat ... flat ... fiat ... fist ... fast

Today in 1593

Izaak Walton, the author of The *Compleat Angler* was born. (Remember the "Sony" ad?)

- The earliest record of people fishing with a rod and hook is in a 4,000-year-old Egyptian picture.

- The heaviest catch on a rod was a 2,664-lb. (1,208-kg) white pointer shark, caught near Ceduna, South Australia, in 1959.

- The longest freshwater cast in a competition was 574 ft. (175 m) in Switzerland in 1968.

Word
of the day

angling To fish with a hook and line; from the Old English *angel* (a hook).

Imagine...

Geeze, the jobs comedy writers get these days! Okay, so they want a TV debate on the subject, "fishing is boring." And I have to provide ten funny reasons for or against.—Five for each. Hey, this shouldn't be hard!

Quote
of the day

"Angling . . . I can only compare to a stick and a string, with a worm at one end and a fool at the other."

Samuel Johnson

Activity
of the day

Angling Find-a-word

Locate the words listed below. The letters left over spell the name of an important fishing manual from the 17th century.

angle, cast, fly, freshwater, hook, lakes, line, lure, ponds, reel, river, rod, trout, worm

```
          R           T
    R I V E R     U L
  T Y H E E C O   O U M
P L ■ T L L D O R R E A
F R E S H W A T E R
T A A N G L E H N
G L C E I R A W O
  P O N D S   K O O
    E           E R K
                S M
```

Today in 1646

the Smithsonian Institution was founded and formally named after James Smithson, the Englishman who donated £100,000 to establish it.

- The Smithsonian Institution is the largest museum in the world.
- James Smithson has a mineral named after him: smithsonite.
- In 1984, over 118,437 people visited the Smithsonian Air & Space Museum on one day.

Word of the day

donation A voluntary gift made to some worthwhile cause; from the Latin *donum* (gift).

Imagine...

What's that in your pocket? $200,000! There's more where that came from too—another million in fact. But only if you can give the $200,000 away first to people who really need it. Make a list of five organizations or groups of people who could use a share. Oh, and just to remind yourself when you're writing the checks, a quick note as to why they need it.

Quote of the day

"In charity there is no excess."
Francis Bacon

Activity of the day

In For a Penny, in For a Pound
England used to use pounds, shillings, pennies, and farthings for money.
One pound = 20 shillings
One shilling = 12 pennies (or pence)
One penny = 4 farthings
One guinea = 21 shillings

1. How many shillings did James Smithson donate?
2. How many pennies in one million pounds?
3. How many guineas is 10,500 shillings?
4. How many farthings in one pound?
5. If one pound = $2, calculate how much you have in pocket money in guineas, shillings, pennies, and farthings.
6. Aside from pennies in shillings, what else is counted in twelves?
7. Find out the slang names for some of the old English currency (e.g.,what is a quid?).

Answers: 1. 2,000,000 shillings; **2.** 240,000,000 pennies; **3.** 500 guineas; **4.** 960 farthings; **5.** Answers will vary; **6.** Two examples are months and eggs; **7.** A quid is a pound

Today in 1677

Phobos, the Martian moon, was discovered by Astronomer Asaph Hall.

- March is named after Mars, the Roman god of war.
- Scientists believe Mars' moons are actually asteroids captured by the planet.
- Phobos is slowly "falling" towards Mars at 54 feet (1.8 m) every 100 years. It will crash in about 40 million years.

Word of the day

Phobos The larger and inner-most of Mars' two moons. Named after the son of Aphrodite (the Greek goddess of love).

Quote of the day

"If the Lord Almighty had consulted me before embarking upon Creation, I should have recommended something simpler."
Alfonso X (commenting on astronomy)

Imagine...

"Houston, this is *Mars Rover 13.* We're skirting the edge of the plateau. We're stopping by what looks like an igloo. There's a movement from what could be a door. Someone-or something-is coming out. Houston-I think we have company." What does a Martian look like? Describe one in 100 words or less.

Activity of the day

Mars Plus

The Martian moons might have been hard to find, but Mars isn't. I mean, it's everywhere. It's hidden in tRAMS and SwARM and MAReS. It's also in every word of this puzzle!

F		Cultivated lands
G		Measures of mass
H		Hurts
K		High flying catches
H	H + MARS = MARSH	A swamp
P		Baby carriages
P		Sloping paths
E		Packets of paper
T		Clever

Answers: farms, grams, harms, marks, marsh, prams, ramps, reams, smart

Today in 1992

the American composer John Cage died.

- Cage is famous for changing the sound of instruments. His "prepared piano" had screws, erasers, and other objects woven into the strings.

- His composition *Music for Changes* involves tossing coins to select the notes to be played.

- In *4'33"* the pianist plays no music. Instead, the "music" is the sounds of the environment—the concert hall and the people.

Word of the day

avant-garde Artists or writers whose ideas are ahead of their time; from the French *vanguard* (units at the head of an army).

Imagine...

You're stuck in the elevator at the shopping center. You're not panicking because the voice in the speaker said they'd have you out of there in an hour—tops. But then the music comes on to cheer you up. Oh no; elevator music! What would you least like to hear if you were stuck in an elevator for an hour? Make a list of your ten most-hated songs of all time.

Quote of the day

"The English may not like music—but they absolutely love the noise it makes."
Sir Thomas Beecham

Activity of the day

A Random Tune

You'll need the following:
Two different-colored dice and a tuned musical instrument (xylophone, recorder, etc.)

To Play:
Roll the dice. Write down the notes to play:
First die: 1 = G, 2 = A, 3 = B, 4 = D, 5 = E, 6 = repeat last note
Second die: Even = long note. Odd = short note.
If you roll doubles, don't play anything (a rest).
When you've written down enough notes, play your song!

Today in 1948

the first two-way conversation was held via satellite.

- Communication satellites are in geo-synchronous orbit, 22,281 miles (35,880 km) above Earth.

- The longest terrestrial (Earth) call was one of over 98,118 miles (158,000 km) during a lecture in London in 1985. Two satellites were used.

- Most international calls only use one satellite as the time lag to send the signals "up and back" can become greater than one second. Annoying when you want to interrupt someone!

Word of the day

satellite An artificial object orbiting the Earth; from the Latin *satellitis* (attendant).

Imagine...

"Hello? Yes, that's me. You're—Oh, the principal. I hope that my daughter isn't—Oh. She is. What is it this time? She did what? To whom? Really! Yes, I can understand you'd be—Yes, I'll speak to her when she gets home. Thank you for calling."
Click.
Ring. Ring.
"Hello? Jennifer, is that you?"
Finish off the phone call. Remember, you can only hear the parent's side!

Quote of the day

"Well, if I called the wrong number, why did you answer the phone?"
James Thurber

Activity of the day

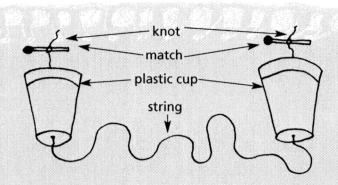

knot
match
plastic cup
string

Plastic Cup Phone Line

Materials: Two plastic cups, two matchsticks, a long piece of fishing line or string

Instructions: Pierce a hole in the bottom of each cup. Thread the line through. Tie (or hot glue) to a matchstick. Speak into one cup as a friend holds the other to his/her ear. Be sure to keep the line taut. Experiment with different types/thicknesses/lengths of string or line.

Today in 1903

John Ringling North, circus president and last in the Ringling family to head The Greatest Show on Earth, was born.

- Beginning their tented circus in 1884, the seven Ringling brothers of Baraboo, Wisconsin became known as "Kings of the Circus World."
- In 1907, they bought the combined circus of P. T. Barnum and James A. Bailey, known as The Greatest Show on Earth, and thus became Ringling Brothers and Barnum & Bailey The Greatest Show on Earth.
- On July 16, 1956, in Pittsburgh, Pennsylvania, having trouble keeping pace with the changing times, the financially troubled circus put on its last show under the "big top."
- Irvin Feld would rescue Ringling Bros. and Barnum & Bailey later that year by taking the circus from tents to arenas and offering a new vision of creative ideas for the circus.

Word of the day

big top The main tent of a circus; the life or the work of circus performers.

Imagine...

If you could be in a circus act, what would you do? Would you be an acrobat? A motorcycle rider whirling around inside a metal ball? Or would you just be a clown, amusing patrons of all ages? Describe your job.

Quote of the day

"The tented circus that exists today (1956) is, in my opinion, a thing of the past."
John Ringling North

Activity of the day

Clown College Cookies

Did you know that the clowns in the Ringling Bros. and Barnum & Bailey Circus are all graduates of the Clown College? Oh yes, in clown college, prospective clowns are put through intensive training. How else will they learn how to tumble, juggle, flip, and fall? Oh, and also, how to put on clown makeup.

Practice making clown faces by decorating cookies!

You will need: round sugar cookies, white frosting, assorted candy decorations (gumballs for noses, candy-coated chocolates, gummies of all kinds, licorice strings for hair, etc.)

To make a clown face: Use a craftstick or plastic knife to spread the frosting onto the cookie, then use your imagination (and the candies) to make the funniest clownface ever!

Today in 1914

the U.S. officially opened the Panama Canal to shipping.

- The first working plan for the canal was drawn up in 1529.
- Ferdinand de Lesseps (whose company dug the Suez Canal) attempted to dig a canal but ran out of money in 1889.
- The canal is about 40 miles (64 km) long and saves a trip round South America—some 1,118 miles (18,000 km).

Word
of the day

canal Long and narrow strip of water made for boats or for irrigation; from the Latin *canalis* (channel)

Quote
of the day

"Oh, Mr. President, do not let so great an achievement suffer from any taint of legality!"

Philander Knox (his reply when Theodore Roosevelt requested legal justification for the U.S. acquisition of the Panama Canal Zone)

Imagine...

The Panama and Suez Canals are both shortcuts. Write about:

- a shortcut you or your family take when traveling.
- how taking a shortcut got you into trouble.
- a shortcut you'd like to create yourself—maybe a straight line from home to school.

Activity
of the day

Short Cuts

You'll need three pieces of scrap paper and a pair of scissors.

1. Fold each piece of paper in half, top to bottom.
2. Fold them again, right to left, so each is four thicknesses of paper.

Now look at the three diagrams. If you were to cut along the dotted line how many separate pieces of paper would you create? Try to work out the answers before you cut.

a

b

c

1

2

Answers: Cut a: 3 pieces; Cut b: 2 pieces; Cut c: 9 pieces

Today in 1934

Charles William Beebe, a zoologist and explorer, descended in a bathysphere to a new record depth of 3,028 feet (923 m).

- Bathyspheres are attached to a ship by steel cables. Bathyscapes use gasoline for ballast, so they can refloat by themselves.

- One bathyscape (the *Trieste*) reached a depth of 35,802 feet (10,912 m) in 1953.

- Fish have been discovered living at depths of over 2,297 feet (7,000 m).

Imagine...

You're descending through the inky depths of the ocean. There's no sound but the steady hum of the air pump. You activate the servo spot-light and peer out of the reinforced porthole. And that's when you see it. What is it? A previously undiscovered species of fish? A monstrous denizen of the deep? A mermaid? A submerged city? Write of or draw your experiences.

Word of the day

bathysphere Spherical deep diving "submarine" (lowered by a cable) for underwater exploration; from the Greek *bathus* (deep) and *sphere*.

Quote of the day

"They that go down to the sea in ships, that do business in great waters; These see the works of the Lord, and his wonders in the deep."
The Bible (King James Version)

Activity of the day

Submarine Trail

The words below can all be found in the puzzle. What's more, they all follow each other (though not in the order given). Start from the first B and draw a continuous line through each square until you arrive at the second B. Good luck!

SUB, PERISCOPE, ESCAPEHATCH, BATHYSPHERE, BATHYSCAPE, ECHO SOUNDER, SUBMERSIBLE, DIVING, CONNING TOWER, BRIDGE

B	A	P	E	H	A	T	C	H
A	C	B	U	S	E	L	B	P
T	S	E	R	E	D	N	I	E
H	I	V	I	N	G	U	S	R
Y	D	R	E	W	B	O	R	I
S	N	G	T	O	R	S	E	S
C	I	N	N	O	I	O	M	C
A	E	R	E	C	D	H	B	O
P	H	P	S	Y	G	C	U	P
E	B	A	T	H	E	E	S	E

Today in 1969

the three-day Woodstock rock music festival ended.

- 400,000 people attended the event.
- Three people died, and two children were born over the three days.
- Headline acts included Jimi Hendrix, the Who, Santana, and Creedence Clearwater Revival.

Word of the day

headliner A star performer at a concert; from *headline* (the heading at the top of a newspaper page).

Imagine...

Woodstock featured a line-up of some of the biggest and most popular bands of the sixties. Imagine that a three-day Woodstock festival is being held this year and you are in control of the program. Create a poster advertising the festival and the bands that will appear. Where would the festival be held? What bands would appear? Who would headline (be the main act in) the festival?

Quote of the day

"There is always a little heaven in a disaster area."
(Stage announcement during the 1969 Woodstock Festival after torrential rain fell.)

Activity of the day

Jumbled Music Styles

Remove the indicated letters then unjumble the remaining ones to spell out a musical style(e.g., AWNINGS-AN= WINGS = swing)

1. BUGLES – G = _____
2. CHIP SHOP – CS = _____
3. CODFISH – FH = _____
4. CROAK – A = _____
5. CRYING OUT – GI = _____
6. FLOCK – C = _____
7. FOURS – O = _____
8. HIPPO – HI = _____
9. LOCK, STOCK AND BARREL – ABCEKST = (three words) _____
10. MISCALCULATES – EMTU = _____
11. NOTCHED – D = _____
12. THAMES VALLEY – LS = (two words) _____
13. UNPACK – AC = _____

Answers: 1. Blues; **2.** Hip Hop; **3.** Disco; **4.** Rock; **5.** Country; **6.** Folk; **7.** Surf; **8.** Pop; **9.** Rock and Roll; **10.** Classical; **11.** Techno; **12.** Heavy Metal; **13.** Punk

Today in 1933

the film *King Kong* (starring Fay Wray) premiered at the Star Theatre in Sydney.
- The movie was one of the first to have a musical soundtrack synchronized to the action on screen.
- The movie had several working titles including The Beast, The Eighth Wonder of the World, King Ape, and Kong.
- The model of Kong in the film was 18 inches (45 cm) high.

Word of the day

premiere The first public performance of a play or movie, from the Latin *primus* (first).

Imagine...

Moviemakers love having giant creatures creating havoc in cities with people screaming and running from them. But how does the monster feel about it all? Choose a movie monster and rewrite the story from that viewpoint. How does it feel about the humans? Does it get scared when the aircraft fly over? Does it just want to get home?

Quote of the day

"Simia, quam similis turpissima bestia, nobis." (How like us is the ape, most horrible of beasts.)

Quintus Ennius

Activity of the day

King Kong Gorilla Math

Here are some statistics about King Kong and his height, weight, reach, etc. But being made in 1933, they're all in Imperial measurements. Convert them into metric. Use the following information:

One foot = 30.48 cm   One inch = 2.54 cm   One pound = 0.45 kg

	Imperial	Metric
Height of model	18 inches	
Height in New York	24 feet	
Height on posters	50 feet	
Height on Skull Island	18 feet	
Weight	47,120 pounds	
Reach	27 feet	
Waist	11 feet	
Neck	9 feet	

Answers:
Model: 45.72 cm
New York height: 731.52 cm (approx 7.3 m)
Poster height: 1,524 cm (approx 15 m)
Height on Skull Island: 548.64 cm (5.5 m)
Weight: 21,204 kg (approx 21 tonnes)
Reach: 822.96 cm (approx 8.2 m)
Waist: 335.28 cm (approx 3.3 m)
Neck: 274.32 cm (approx 2.7 m)

Today in 1950

the American Broadcast Company (ABC) began the tradition of airing Saturday morning shows for children.

- The network introduced two new shows: "Animal Clinic," which featured live animals, and "Acrobat Ranch," a western-themed variety show starring acrobats Tumbling Tim and Flying Flo.

- The Columbia Broadcasting Company (CBS) aired the first animated cartoon in 1955 with "The Mighty Mouse Playhouse."

- In the 1960s, cartoons showed up every Saturday morning (along with advertising aimed at kids), and the several hours of kids" programming fast became a weekend ritual in many homes.

- Today, with the wide availability of cable, several 24-hour networks are devoted just to kids and consist of cartoons, kid's movies, game shows, and educational programs.

Word of the day

show A presentation of entertainment such as a television program or movie; from the Old English *sceawian* (to look).

Quote of the day

"It's never too late to have a happy childhood."
Tom Robbins, *Still Life with Woodpecker*

Imagine...

You have been asked by a major studio to develop a new television program for kids your age. You should already be an expert on that. Chances are, whatever you like, there are bound to be other kids your age who like the same thing. So, will it be a cartoon? a game show? an adventure program? a how-to show for kids? Make your decision and write about it.

Activity of the day

Homemade TV

Make your own television and television show to go with it.

You will need: a shoebox, two paper towel rolls, plain white shelf paper, crayons or markers, transparent tape

To make the TV: Cut a square opening in the middle of the lid. as shown. Then using the round ends of the paper towel rolls as a guide, cut two sets of holes in the sides of the box.

To make the TV program: Cut a long piece of the shelf paper as long as you want your show to be. (You may have to cut the paper width-wise, too, to fit the box.) Tape one end of the paper to the side of the roll. Roll up the paper and then secure the end to the other side of the roll. (See diagram for finished product.)

Now you can draw your TV program and write the dialogue right onto the prepared shelf paper. You can you your idea from the "Imagine . . ." section above or think up a new one.

Today in 570

Muhammad, the founder of Islam, was born in Mecca.

- Mecca's name in Arabic is Umm Al Qura (mother of cities).
- Two million Muslims make a pilgrimage (hajj) to Mecca each year.
- All Muslims are expected to make the journey at least once in their lifetime.

Imagine...

What place would you like most to visit in the world? Perhaps a sports stadium (like The Coliseum in Los Angeles, CA), a building (like the Taj Mahal in India), or a natural wonder (like the Grand Canyon in the U.S.). Well, today's your lucky day! Just write, in 50 words or less, why you should win the first prize of a trip to anywhere in the world.

Word of the day

Mecca A place that attracts many visitors; from *Mecca* (birthplace of Muhammad.)

Quote of the day

"New York . . . is not Mecca.
It just smells like it."
Neil Simon

Activity of the day

Mecca Cross-Quiz

Complete the crossquiz using the clues below. An encyclopedia may help!

1. The leader of a Muslim state
2. Followers of Islam
3. Religion based on the teaching of Muhammad
4. A person who journeys to a sacred place
5. A slender tower with balconies
6. A country on the Arabian Peninsula
7. A Muslim place of worship
8. The prophet who founded Islam
9. To surround and attack a city
10. The birthplace of Muhammad

Answers: 1. Caliph; 2. Muslim; 3. Islam; 4. Pilgrim; 5. Minaret; 6. Saudi Arabia; 7. Mosque; 8. Muhammad; 9. Besiege; 10. Mecca

Today in 1911

the *Mona Lisa* was stolen from the world's largest national art gallery, the Louvre (in France).

- The *Mona Lisa* is also known as La Gioconda.
- Rumour has it that the *Mona Lisa* now on display is a forgery.
- Leonardo da Vinci used to carry the portrait with him when he traveled.

Word of the day

forgery A copy that is presented as the original (often with criminal intent); from the Latin *fabricare* (to fabricate or make).

Imagine...

The *Mona Lisa* has an enigmatic or puzzling smile . For hundreds of years the world has wondered just what she's smiling at. Now the truth can be revealed, for you have discovered a letter from her to her best friend, written after she sat for the portrait. Write the letter, describing the experience (sitting for a portrait can be very boring!). What was Leonardo da Vinci like? Did he tell jokes? Look peculiar? Tell her a secret? Just why is she smiling anyway?

Quote of the day

"A lotta cats copy the Mona Lisa, but people still line up to see the original."

Louis Armstrong

Activity of the day

Portrait Painting

Drawing portraits is easier if you start with the basic proportions of the face.

1. Draw an oval that nearly fills your page (leave room for the hair).
2. Draw a faint vertical line down the center. Draw a horizontal line across the center, and another halfway between the center and the bottom.
3. Place the eyes on the central horizontal line (one eye-width apart). Draw the mouth on the second line. Draw the nose in between. Add the ears, level with the central horizontal line.
4. Now add in the other details.

Today in 1741

George Frideric Handel began work on his famous oratorio, the *Messiah*.

- The "Hallelujah Chorus" is the best known section of the *Messiah*.
- Handel was a child prodigy, and from the age of eight played the organ, violin, and clavier and composed.
- Handel studied law at university before deciding to make his living by music.
- The *Messiah* was the last musical performance he heard before he died in 1759.

Imagine...

Choosing a career can be difficult and people often change their minds. Handel did. But what if you were the Prime Minister and thought that plumbing was more interesting? Or if you were Queen and decided to try out hairdressing? Choose a famous person and imagine what would happen if he or she changed jobs to something very, very different

Word of the day

messiah An expected deliverer; from the Hebrew mashiah (the anointed one).

Quote of the day

"Just a little more reverence, please, and not so much astonishment."
Sir Malcolm Sargent (rehearsing a female chorus in "For Unto Us a Child is Born" from Handel's *Messiah*)

Activity of the day

The Operatic Occupation Word Puzzle

If Handel had struck out at being a composer, maybe one of these other jobs in opera may have suited him.

1. A player of a violin-shaped instrument with a spike
2. A player of a particular wind instrument
3. A person who plays music
4. A person who ensures pianos are in tune
5. A player of an air-operated keyboard with pipes
6. A female singer with a high voice
7. A person who entertains
8. A person who works above the ground with cables

C	O	M	P	O	S	E	R

Answers: cellist, oboist, musician, piano-tuner, organist, soprano, entertainer, rigger

Today in 1977

Bryan Allen became the first person to complete a 1.2-mile (2-km), figure-eight course in an aircraft (the *Gossamer Condor*) powered by human muscles.

- The plane had a 97 foot (32 m) wingspan.
- The course took 6 minutes and 22 seconds to complete.
- In 1979 he flew the *Gossamer Albatross* across the English Channel.

Word
of the day

gossamer Delicate, fine-textured, silky fabric; from the Middle English goose summer (a time of the year when geese were eaten and gossamer threads from spiders were common).

Quote
of the day

"If God had intended us to fly, he'd never have given us the railways."
Donald Swann

Imagine...

What if everyone rode pedal-powered skycycles instead of ordinary bicycles? What advantages would there be? Disadvantages? How would roads change? What would the police use? What if you got tired when skyriding? Where would the bike rack be at school? Write about a day out on your skycycle.

Activity
of the day

Figure-eight Math

Complete the figure-eight circuit:

ACROSS	DOWN
1. 43 – 15	1. 76/2
2. 9 x 2	2. 11 x 8
3. 39+26+20	3. 100 – 11
	4. 21 + 27

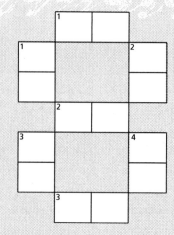

Answers: Across: 28, 18, 85; Down: 38, 88, 89, 48

Today in 1875

English swimmer Captain Matthew Webb, 27, crossed the English Channel from Dover to Calais in 22 hours and was the first to accomplish the feat.

- Gertrude Ederle, 19, New York Olympic champion, became the first woman to swim the English Channel in 1926.

- In 1950, Florence Chadwick, 31, a San Diego, California, stenographer, swam the English Channel August 20, beating the record set by Ederle.

- U.S. Olympic swimming champion Johnny Weissmuller, 25 in 1928, retired after having set 67 world records and having won three Olympic gold medals.

Word of the day

swim To move through the water by means of the limbs, fins, or tail; from Old English *swimman*.

Imagine...

One Chinese folk tale tells of Buddha holding a race for the animals to determine their order of appearance in the Chinese Zodiac. Now, the star signs are going to also have a race to establish their importance. Who will win? Will it be Leo the lion? Pisces the fish? Will the Gemini twins have the advantage? Tell the story of the Star Signs 500.

Quote of the day

"To me, the sea is like a person—like a child that I've known a long time. It sounds crazy, I know, but when I swim in the sea I talk to it. I never feel alone when I'm out there."

Gertrude Ederle (remark made 30 years after becoming the first woman to swim the English Channel)

Activity of the day

Snail Race

Seven snails competed in the Compost Heap to the Vegetable Garden race. Use the information below to work the order in which the snails finished.

1. Edward finished before Francis but after Denise.
2. Bernard could only see Abigail in front of him at the finish.
3. Gabby got fed up seeing Francis's shell for the whole race.
4. Cathryn finished before Denise.

Answers: 1. Abigail, 2. Bernard, 3. Cathryn, 4. Denise, 5. Edward, 6. Francis, 7. Gabby

Today in 1966

the first photograph of Earth, seen from the moon, was taken. The photographer? A spacecraft called *Orbiter 1*.

- February 1865 is the only month in recorded history not to have had a full moon.
- The volume of the earth's moon is the same as the volume of the Pacific Ocean.
- The moon has over 3 million craters larger than 3.2 feet (1 m) in diameter.

Word of the day

camera A light-proof box with a lens at one end and light-sensitive film at the other; from the Greek *kamara* (an arched chamber).

Imagine...

You bought the camera at a second-hand store. It was old, but obviously well looked after. After you'd used up the last few shots on the film; you had it developed. It wasn't until you got the pictures back that you realized there was something very different about this camera. Very, very different! So, what was on the film? What was unusual about the photos? Did the camera do something peculiar to your pictures? Write about or draw the unusual photographs.

Quote of the day

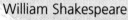

"The moon's an arrant thief, and her pale fire she snatches from the sun . . . ."
William Shakespeare

Activity of the day

Moons of Saturn Find-A-Word
Saturn has some 20 moons, compared to Earth's one. In the puzzle, find these ten moons:
Dione, Enceladus, Hyperion, Iapetus, Janus, Mimas, Phoebe, Rhea, Tethys, Titan
and this space probe:
Pioneer 11
The letters left over spell out the name of the scientist who, first discovered that Saturn's rings were separate from the planet.
P.S.: One moon appears twice — it orbits Saturn in the opposite direction to all the others.

E	P	I	O	N	E	E	R	11
N	N	A	T	I	T	B	C	H
O	O	C	R	I	M	E	S	I
I	I	T	E	I	I	O	A	A
D	R	A	N	L	M	H	J	P
A	E	H	R	H	A	P	A	E
U	P	Y	G	E	S	D	N	T
S	Y	H	T	E	T	N	U	U
P	H	O	E	B	E	S	S	S

Answers: The scientist is Christiaan Huygens; Retrograde moon: Phoebe

Today in 1933

the Niagara Falls Power Company transmitted the first commercial electric power from the Falls.

- June 30, 1859, French tightrope walker Charles Blondin, 35, crossed Niagara Falls on a tightrope.
- Niagara Falls was discovered by French Franciscan missionary—explorer Louis Hennepin. He was so moved by the sight that he fell on his knees and later wrote, "The universe does not afford its parallel."
- Goat Island is an island of western New York in the Niagara River, dividing Niagara Falls into the American and Canadian Falls.

Imagine...

You have a new boat, one that can travel on any kind of water—ocean, lake, river. It is your desire to travel by boat throughout and around the United States. How many states could you visit without removing your boat from the water? Get a U.S. map and plot your journey. Decide where your major ports of call will be. Make a list of all the states you will visit. Then, write the directions for the trip so that someone could follow them and make the same trip you plan to make.

Word of the day

cataract A large or high waterfall; from Greek *katarassein* (to dash down).

Quote of the day

"We'll never know the worth of water till the well goes dry."
Scottish Proverb (18th century)

Activity of the day

Travel Records

You have your map for your boat trip from "Imagine . . . ." Use it to figure out the following information:

Your boat can travel an average of 10 knots (1 knot = one nautical mile per hour, approximately 1.85 kilometers [1.15 statute miles]) per hour.

How many miles/kilometers will your journey be?

Approximately how long will it take you to complete your journey? (Plan how many hours each day you will travel.)

If the fuel for your boat's engine costs an average of $2 per gallon and your boat can travel 20 miles on a gallon of fuel, approximately how much is the fuel for the trip going to cost you?

If your costs for food are approximately $20 a day, how much will you spend for food for your entire trip?

Today in 1883

volcanic eruptions on the island of Krakatoa (in Java) tore the island apart.

- Huge tsunamis, (some 197 feet [60 m] high) caused by the eruptions drowned over 36,000 people.

- One of the explosions was heard over 2,981 miles (4,800 km) away!

- More volcanic eruptions in 1928 created a new island, named Ana Krakatoa (son of Krakatoa).

Word
of the day

tsunami A huge destructive wave; from the Japanese, *tsu* (harbor) + *nami* (wave).

Quote
of the day

"Nous dansons sur un volcan." (We are dancing on a volcano.)
Narcisse Salvandy

Imagine...

Some holiday this turned out to be! First there are earth tremors, then the sky fills with dark clouds of soot, and then a volcano erupts. To make matters worse, room service has been terrible! Besides, what sort of name is "Krakatoa" for a holiday resort? Write a diary of your vacation stay at Club Krakatoa.

Activity
of the day

The Krakatoa Dash
Complete each math problem. Eight answers have the numeral 4 in them; they show the only safe way across the island.

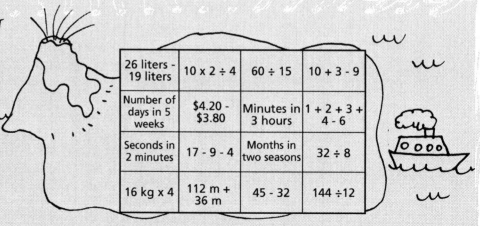

26 liters - 19 liters	10 x 2 ÷ 4	60 ÷ 15	10 + 3 - 9
Number of days in 5 weeks	$4.20 - $3.80	Minutes in 3 hours	1 + 2 + 3 + 4 - 6
Seconds in 2 minutes	17 - 9 - 4	Months in two seasons	32 ÷ 8
16 kg x 4	112 m + 36 m	45 - 32	144 ÷12

Answers: Row 1: 7, 5, 4, 4; Row 2: 35, 40 ¢, 180 mins, 4; Row 3: 120 secs, 4, 6, 4, Row 4: 64 kg, 148 m, 13, 12

Today in 1922

The first radio commercial was broadcast on radio station WEAF in New York City.

- The commercial lasted ten minutes and cost $100.
- The station also featured some of the earliest advertising jingles including "Gold Dust Washing Powder" that "brightened the corners."

Word of the day

copywriter A person employed to write advertising copy; from the Latin *copia* (abundance) and the Old English *writan* (engrave, draw, write).

Imagine...

What if all products were exactly as they are portrayed in advertisements? Soap powders did wash "whiter-than-white." Cartoon characters did appear whenever you ate certain candies. What would life be like? Write a story about the "Advertisement That Was True."

Quote of the day

"Where star-cold and the dread of space
in icy silence bind the main
I feel but vastness on my face. I sit, a
mere incurious brain, under some out-
cast satellite . . . "

Christopher Brennan

Activity of the day

Promoting Your Least-favorite Subject

Be a copywriter and write a radio commercial for your least favorite school subject. The commercial must persuade students to study the subject. (That's hard when you don't like the subject, but hey, ad agencies have to do it all the time!) Write the script and perform or record it. Can you use sound effects or music to make it more interesting and appealing?

Today in 1930

the Reverend William Archibald Spooner died.

- The Reverend Spooner was famous for mixing up his sentences. Some famous Spoonerisms (some of which are of doubtful attribution):

"Work is the curse of the drinking classes" (Drink is the curse of the working classes.)

"A half-warmed fish" (a half-formed wish).

"You have hissed my mystery lectures; you have tasted the whole worm." (You have missed my history lectures; you have wasted the whole term.)

Word
of the day

Spoonerism The transposition of the initial consonants in a pair of words, either accidentally or for humorous effect. Named after the Reverend Spooner.

Quote
of the day

"Kinquering Congs Their Titles Take." (Announcing a hymn: actually Conquering Kings Their Titles Take)"
William Spooner

Imagine...

Make up some Spoonerisms of your own from proverbs. What can you make from:
- A rolling stone gathers no moss.
- A stitch in time saves nine.
- Out of the frying pan into the fire.
Remember, they don't have to make sense!

Activity
of the day

Pig-Latin Limerick
In pig Latin, the first letter of a word is moved to the end and the letters 'ay' are added (if the first letter is a vowel the letters yay are added). Can you translate this pig-Latin limerick?

heretay onceyay asway ayay adylay amednay Ynnlay
howay asway osay uncommonlyyay hintay
hattay henway hesay assayedyay
otay rinkday emonadelay
hesay lippedsay hroughtay hetay trawsay andyay ellfay inyay!

Answers:
There once was a lady named Lynn
Who was so uncommonly thin
That when she assayed
To drink lemonade
She slipped through the straw and fell in!

Today in 1901

the first vacuum cleaner (powered by a gasoline motor) was patented in Great Britain.

- A vacuum cleaner doesn't "suck" up dirt.—A fan inside creates a vacuum which causes outside air to rush in, carrying the dirt with it.

- The first portable vacuum cleaners were marketed in America by William Hoover. After about 1908, the machines were often known as Hoovers.

Word of the day

vacuum To clean by suction; from the Latin *vacuus* (empty).

Imagine...

You knew the new vacuum cleaner was strong, but it wasn't until your blankets got sucked up that you realized just how strong. But the trouble really began when the cat ran past and disappeared up the nozzle. And should you really have peered so closely down it to see where the cat had gone?

Quote of the day

"Nature abhors a vacuum."
François Rabelais

Activity of the day

blow

Spray Painting

Warning: Messy art activity ahead. Proceed with caution! This art activity uses the vacuum effect to paint.

You'll need these: drinking straws, small containers, thin paint; and somewhere that can get messy.

- Measure 2 inches (5 cm) from the end of the straw.
- Cut halfway through the straw with scissors.
- Fold the straw back to a right angle.
- Insert the longer end into the paint.
- Blow through the shorter end at a vertical piece of paper.

Answer: The airstream across the top of straw creates an area of lower pressure. The paint rises up the straw then is propelled away in a spray.

Today in 1955

the first solar-powered car was driven in a U.S. demonstration.

- Plans have been made for a solar collector to be placed in orbit that would produce as much power as five nuclear power plants (one billion watts).

- Solar cells aren't very efficient; they can only convert about 10% of sunlight into energy. However, they are environmentally friendly.

Word of the day

solar Using the energy of the sun; from the Latin *sol* (sun).

Imagine...

Eventually we're going to run out of oil and gasoline for our cars. What will we use then? Solar power? Steam engines? Nuclear power? Guinea pigs on little treadmills? Create an advertisement for the car of the future, powered exclusively by . . . what?

Quote of the day

"I know a man who has a device for converting solar energy into food. Delicious stuff he makes with it, too. Been doing it for years . . . . It's called a farm."
David Stenhouse

Activity of the day

pole

paper

Tracking Shadows

Track the sun's movement and the shadows it creates through a school day. You'll need a narrow pole about 3 feet (1 m) tall, a large sheet of paper, and an open area that faces north.

★ Push the pole into the ground.
★ Place the paper to the south of the pole (see diagram)
★ Every half hour, mark the position of the shadow on the paper.

Discuss these:

★ What pattern do you see?
★ When were the shortest shadows? the longest?
★ What does the pattern show?
★ What moves — us or the sun? How do we know?

Today in 1853

the first triangular stamp was issued in the Cape of Good Hope.

- Rowland Hill first suggested the idea of postage stamps in 1837.

- In 1980, a single octagonal British Guiana stamp sold for (U.S.) $935,000.

- The Penny Black was the first officially printed postage stamp in the world.

Word of the day

philatelist A collector and student of postage stamps; from the Greek *philos* (lover, loving) and *ateleia* (exemption from payment).

Imagine...

Design a set of commemorative stamps. What might be worth commemorating? Your family members' birthdays? school holidays? your pets? Your collection of odd socks? Make sure your stamp has perforations, a price, and the country of origin.

Quote of the day

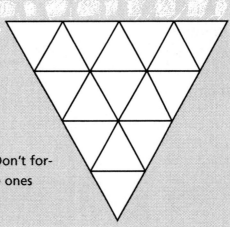

"What should I do? I think the best thing is to order a new stamp to be made with my face on it."

Charles Joseph (on becoming Emperor of Austria)

Activity of the day

Triangular tabulations

How many triangles are there? Don't forget the upside-down ones or the ones made from other triangles.

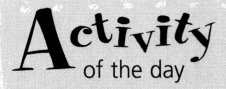

Answers: Small: 16; Medium: 7; Large: 3; Biggest: 1

Today in 1752

England's calendar changed. The new system (called the Gregorian calendar) resulted in September 2nd of that year becoming September 14th.

- The problem occurred because the Julian calendar; in use at the time, was 11 minutes and 14 seconds longer than the solar year.

- In the Gregorian calendar, century years divisible by 400 are leap years.

- An International fixed calendar has been proposed with an extra month called "Sol."

Word of the day

calendar A timekeeping system that defines the beginning, length, and divisions of the year; from the Latin *kalendarium* (account book).

Quote of the day

"Thirty days hath September,
April, June, and November.
All the rest have thirty-one,
excepting February alone,
And that has twenty-eight days clear
And twenty-nine in each leap year."

Folk saying

Imagine...

Create an entirely new calendar to replace the Gregorian Calendar. Aside from having 365 days (changing Earth's orbit is tricky) you can have any number of months and call them whatever you please. (What will the months be named after? Famous people? Cartoon characters? Animals?) Will your calendar be logical and easy to use or weird and wacky? Will there be a special day for your birthday?

Activity of the day

The French Revolutionary Calendar

See if you can calculate what the date of your birthday would be under the calendar adopted by France after the revolution. It had 12 months of 30 days each and there were five days of national holidays from September 17-21.

Autumn Months
(starting September 22)
Messidor: the harvesting month
Thermidor: the heat month
Fructidor: the fruit month

Winter Months
(starting December 21)
Vendémiaire: the vintage month
Brumaire: the fog month
Frimaire: the frost month

Spring Months
(starting March 21)
Nivôse: the snow month
Pluviôse: the rain month
Ventôse: the wind month

Summer Months
(starting June 19)
Germinal: the seeds month
Floréal: the blossoms month
Prairial the meadows month

Today in 1900

the book *The Wizard of Oz* by L. Frank Baum, was first published.

- He wrote 14 books about the land of Oz.
- If you have a pair of the ruby slippers from the film, keep them safe; they're worth about $1.5 million dollars!
- Author L. Frank Baum named his magical land after his eye fell on a pair of file drawers labeled "A-N" and "O-Z."

Word
of the day

wizard A person who practices magic or sorcery; from the Middle English *wise* (originally from the German *wis*, meaning wit).

Imagine...

You're the editor of the *Munchkin Daily News*. Write a news report on the momentous happenings starting with the house landing on the wicked witch. You could feature interviews with eye-witness munchkins, the good witch, and Dorothy and include "photos" of the house, and the ruby slippers.

Quote
of the day

"Somewhere over the rainbow, Skies are blue,
And the dreams that you dare to dream
Really do come true."

E.Y. ("Yip") Harburg

Activity
of the day

Follow the Metric Brick Road

Information:

Each brick in the metric brick road is 30 cm long by 15 cm wide by 10 cm deep.

Each brick weighs 3.5 kg.

Each brick (being gold and all) is worth $585.

Calculate:

1. How many bricks would be needed to create a path approximately 9 m long by 3 m wide?
2. The road to the Emerald City is about 40 km long and 3 m wide. How many bricks would be needed?
3. What would its area be?
4. How much would it be worth?
5. If the bricks were piled one on top of each other, how high would the pile be?
6. How much would they weigh?

Answers:

1. 9 m x 3 m = 30 bricks x 20 bricks = 600 bricks

2. 40 km x 3 m = 133,333 bricks x 20 bricks = 2,666,660

3. 40,000 m x 3 m= 120,000 m²

4. 2,666,660 bricks x $585 = $1,559,996,100

5. 2,666,660 x 10 cm = 266,666 m (266.67 km)

6. 2,666,660 x 3.5kg = 9,333,310 kg (9333.31 tons)

Today in 1666

most of the Great Fire of London was extinguished.

- The fire started in Pudding Lane, near the site of the old London Bridge.

- St. Paul's Cathedral, destroyed in the fire, was rebuilt from a design by Sir Christopher Wren.

- The Royal Navy used gunpowder to destroy homes in an (unsuccessful!) attempt to create a firebreak.

Word of the day

extinguish To put out or quench; from the Latin ex + *stinguere* (quench).

Quote of the day

"But methought it lessened my esteem of a king, that he should not be able to command the rain."
Samuel Pepys

Imagine...

Samuel Pepys lived in London at the time of the fire. He was one of the first people to realize how much of the city was burning and much of what we know is from his diaries of the time. Imagine a wildfire is threatening your town. Write a series of diary entries describing what happened.

Activity of the day

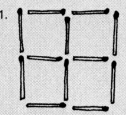

1.

Playing with matches

Place 12 matches as shown in the picture.

1. How many squares are there?
2. Take away 1 match to make 3 squares.
3. Move 4 matches and make 3 squares.
4. Move 2 matches to make 7 squares.
5. Move 3 matches and make 3 squares.

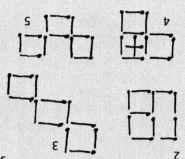

Answer: 1. 4 small + 1 large = 5.

Today

is National Be Late for Something Day in the United States.

- The date was established by the Procrastinators Club of America.

- Suggestions for celebrating the day include sleeping in, not turning up for work, or just ignoring everything you planned to do.

Imagine...

All clubs have a set of rules for their members. What rules would a procrastinators club have? When (if ever!) would they have meetings? Would they keep putting them off? Write rules for the Procrastinators Club or for one of these: The Apathy (can't be bothered) Club, The Good Excuses Club, The Whining Club.

Word of the day

procrastinate To postpone doing what one should be doing; from the Latin *crastinus* (of tomorrow).

Quote of the day

"Never do today what you can put off till tomorrow."
Punch Magazine

Activity of the day

Procrastination Rules!

Here are a bunch of scrambled words that all mean to procrastinate, delay, hold back, or ignore. How many can you figure out? Or should you just put it all off until later?

Answers: putoff, defer, postpone, discontinue, linger, detain, arrest, retard, impede, hinder, dawdle, stay, loiter, overlook, suspend

FFOTUP

DEEFR

PONESTOP

TINDISCONUE

GERNIL

NETIDA

TRESRA

TARRED

EMIPED

DRIHEN

DELWAD

YATS

ROITEL

OOOVERKL

SSUPDEN

P
R
O
C
R
A
S
T
I
N
A
T
I
O
N

Today in 1966

in 1966 *Star Trek* appeared for the first time on the U.S. NBC television channel.

- The transporter was used to save time and money in showing the *Enterprise* taking off and landing.

- Leonard Nimoy's father had a barber shop where one of the more popular haircuts given was the "Spock cut."

Word of the day

frontier A wilderness at the edge of a settled area of a country; from the Latin *frontis* (front).

Quote of the day

Captain Kirk: "I suspect you're becoming more and more human all the time."

Spock: "Captain, I see no reason to stand here and be insulted."

From the *Star Trek* television series

Imagine...

Now wouldn't the *Star Trek* transporter beam be handy? It could beam you from home to school, overseas, anywhere! Write about a world where everyone uses the transporter beam for travel. What disadvantages might there be? What would happen to roads? vehicles? crime? tourism?

Activity of the day

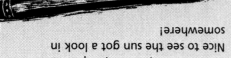

Answer: Notice the beginning letters of Saturn, Uranus, Neptune. Nice to see the sun got a look in somewhere!

Solar System Mnemonics

You can hardly be exploring the frontiers of space if you don't even know the planets of your own solar system. But there are nine of them and it's easy to mix them up. So what you need is a mnemonic, a memory aid that uses the first letter of each word in a phrase or sentence.

How about these:

"Many Various Elephants Munch Jam So Underwater Numbats Purr"

Each initial letter represents the initial letter of a planet. So, Many = Mercury, Various = Venus, and so on.

Still don't think much of munching elephants? Fine! Make up your own! Here are the planets (in order), just in case you'd forgotten:

Mercury, Venus, Earth, Mars, Jupiter, Saturn, Uranus, Neptune, Pluto

The sillier the better, so go for it!

Challenge: What other member of the solar system can you spot hidden in the list?

Today in 1936

Buddy Holly (actually Charles Hardin Holly) was born in Texas.

- He died (along with Ritchie Valens and the "Big Bopper") in a plane crash in 1959.

- His support band was called "The Crickets."

* His hits included "That'll Be the Day" and "Peggy Sue."

Word of the day

band A group of musicians playing popular music for dancing; from the Latin *banda* (to unite).

Imagine...

I don't know, the weird names bands have these days! What sort of name is "Silverchair" or "Green Day" anyway? Back in my day, bands had proper names—like "Beatles" and "Crickets" and "Country Joe and the Fish." Create a new band. Give them a name. Or make a list of the weirdest band names you can find.

Quote of the day

"All the good music's already been written by people with wigs and stuff."
Frank Zappa (rock musician)

Activity of the day

Top 10 Math

Here's this week's top 10 Rock 'n' Roll chart. Next to each song is its movement since last week. For example, "Rock Around the Clock" has moved up seven places (and must have been at 8 last week). Use the information to work out all of last week's chart.

Who was top?

1. "Rock Around the Clock" (up 7)
2. "Shake, Rattle 'n' Roll" (up 8)
3. "That'll Be the Day" (down 2)
4. "Peggy Sue" (steady)
5. "Love Potion No. 9" (down 2)
6. "Wild One" (up 3)
7. "Run Around Sue" (down 2)
8. "Heartbreak Hotel" (down 2)
9. "Shakin' All Over" (down 2)
10. "Da Doo Ron Ron" (down 8)

Answer: Last Week's Chart: 1. That'll Be the Day, 2. Da Doo Ron Ron, 3. Love Potion No. 9, 4. Peggy Sue, 5. Run Around Sue, 6. Heartbreak Hotel, 7. Shakin' All Over, 8. Rock Around the Clock, 9. Wild One, 10. Shake, Rattle 'n' Roll

Today in 1921

Harry Secombe of *Goon Show* fame was born. Fellow *"Goon"* Peter Sellers was born on exactly the same date in 1925.

- The *Goon Show* was a comedy radio show broadcast from the UK in the 1950s.

- Characters on the show included Bluebottle, Major Bloodnok, Eccles, Moriarty, Henry Crun, and Minnie Bannister.

- Peter Sellers played Inspector Clouseau in the *Pink Panther* movies.

Word of the day

goon (Slang.) An awkward, stupid person.

Quote of the day

Spike Milligan: How are you at Mathematics?

Harry Secombe: I speak it like a native.

Imagine...

All of us do stupid things at one time or another. The Eccles character in the Goon Show was particularly well-known for the stupid things he did. What if all of the stupid things you've done in your life all happened on the same day? Now imagine they were all broadcast live, around the world. Write about what you did, how you felt, and what the result of your "day of stupidity" was. Was it fame? fortune? or dying of embarrassment?

Activity of the day

How Stupid is He/She?

How stupid? He couldn"t pour water out of a boot with instructions on the heel!

How stupid? He couldn't match up all of these stupid sentences!

1. A few clowns	A. brain bill
2. A few feathers short of a	B. casserole
3. A few fries short of a	C. every branch on the way down
4. A few peas short of a	D. Happy Meal
5. Doesn't have all his cornflakes	E. off the cracker
6. Elevator doesn't go all the way	F. In one box
7. Forgot to pay his	G. remote control
8. Missing a few buttons on her	H. short of a circus
9. Fell out of the stupid tree and hit	I. to the top floor
10. The cheese slid	J. whole duck

Answers: 1H, 2J, 3D, 4B, 5F, 6I, 7A, 8G, 9C, 10E

Today in 1737

Luigi Galvani was born in Italy. He was the first scientist to discover that muscles contracted when an electric current was applied.

- He made his discovery when he accidentally touched a frog with a charged scalpel.

- When we decide to move our bodies, nerve impulses (of thousandths of a volt) are transmitted down our spines to skeletal muscles.

- The *volt* is named after another Italian scientist, Count Alessandro Volta.

Word of the day

galvanize To move to action, as though by an electric shock; from Luigi Galvani.

Imagine...

Sometimes you wonder how some mad scientists stay alive, the way they wire up their monsters in damp cellars, attach lightning rods to roofs in the middle of storms or use large, badly labeled power switches. Write a list of electrical safety rules for mad scientists to follow. Illustrate your rules with pictures showing what not to do.

Quote of the day

"The galvanized iron roofs on their front verandahs dipped in a sudden curve like the brim of a sundowner's hat."
Robin Boyd

Activity of the day

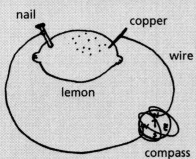

nail
copper
wire
lemon
compass

A Lemon Battery
You'll need these:
a lemon, a galvanized nail, a piece of copper wire 1-1.5 in. (5-6 cm), a piece of plastic-coated wire, and a compass.

1. Push the nail in one end of the lemon.
2. Push the copper wire in the other.
3. Wrap the wire around the compass.
4. Attach the bare ends of the plastic-coated wire to the copper and nail. Does the compass needle move? If not, move the nail and copper closer to each other.

Extra: What other vegetables/fruit will work as a battery? What happens if you attach the plastic-coated wire to the copper and the nail the other way round?

Today in 1869

a Baptist minister invented the rickshaw in Yokohama, Japan.

- Rickshaw runners often traveled 18.5-31 miles (30-50 km) a day.

- The rickshaw is an adaptation of the French brouette or sedan chair.

- The runners were called "hikis."

Word of the day

rickshaw A small two-wheeled cart pulled by one person; from the Japanese *jinrikisha*: *jin* (person) + *riki* (power) + *sha* (vehicle).

Quote of the day

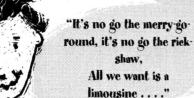

"It's no go the merry-go-round, it's no go the rickshaw,
All we want is a limousine . . . ."
Louis MacNeice

Imagine...

There's always a car chase in an action movie. Imagine though if they had do the chase using rickshaws. Write the screenplay (script) for the chase scene in the new movie thriller *Rickshaw Rampage*. Make sure you include several crashes, the hero climbing from one rickshaw to another and a "hiki"-less rickshaw running amok

Activity of the day

Japanese Words

Find these Japanese words in the puzzle. The leftover letters spell the special name given to Japanese written characters.

BAMBOO
BUNRAKU (form of puppetry)
CHIN (small dog)
HAIKU (poem)
HARI-KARI (form of ritual suicide)

HIROSHIMA
JUDO
KABUKI (theater)
KOTO (musical instrument)
NIPPON (name for Japan)
NOH (theater)
ORIGAMI
SAMISEN (musical instrument)
SAMPAN (boat)
SHINTO (religion)
SHO (musical instrument)
SUSHI
TSUNAMI (tidal wave)
YEN (currency)

O	R	I	G	A	M	I	N	O	H
T	H	I	R	O	S	H	I	M	A
S	A	M	I	S	E	N	P	I	I
U	R	S	U	S	H	I	P	S	K
N	I	S	D	E	H	O	O	H	U
A	K	A	B	U	K	I	N	O	J
M	A	M	G	C	H	I	N	R	U
I	R	P	K	O	T	O	A	T	D
P	I	A	H	B	A	M	B	O	O
B	U	N	R	A	K	U	Y	E	N

Answer: IDEOGRAPH

Today in 1930

Penny the Hen (a New Zealand Black Orpington) died after laying 361 eggs in 364 days.

- On a poultry farm a hen is a female chicken at least one year old. Females less than a year old are called pullets.
- The tail feathers of the male Yokohama chicken are up to 6.5 feet (2 m) long.
- An egg with nine yolks was discovered at a poultry farm in New York in 1971.

Word of the day

pullet A young hen usually less than a year old; from the Latin *pullus* (chicken).

Imagine...

What happened to the poor hen who laid the nine-yolk egg? What did the farmer say when she picked it up? What do you think of a nine-yolk egg? Did the hen get an award? Special seed? Or a day off? Write about what happened on the "Day of the Nine-Yolk Egg."

Quote of the day

"What! all my pretty chickens
and their dam,
At one fell swoop?"
Shakespeare, *Macbeth*

Activity of the day

The Chicken Game

In recent interviews we asked some people why the chicken crossed the road. Unfortunately, their replies became rather confused. Can you match the answers to those given by **the principal, Colonel Sanders, Sir Edmund Hillary, Dr. Seuss, Grandpa, the politician,** and **Captain Kirk?**

1. To boldly go where no chicken has gone before.
   _____
2. I missed one?
   _____
3. Because it's there.
   _____
4. In my day, we didn't ask why the chicken crossed the road. Someone told us that the chicken crossed the road, and that was good enough for us.
   _____
5. Did the chicken cross the road? Did he cross it with a toad? Yes! The chicken crossed the road, but why it crossed, I've not been told!
   _____
6. I have no comment at this time.
   _____
7. What! Without permission?
   _____

Answers: 1. Captain Kirk; 2. Colonel Sanders; 3. Sir Edmund Hillary; 4. Grandpa; 5. Dr. Suess; 6. Politician; 7. The Principal

Today in 1940

five children found priceless Palaeolithic cave paintings in Lascaux, Dordogne, south-west France.

- The main cave is called the "Hall of the Bulls" with some 1,500 paintings.
- The paintings date from between 15,000 BC to 9,000 B.C.
- The caves were opened to the public but closed again when the pictures began to fade and green fungus started to cover them.

Word of the day

Palaeolithic Relating to the second period of the Stone Age (following the eolithic age). From the Greek "palaiós" (ancient) and "líthos" (stone).

Imagine...

Jodi was in the lead when she suddenly disappeared. One moment she'd been complaining about the rain, the bushes, how tired she was. The next, she was gone, slipping out of sight so fast it was scary. We gathered round the hole in the forest path. Jenka shone his torch. "Jodi, you okay?" A pause, and then "Yeah, it wasn't a big drop. Hold on, I'll just try my torch." Another pause. "Hey, guys, you won't believe what's down here. Not in a million years!" Finish the story.

Quote of the day

"Ads are the cave art of the twentieth century."
Marshall McLuhan

Activity of the day

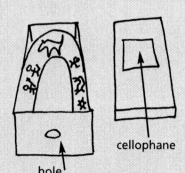

hole   cellophane

Cave Painting Diorama

You'll need: a small enclosed box (shoebox size is ideal), paper, scissors, and paint or felt-tip pens.

1. Bend and then cut a strip of paper so that it fits around three sides of the inside of a box (see picture).
2. Remove the paper and color it gray or brown, for the cave wall.
3. Paint or draw some "cave paintings" on the paper. These were often pictures of animals (deer, elk, etc.) and hunters (with spears or bows). Keep the pictures simple and use earth colors.
4. Put the paper back into the box.
5. Cut a small viewing hole in one end.
6. Cut a rectangular hole in the box lid to let light in. Cover the hole with some clear cellophane.
7. Make a small cave-person for your scene, or make some boulders.
8. View the scene through the peephole.

Today in 1788

New York City became the first capital of the United States.

- The headquarters of the United Nations is in New York.
- Washington, D.C. became the U.S. capital in 1800.

Word of the day

capital The most important town or city in a region; from the Latin *caput* (head).

Imagine...

Poor old New York! It seems like every year it gets hit by meteors, trodden on by huge monsters, or drowned by gigantic waves. Well, in the movies at least. Prepare a report from the city council listing all the calamities that have befallen the city, the cost of damages, and how repairs are being made.

Quote of the day

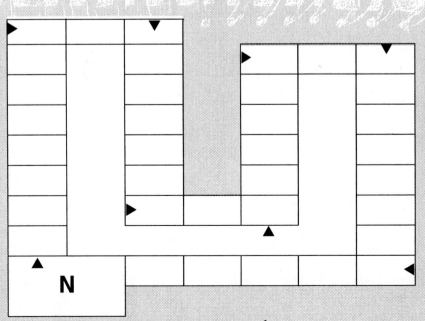

♪"New York, New York–It's a helluva town."

Song, lyrics by Betty Comden and Adolph Green, music by Leonard Bernstein

Activity of the day

City link

Each of these cities begins with the last letter of the previous answer. Join them up in one long city-link.

1. Previous U.S. capital
2. Capital of Kuwait
3. Capital of Japan
4. Capital of Norway
5. Capital of Canada
6. Capital of Greece
7. Capital of South Korea
8. Capital of UK

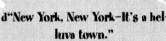

N

Today in 1801

Colonel William Paterson of New South Wales, Australia, was wounded in a duel (Australia's first duel) with John Macarthur.

- Aleksandr Sergeyevich, revered as the founder of modern Russian poetry, died in 1837 at the age of 38 of wounds received in a duel.
- Évariste Galois, though he died at the age of 21 in a political duel, made contributions to the field of mathematics, including inventing the Galois theory, a critical area of modern algebra.
- The most famous U.S. duel took place in 1804 between political enemies Aaron Burr and Alexander Hamilton.

Word of the day

duel A prearranged, formal combat between two person, usually fought to settle a point of honor; from Latin, variant of *bellum* (war).

Quote of the day

"In honor I gained them and in honor I will die with them."
Lord Nelson, referring to the stars on his uniform

Imagine...

You are a news reporter in the year 1780. The Marquise de Saveloy has challenged the Duke of Hamburger to a duel to satisfy his code of honor. They are to meet at dawn in the shadow of the Eiffel Tower. The weapons they have chosen are custard pies—at 20 paces. Write the headline and the story—with a play-by-play account.

Activity of the day

Pair the Pairs

It takes two to duel—or at least a couple—or a twosome. Match these definitions with their correct pairs.

DEFINITIONS	WORDS
1. A pair of performers	duo
2. A half-tone illustration in two colors	twosome
3. A performance by two musicians	two
4. Double	pair
5. Two of a kind, especially in hunting	duotone
6. A pair of partners	duologue
7. Two rhyming lines of verse	duet
8. A set of two objects used together	dual
9. One more than one	deuce
10. Two people together	couplet
11. The two on a dice or a playing card	couple
12. A conversation between two people	brace

Answers: 1. Duo 2. Duotone 3. Duet 4. Dual 5. Brace 6. Couple 7. Couplet 8. Pair 9. Two 10. Twosome 11. Deuce 12. Duologue

Today

is Old People's Day in Japan.

- Shigechiyo Izumi had reached an authenticated age of 120 years and 237 days when he died in 1986.

- He was born in June of 1865!

- France was the first country to provide old-age pensions.

Word
of the day

geriatric Relating to aged people; from the Greek *gêras* (old age) and *iatrikós* (of medicine).

Imagine...

You're 120 years old and some young whippersnapper from the local primary school is annoying you about an interview. Write an interview between the two of you. How will things change in this country over the next 110 or so years? What will you be able to remember? What will you want to forget?

Quote
of the day

"Old age is a second childhood."
Aristophanes

Activity
of the day

Who's Oldest?

The reporter from the newspaper was interviewing Old Jack, Old Tom, Old Sam, and Old Angus.
"I know all of you are over ninety," said the reporter, "but which of you is the oldest?"

"I'm younger than Old Tom but older than Old Sam," said Old Jack.
"Eh, what?" said Old Tom.
Old Angus added, to make it clearer "I'm younger than Old Tom but older than Old Jack."
"Zzzzz," snored Old Sam.

Answer: Old Tom

Who is the oldest?

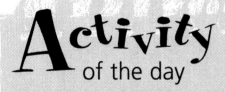

Today in 1840

one of the earliest uses of the word "okay" is recorded with the founding of the OK Club (a political group) in New York City.

- Another suggestion is it stands for All Correct (poorly spelt as "Orl Korrect").
- Some other two-letter combinations that didn't endure from the same time are: KY (know yuse = no use), KG (know go = no go) and NF ('nuff sed = enough said).
- One of the most famous Western gunfights took place in the OK Corral.

Word
of the day

colloquial Informal spoken language or conversation; from the Latin *loqui* (speak).

Imagine...

Everybody uses informal words in their speech such as "ok," "cool," or (even!) "groovy." Not everybody uses the words in the same way, and sometimes it can become confusing when two words that usually mean the opposite (e.g., cool and hot) can mean the same thing (excellent). Write a conversation between a parent and a child who are using all the latest hip, happening, chill-out, radical, sick, groovy, funky words you know.

Quote
of the day

"OK, Houston, we have had a problem here . . . Houston, we have a problem."
James Lovell (After the explosion on board *Apollo XIII*, which put the crew in serious danger)

Activity
of the day

Abbreviations

OK is an abbreviation of "okay" that most people recognize. Here are some abbreviations from e-mails and computing. How many can you work out? Each has a clue to its meaning.

1. WYSIWYG: this will print out how you can see it.
2. B4: previously
3. 2nite: this evening
4. EZ: not difficult
5. Cos: for that reason
6. \<g>: smile
7. \<s>: breathe out deeply
8. THX: expression of gratitude
9. ROTFL: Expressing amusement
10. OTOH: Alternatively
11. LTNS: haven"t seen you in a while
12. BTW: introducing a different topic
13. CU: goodbye.

Answers: 1. what you see is what you get; 2. before; 3. tonight; 4. easy; 5. because; 6. grin; 7. sigh; 8. thanks; 9. rolling on the floor laughing; 10. on the other hand; 11. long time no see; 12. by the way; 13. see you

Today in 1933

33 1/3 rpm phonograph records were first used for the first time.

- rpm is the abbreviation for "revolutions per minute."
- Thomas Edison invented the first record player. It used wax-coated cylinders.
- The flat phonograph record was invented by Emile Berliner in 1887.
- Other speeds for records include 45 and 78 rpm.
- A gramophone player was invented in France that played from the inside to the outside at a speed of 90 rpm. Modern CD players also play from the center out.

Word of the day

phonograph A mechanical or electrical device in which rotating records cause a stylus to vibrate to create sound; from the Greek *phone* (voice or sound).

Imagine...

The great debate: Phonograph players are better than CD players. Choose one side of the argument and state your case or list at least three reasons for and against.

Quote of the day

"To invent, you need a good imagination and a pile of junk."
Thomas Edison

Activity of the day

Recording Time Line

The past 100 years have seen sound recording progress from the wax cylinders of Edison's original phonograph through to the DVDs being installed in many computers. Use the clues to place all these recording inventions on the circular time line.

Cassette: Invented just in time to record the Beatles.

CD: Wow! They're about 20 years old!

DAT: Digital Audio Tape. Mainly found in videos, invented 93 years after the phonograph.

DVD: The latest and greatest!

Gramophone: The first flat record.

LP: Long-playing record. Invented 50 years after the tape recorder.

Phonograph: The first sound recording device.

Tape recorder: Only just got invented in the 19th century.

Answers: phonograph-1877; gramophone-1887; tape recorder-1898; LP-1948; cassette-1960; DAT-1970; CD-1980; DVD-1997

Today in 1819

Jean Foucault was born. He was the first person to prove that the earth turns on its axis.

- He demonstrated the rotation of Earth by suspending a huge, 200 feet (67 m) tall pendulum from the dome of the Panthéon in Paris.

- He also invented the gyroscope, an important part of aircraft autopilots.

- He was the first scientist to accurately measure the speed of light.

Word of the day

gyroscope A mounted spinning wheel that resists turns in any direction. From the Greek "gûros" (ring).

Quote of the day

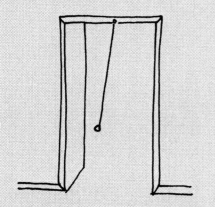

"The motion of the earth, which forever rotates from west to east, will become appreciable in contrast with the fixity of the plane of oscillation."
Jean Foucault

Imagine...

The gyroscope helps planes and spacecraft keep "upright." Imagine you had a special gyroscope attached to you so you could walk up walls, across ceilings — all without falling! Would you use your gyroscope for good or just for fun? What tricks could you play on people? Write all about the adventures of the GyroKid!

Activity of the day

Pendulum Puzzles

You'll need: a length of thin string (approx. 6.5 ft [2 m] long), a pin, a small lump of clay, a doorway (to hang it in), and a watch with a second hand.

1. Wrap the clay around one end of the string to make a bob.
2. Pin the other end of the string to the top of a doorway so that about 3 feet (1 m) of string is swinging free.
3. Pull the bob (clay) back about 12 in. (30 cm) from the vertical and release it. Time how long it takes to return ten times to its original position.

Questions:

1. Pull the bob back further (say 47 in. [50 cm]). How does this affect the time to complete ten swings?
2. Release the bob from only 6 in. (15 cm). What effect does this have?
3. Add more clay to the bob. How does this change the timing?
4. Make the string longer (say 5 feet [1.5 m]). How does this change the timing?
5. Make the string shorter. What happens now?

Challenge: Can you make the pendulum swing exactly 60 times in one minute (one-second swings)?

Answers: 1–3. The timing should remain the same; 4. With a longer string the time should increase; 5. With a shorter string the time should decrease.

Today in 1928

Mickey Mouse made his screen debut in *Steamboat Willie*.

- Walt Disney's first cartoon company was called Laugh-O-Grams.
- Mickey was going to be called Mortimer Mouse but Mrs. Disney though that "it lacked charm."
- Mickey lost his tail in the Second World War because it was hard to animate (and also to save money!).

Imagine...

In the real world, if you step off a cliff you fall. In the cartoon world you keep walking until you realize there's nothing below you! And when you fall, anything heavy will fall slower and land on you! What other "laws" are different in the world of cartoons? Make a list! (Hint: think especially of the Road Runner and Wylie Coyote.)

Word of the day

cartoon A film made by photographing a series of drawings; from the Italian *cartone* (card).

Quote of the day

"I'd rather entertain and hope that people learn, than teach and hope that people are entertained."
Walt Disney

Activity of the day

A Bouncing Ball Flip Book

You'll need: 20 small sheets of paper (e.g., five pieces of copy paper cut into quarters), a stapler, a pen, and a copy of one of these pictures (enlarged).

1. Join the 20 sheets into a small booklet.
2. Slip the picture under the first page. Trace the first ball.
3. Slip the picture under the second page. Trace the second ball.
4. Continue until you have one ball drawn on each page. (Remember to keep the picture in the same position for each page.)
5. Hold the stapled edge of the book. Flip the pages. The ball should appear to "bounce" up and then down.

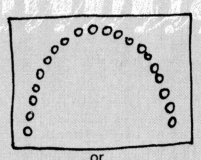

or

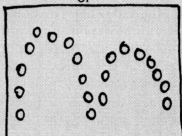

Today in 1896

projection machines were developed in the U.S. and first used in New York City in 1896.

- The first motion pictures made with a single camera were by E. J. Marey, a French physician, in the 1880s.
- The first U.S. movie theater was built in Pittsburgh in 1905.
- U.S. movie theaters began showing double features in 1931 to boost business. Many unemployed executives spent their afternoons at the movies.
- Hollywood became the American movie capital after 1913 and gave employment in its heyday to a host of talented actors.

Word of the day

screen The white or silver surface on which a picture is projected for viewing; from Middle English *screne* (screen).

Quote of the day

"The movies are the only business where you can go out front and applaud yourself."

Will Rogers

Imagine...

Make a list of your top ten favorite films of all time. Which film is at the top of the list? What makes this film so special? Write a "blurb" for the film (describing the plot and characters) that would make other people want to see it.

Activity of the day

Filming by the Numbers

All you have to do is put these ten films in order. The only problem is that the missing word is what you have to order them by. So, to make it easier, here are the missing words:

one, two, three, four, five, six, seven, eight, nine, ten.

And here are the films:

_____ Days A Week

_____ Days, Seven nights

_____ Hundred and _____ Dalmatians

_____ on Treasure Island

_____ Thousand and One: A Space Odyssey

_____ Weddings and a Funeral

Snow White and the _____ Dwarfs

Star Trek: Deep Space _____

The _____ Amigos

The _____ Commandments

Answers: *One hundred and One Dalmatians; Two thousand and One: A Space Odyssey; The Three Amigos; Four Weddings and a Funeral; Five on Treasure Island; Six Days, Seven Nights; Snow White and the Seven Dwarfs; Eight Days A Week; Star Trek: Deep Space Nine; The Ten Commandments*

Today in 1973

Jackson Pollock sold his *Blue Poles* painting to Australia for $2,000,000.

- Pollock developed a form of painting called action painting where he dripped paint from trowels and sticks onto huge canvases stretched on the floor.

- *Blue Poles* is now worth more than $40 million.

- Scientists have analyzed the patterns of the paint and believe they are made up of fractals, the same patterns that occur in coastlines, tree silhouettes, and the edges of snowflakes.

Imagine...

You've entered a piece of artwork in a local art gallery show and amazingly enough, it's won first prize. Even more amazing, a mysterious collector wants to purchase it for $10,000! The only problem is, you didn't paint it. It was your artistic cat, Alice, who did it. Will you tell? Can Alice keep up the good work? How did you find out she could paint? Write all about it.

Word
of the day

canvas Heavy, closely woven fabric, often used for painting on; from the Latin *cannabis* (hemp).

Quote
of the day

"Life is a great big canvas, and you should throw all the paint on it you can."
Danny Kaye

Activity
of the day

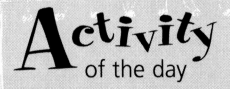

Action painting

You"ll need an area that can get a bit messy, some clothing that can get messy, some paper that can get messy, and some paints and brushes.

1. Place a sheet of paper on the floor. Put lots of newspapers around it to catch spillage.
2. Choose a paint and dip your brush in.
3. Stand above the paper and let the paint drip from your brush onto the paper from a height.
4. Choose new colors and repeat.

Tips: Try dripping … dropping … dribbling … swaying … to see what effects those actions have on the texture and patterns you make.

Today in 1985

the French government admitted responsibility for the sinking of the Greenpeace Organization's *Rainbow Warrior*.

- The ship is now a reef off the coast of New Zealand.
- Greenpeace has 4.5 million members worldwide and works to protect the environment.
- Among other campaigns, Greenpeace helped to slow or stop nuclear testing in the Pacific, commercial whale-hunting, and the disposal of toxic wastes at sea.

Word of the day

environment The area in which something exists or lives; from the Old French *environ* (surroundings).

Quote of the day

"France put agents into New Zealand. France put spies into New Zealand. France lets off bombs in the Pacific. France puts its president in the Pacific to crow about it."

David Lange

Imagine...

Humans seem to find the sea a handy place to dispose of their waste: "out of sight, out of mind." But for the creatures of the oceans, it isn't out of sight — it's in their environment, in their home. Write a poem describing how they feel about it.

Activity of the day

It's Not That Easy Being Green
Each of the words or phrases starts with green — work them all out and your friends will be green with envy!

	F	L	Y			Greenish pest on garden plants
	B	E	A	N		A vegetable
G						A large, cold island to the north.
R						American slang for paper money
E						A building with glass walls
E						A signal to proceed
N						A special ability to make plants grow
						The moon was thought to be made of this.
						A merchant who sells fresh foodstuffs
						Someone in charge of lawns and grounds.

Answers: greenfly, green bean, Greenland, greenback, greenhouse, green light, green thumb, green cheese, greengrocer, green(s) keeper

Today

is the Autumnal Equinox.

- Day and night are of equal length at two times during the year, at the vernal equinox (March 21) and the autumnal equinox (September 23).

- These equinoxes are reversed in the Southern Hemisphere: their vernal equinox is on September 23, and autumnal equinox is on March 21.

- In between the two equinoxes are the two solstices, with the year's longest and shortest days.

Word
of the day

equinox Either of two times of the year when day and night are of equal length; from the Latin *æqui* (equal) and *noctis* (night).

Imagine...

Uh oh. The earth's orbit has changed, just a teensy weeny bit. Oh, all right, a heck of lot. Result?—23 hours of sunlight and one hour of night. Or is it the other way round? Anyhow, there's a lot of one and not much of the other. Would it make any difference? How? Write about it.

Quote
of the day

"The night of time far surpasseth the day, and who knows when was the equinox?"
Sir Thomas Browne

Activity
of the day

Changing Winter into Summer
Change the winter into summer one letter at a time.
Use the clues to help.

W	I	N	T	E	R	
						Mechanical device for winding
						Get in the way
						Stroke in tennis: back-
						Stronger, more firm
						First name of author of *To Kill a Mockingbird*
						A basket of food
						A bread without yeast
						A wave that crashes violently down
						Extraordinarily abundant crop
						Unfortunate (slang)
S	U	M	M	E	R	

Answers: WINTER, winder, hinder, hander, harder, Harper, hamper, damper, dumper, bumper, bummer, SUMMER

Today in 1991

Theodor Geisel, better known as Dr. Seuss, died at age 87.
- He was born in Springfield, Massachussetts on March 2, 1904.
- He began work in the advertising business drawing cartoons. He used his middle name of Seuss and added the "Dr." to it when he did work on a humor piece on science experiments and wanted his name to sound more scientific.
- His first book *And to Think That I Saw It on Mulberry Street* was published in 1937. In 1955, in an effort to promote literacy among school children, he used 220 basic words to write the *The Cat* in the Hat.
* He won the Pulitzer Prize in 1984 for his contribution to literature and three Academy Awards.

Word of the day

Seuss-ism The wit and witicism of Dr. Seuss.

Quote of the day

"I like nonsense-it wakes up the brain cells. Fantasy is a necessary ingredient in living. It's a way of looking at life through the wrong end of a telescope . . . and that enables you to laugh at all life's realizations."

Theodor Seuss Geisel

Imagine...

Dr. Seuss often used his whimsical style of rhyme to get across a message. Can you figure out his message here? Now, can you write your own Dr. Seuss poem? Take one of the pages from The Cat in the Hat or *Green Eggs and Ham* and make your own message, replacing his words with your own (and don't forget to rhyme).

You have brains in your head.
You have feet in your shoes,
You can steer yourself
Any direction you choose.
You're on your own
And you know what you know.
And YOU are the guy who'll decide where to go.

—*Oh, The Places You'll Go*

Activity of the day

Characters and Creatures
Can you match up these characters and creatures to the Dr. Seuss books from which they come?

Character/Creature	Book Title
1. Whos Little Cindy Lou	A. *McElligot's Pool* (1947)
2. Gack	B. *Horton Hears a Who* (1954)
3. The Elephant	C. *How the Grinch Stole Christmas* (1957)
4. Dogfish	D. *One Fish, Two Fish, Red Fish, Blue Fish* (1960)
5. Fiffer-feffer-feff	E. *Green Eggs and Ham* (1960)
6. Sam I Am	F. *Dr. Seuss's ABC* (1963)

Answers: 1. C, 2. D, 3. B, 4. A, 5. F, 6. E

Today in 1888

the Sherlock Holmes adventure *The Hound of the Baskervilles* (written by Sir Arthur Conan Doyle) was first serialized.

- *The Hound of the Baskervilles* saw the return of Sherlock Holmes after his "death" in a previous adventure.
- The Sherlock Holmes character was based on one of Conan Doyle's professors in college.

Word of the day

serial A story that appears at regular intervals; from the Latin *serere* (join or connect).

Imagine...

Sherlock Holmes solved many mysteries by observation and attention to small clues. Write about how you solved the *Mystery of the Green Man* by using the following clues: a dog collar with a missing stud, a scratched ten-cent coin, and a knotted ribbon.

Quote of the day

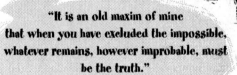

"It is an old maxim of mine that when you have excluded the impossible, whatever remains, however improbable, must be the truth."

Sir Arthur Conan Doyle

Activity of the day

Whodunit?

Ah, a case worthy of the great Sherlock Holmes himself! Read the mystery story and see if you can figure out "whodunit."

When Harry left his house, it was early on a fine warm day. He fished at his favorite hole for most of the morning and then drove into town to pick up some supplies. It was almost dark when he returned home to discover his home had gone. Vanished. Stolen? Perhaps, but most certainly missing.

At the police station the officer on duty was a little bemused.

"It was there this morning, sir?"

"Yes! Of course it was! Would I not see my own house?"

"Er, were there any tracks—footprints, tire tracks?"

"Only from my vehicle."

"Any other clues that might help us, sir?"

"Well, I had left the fire going and—"

"And what, sir?"

"The ground where it had been was very wet when I got back."

"Ah," said the officer. "That explains it all!"

It does? Can you figure out where Harry's house went?

Answer: Harry's house was an igloo and it melted.

Today in 1986

the film *Crocodile Dundee* opened in the U.S.

- The film took $100 million in the first three months.

- Quote marks were used around to the word "Crocodile" for the American release so they wouldn't think that Dundee was a crocodile.

- How do you tell the difference between a crocodile and an alligator? (You can't see the alligator's teeth when its mouth is shut.)

Word
of the day

crocodile A large lizard-like reptile; from the Greek *krokodilos* (worm of the stones) — *kroke* (pebble) and *drilos* (worm).

Quote
of the day

"How doth the little crocodile improve his shining tail,
And pour the waters of the Nile on every golden scale!
How cheerfully he seems to grin, how neatly spreads his claws,
And welcomes little fishes in with gently smiling jaws!"

Lewis Carroll

Imagine...

I turned to my left. "See yer later, alligator." It winked. I turned to the right. "In a while crocodile." It smiled. I didn't. Is this the end of a story? The beginning? The middle? Decide and finish it off.

Activity
of the day

Simian riddle

Employees have recently been given a new safety instruction. Find out what it is by coloring in all the odd numbers in the puzzle. Write the remaining letters below:

_ _ _ _ _ _ _ _ _ _ _ _ _

_ _ _ _ _ _ _ _ _

N-2	M-3	N-5	B-19	V-21	C-23	X-31	Z-9
A-11	S-15	E-8	V-14	D-91	E-26	F-23	G-71
H-3	J-7	K-11	L-91	P-15	R-18	O-15	U-91
Y-87	S-94	T-65	M-56	R-31	E-33	W-3	I-20
Q-11	J-9	L-8	E-10	U-45	A-6	O-43	T-24
A-22	A-21	C-80	C-81	Y-17	R-60	R-43	S-85
I-91	O-10	C-14	G-11	H-15	O-12	D-27	F-21
E-43	R-41	D-16	S-17	I-46	T-15	L-88	E-52

Answer: Never smile at a crocodial.

Today in 1932

New York City's first real skyscraper opened at 50 Broadway.

- Architect Bradford Lee Gilbert climbed to the top of the 13-story building and let down a plumb line during a hurricane to show crowds who had gathered in anticipation of the building's collapse that it was as steady as a rock.
- The Sears Tower rises 110 stories to a height of 1,454 feet (443 m). It is 104 feet (32 m) taller than New York City's World Trade Center.
- In 1884, the world's first skyscraper, a ten-story marble structure, went up in Chicago.
- However, the ten-story Wainwright building (1890) in St. Louis is considered the first true skyscraper.
- On April 30, 1931, the 102-story Empire State Building opened; it was the world's tallest building for 40 years.

Word of the day

batophobia An abnormal fear of being near an object of great height, such as a skyscraper or mountain; from Greek *batos* (to do) + *phobia*.

Imagine...

You have just been hired to design a skyscraper for the city you live in. Think about what you would like your building to look like. Will it be an architectural feat with dramatic features that no one has dared attempt? Or will it be a work of art with flowing lines and curves? To make your building more realistic, decide on a scale (e.g., 1 inch equals 10 feet) and indicate what materials you want your building to be made of. You can even add the landscaping, too.

Quote of the day

"The job of buildings is to improve human relations: architecture must ease them, not make them worse."

Ralph Erskine, British architect

Activity of the day

Architecture and Environment

Describe the kinds of living spaces that are predominate in the following areas and give a brief explanation of the inhabitants' choices

1. Coast of North Carolina
2. Singapore
3. The U.S. Southwest
4. South American jungles
5. Pacific islands
6. Swiss Alps
7. Florida Everglades
8. Greek islands

Today in 1973

the Sydney Opera House was opened.

- It took 16 years to build and was designed by Danish architect Joern Utzon.

- He resigned when engineers declared his design "unbuildable."

- The first performance given in the Opera House was of Prokofiev's "*War and Peace.*"

Word of the day

Opera House A building for the performance of opera; Italian *opera*, from Latin *opera* (work or labor).

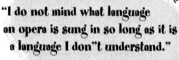

Quote of the day

"I do not mind what language an opera is sung in so long as it is a language I don"t understand."
Sir Edward Appleton

Imagine...

As caretaker at the Grand Opera House you've heard the stories about the ghostly apparition haunting the theater. Of course, you don't believe them, do you? But tonight, as you do your rounds, you're not so sure. Suddenly there's a noise and—what? Describe the old, gloomy theater, the dusty hidden stairway, and what happens when the caretaker turns around.

Activity of the day

Opera Rules, Okay!

Put on an opera! Use the plot below to create a mini-opera. Remember, in an opera:

1. Everyone must sing his/her lines (no matter how badly!)

2. Emotions—love, anger, sadness, etc.—must be over-emphasized. Heaps!

3. Anyone dying must take a long time—and sing while they do so.

4. Participants must use large hand-movements and gestures.

Opera plot: Artolia is drinking in a tavern with his friends. They toast Artolia's true love, Gwendolina. She enters. She and Artolia vow their undying love to each other. Gwendolina's maid enters to warn them that Gwendolina's father is coming to take his daughter away. Gwendolina and Artolia pledge never to be separated. The father enters, very angry. Gwendolina and Artolia tell him of their love. The father scoffs and draws his sword to strike Artolia. Gwendolina throws herself in front of him and the sword strikes her. She dies. Everyone weeps. The undertaker arrives and takes her away.

Today in 1829

the first metropolitan police force was established in London by Sir Robert Peel.

- The policemen were named "bobbies" after their founder's first name, Robert.
- An earlier group of police officers was called "Robin Redbreasts" because of the waistcoats they wore.

Word of the day

constable A policeman or policewoman; from the Latin *comes stabuli* (head officer of the stable).

Imagine...

A police officer has to carry lots of equipment (e.g., handcuffs, a truncheon, a notepad, first-aid kit, whistle, radio, and more). Design a police robot that would carry it all for them. Draw a plan and label all the parts. What else might the police officer appreciate on the beat? A comfortable chair? Hot coffee? Include them in the design.

Quote of the day

"My father didn't create you to arrest me!"
Arthur Peel (son of Robert Peel)

Activity of the day

International Police

Police forces exist in almost every country of the world, and it's handy to know who to ask for (or avoid?) when you're traveling. So here are the names of six police forces. Take away the extra letters and unscramble the others to find out what nationality the force is. Get on the beat!

polizei: manger - s = __German__

politie: touched - oe = _____

polizia: mail train - mr = _____

policía: happiness - ep = _____

gendarme: arch-felon - alo = _____

mounties: ball and chain - bhll = _____

Answers: German, Dutch, Italian, Spanish, French, Canadian

Today in 1846

ether was first used to anesthetize a dental patient.

- The Sumerians (5,000 B.C.) believed dental decay was caused by worms in the teeth.
- The Ancient Egyptians had special "tooth-doctors."
- Nitrous oxide was first used as an anesthetic in 1844.

Word of the day

anesthetic A drug that causes temporary loss of bodily sensation; from the Greek *anaisthesia* (loss of sensation).

Imagine...

As an animal dentist, you've had to pull teeth from some pretty strange creatures—that elephant last week certainly wasn't too cooperative! So when you got the call to visit the local zoo, you weren't too fazed. But you felt a little different when you got there. How on earth did they expect you to extract a tooth from a . . . what? Write the story.

Quote of the day

"I'd be equally as willing for a dentist to be drilling than to ever let a woman in my life."
Alan Jay Lerner

Activity of the day

Riddle: What do dentists in court trials have to swear?

1. Assemble the three-letter groups into one long line following the order of the spiral (starting from DYU).
2. Add 12 letter "O"s.
3. Answer the riddle!

DYU	NTH	AND	TTH
PRM	ING	TTH	HLE
ISE	BUT	THE	HEW
TTE	LLT	HET	THT

Answers: Do you promise to tell the tooth, the whole tooth, and nothing but the tooth?

Today in 1869

the first tourist postcard was issued in Austria.

- Mario Morby of the UK has a collection of over one million postcards.
- In 1984, a Mucha Waverly Cycle postcard sold for $4,400.
- 5,998 — the number of words an Englishman managed to write on the back of a standard postcard in 1988.

Word of the day

deltiology The collection and study of postcards; from the Greek *deltion*. (writing tablet).

Imagine...

You're are on the best holiday you've ever had. Your parents tell you to send a post-card to your granny—the one who doesn't like you. At the bottom of the postcard you write: "Having a great time. Wish you were here." And then suddenly she is. What happens now? How do you get rid of her? What would you do with a postcard with those sorts of powers?

Quote of the day

"See what will happen to you if you don't stop biting your fingernails."
Will Rogers
[Message to his niece on a postcard of the Venus de Milo]

Activity of the day

Postcard Rebus

Your (lucky!) friend is on a round-the-world trip. You've received lots of postcards, but sometimes it's tricky working out just where in the world they've come from. Can you decode these countries' names?

Answers: 1. Turkey; 2. New Zealand; 3. Britain; 4. Iran; 5. France; 6. Wales; 7. Canada; 8. Israel; 9. Peru

Today in 1950

the comic strip *Peanuts* began.

- *Peanuts* was originally called *Li'l Folks*.
- *Peanuts* is set in the town of Sebastopol.
- Charlie Brown shares the same first name as his creator, Charles Schulz.

Word
of the day

cartoon A humorous drawing published in a newspaper or magazine. Also a full-size drawing on paper as a preliminary design for an artwork; from the Italian *cartone* (card).

Quote
of the day

"I love mankind—it"s people I can't stand."
Charles Schulz

Imagine...

What if you could live a day in your favorite cartoon? Which would it be? How would the cartoon characters react to finding you there? Write about your "visit," the things that happened and how you finally got out.

Activity
of the day

Peanuts Word Search

How many of these *Peanuts* words can you find? The left over letters make the phrase most often used in this comic strip.

Baseball
Beethoven
Brown
Charlie
Kennel
Linus
Lucy
Marcie
Patty
Peppermint
Schroeder
Snoopy
Woodstock

P	G	O	O	L	R	D	G	B	W
A	E	Y	R	L	E	E	I	E	O
T	I	P	E	A	D	I	F	E	O
T	L	O	P	B	E	C	C	T	D
Y	R	O	H	E	O	R	S	H	S
C	A	N	B	S	R	A	U	O	T
U	H	S	R	A	H	M	N	V	O
L	C	A	O	B	C	R	I	E	C
L	I	E	W	B	S	R	L	N	K
K	E	N	N	E	L	O	W	N	T

Today in 1985

the first Adelaide Grand Prix (Australia) was won by Keke Rosberg of Finland.

- The title Grand Prix was first used for a French horse race, "Grand Prix de Paris," run in 1863.
- The first motor-racing Grand Prix was held in 1906.
- Points scored by the Grand Prix winners determine the world champion drive.

Imagine...

You are in charge of waving the winner's flag at the end of each Grand Prix race. What do you do in your spare time? Where do you practice flag-waving? How did you become a flag-waver? What training was involved? Where else might you use your talents? Write the Grand Prix Flag-Waver's Manual.

Word of the day

Grand Prix An international race; from the French *grand prix* (great or chief prize).

Quote of the day

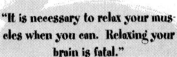

"It is necessary to relax your muscles when you can. Relaxing your brain is fatal."

Stirling Moss (British race car driver)

Activity of the day

START

Pencil Grand Prix

Rev up your pencils and play the high-octane Pencil Grand Prix!

1. Draw a wide racetrack winding around a piece of paper. Include a starting line, dangerous bends, oil spills, water hazards, shortcuts, etc.

2. To play, you'll need a pencil and a partner.

3. Place your pencil upright on the start line. Hold the pencil steady with the tip of your finger. When it's your turn, slowly move your finger back until the pencil begins to slip. As it does, push it forward, trying to keep on the track. As soon as the pencil drops, it is your partner's turn. Your next turn starts from the end of your last pencil mark.

4. Additional rules: If you "crash" off the track, hit an oil spill, water hazard, etc., your partner gets an extra turn. The first to the finish line wins!

Today in 1869

the famous silent movie comedian Buster Keaton was born in Pickway, Kansas.

- He was born Joseph Keaton, but his name was changed to "Buster" after he fell down a flight of stairs when he was six months old.

- His nickname was given to him by the magician Harry Houdini, who picked him up off the floor after the fall!

- He received a special Oscar in 1959 for his work in comedy.

Word of the day

comedian A performer who tells jokes and performs comic acts; from the Latin *comœdia* (comic poet).

Imagine...

You're the writer for a world famous comedian. She's asked you to come up with a really funny story for her next show. This normally wouldn't be a problem, but she's asked that the funny story involve a baby, a roll of transparent tape, and the number thirteen. Oh, and nothing too wild—she's telling the joke at the president's birthday party.

Quote of the day

"No man can be a genius in slapshoes and a flat hat."
Buster Keaton

Activity of the day

Brain Buster Math Squares

What are the missing numbers? As you work them out, circle the letter above the number in the decoding strip. Rearrange the letters to answer the question: What did Buster Keaton's mother change his name to when he was found cleaning the furniture?

12	10	28
6	2	
2	5	4

0	11	11
8		16
9	15	24

14		19
3	6	8
11	6	11

4	6	
6	3	9
24	18	27

1	2	3
4	5	9
	7	13

24	50	19
16	15	
40	65	29

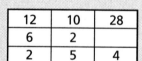

A	W	S	M	U	R	E	D	M	T
1	2	3	5	6	7	8	10	11	12

Today in 1964

Janice Salt married Francis Pepper.

- Giovanni Viglotti managed to illegally marry over 104 women between 1949 and 1981 before he was jailed for fraud and bigamy.

- The oldest recorded groom was 103 when he married his sprightly bride of 84.

- Nearly 6,000 couples were married at one time in South Korea in 1982. The wedding ceremony was held in a gymnastics stadium.

Word of the day

marry To take in marriage; from the Latin *maritus* (husband).

Imagine...

Your newspaper editor warned you that it would be a strange wedding. Well, the bride did wear white—but not a dress. The groom wore a suit—kind of. And there sure was something old, something new, something borrowed, and something blue—but not what anyone, especially the guests; would ever have guessed. Describe this strange wedding.

Quote of the day

"I have always thought that every woman should marry – and no man."
Benjamin Disraeli

Activity of the day

1. He gave her a pair of red slippers in 1989 and told her to "click your heels together." When were they married?

2. In what year did she receive a red flag with yellow stars?

3. Why did he buy his wife mothballs in 1974?

4. In which year did they dine out at a seafood restaurant?

5. In 1999, Mrs. Nuptial cleaned out the fish tank. What was she expecting?

Anniversary Fun

Mr. Nuptial likes to give his wife unusual wedding anniversary gifts.

Challenge:
There are no "official" anniversary gifts for years 31-39, so invent your own!

Year	Anniversary gift	Year	Anniversary gift
1st	Paper	9th	Pottery
2nd	Cotton	10th	Tin/Aluminium
3rd	Leather	20th	China
4th	Fruit/Flowers	25th	Silver
5th	Woodenware	30th	Pearls
6th	Candy	40th	Ruby
7th	Wool	50th	Gold
8th	Bronze		

Answers: 1. 1949 (1989 was their ruby wedding) 2. 1969 (China) 3. For the silver-fish 4. 1979 (Pearl) 5. Gold fish (50th)

Today in 1927

the movie *The Jazz Singer* opened in New York's Warner Theatre.

- *The Jazz Singer* was the first commercial "talking" movie.

- Before "talkies," the actors' words were shown on the screen and the music was provided by a live orchestra or organist in the theater.

- *The Jazz Singer* was remade in 1952 and again in 1980 (with Neil Diamond).

Word of the day

silent In films, having no spoken dialogue or soundtrack; from the Latin silere (to be silent).

Imagine...

Imagine you were at the first screening of *The Jazz Singer*. How would you have reacted to seeing "talking" pictures? What would you tell your friends? Would they have believed you? Write a report for the local paper telling us about this amazing new form of entertainment. Include some predictions for your readers of how you think the movies may change in the future. Maybe one day people will even show movies at home to their families—and in color, too!

Quote of the day

"Wait a minute, wait a minute, you ain't heard nothing yet."

Al Jolson (the first words in *The Jazz Singer*)

Activity of the day

Silent Movie Storyboard

1. Cut out from the newspaper ten interesting photographs of people.
2. Arrange them on a large sheet of paper.
3. Think how the pictures might be linked together like scenes from a movie. Glue them to the sheet in order.
4. Cut out some "speech bubbles" like the ones shown and glue them to the mouths of the people in the pictures. Now write in the words. Print neatly!
5. Write subtitles beneath the pictures where necessary to explain how the story develops.
6. Share your silent movie storyboard with a partner.

Today in 1806

carbon paper was first patented by Roger Woodward.

- Carbon paper is thin paper coated with a mixture of wax and "ink." It is placed between two sheets of paper to make a copy of the top document.

- Woodward invented the paper as part of a design for a machine that would allow blind people to write.

- The abbreviation "cc" in e-mails stands for "carbon copy."

Imagine...

Have you ever had to write out "lines" as a punishment at school? You know, 100 identical sentences reminding you how to (or how not to!) behave. Carbon paper might be one way to speed this process up. Or perhaps tying a bunch of pens together. Or—well, what can you think of? Write out a list of your top five ways to reduce the time taken to write: "I must not cheat ever, ever again."

Word of the day

copy An imitation or reproduction of an original; from the Latin *copia* (abundance)

Quote of the day

"Copy from one, it's plagiarism; copy from two, it's research."
Wilson Mizner

Activity of the day

Carbon Copy

Make your own carbon paper.

You'll need these:
- a sheet of copy paper
- crayons
- newspaper

1. Place the copy paper in the middle of a sheet of newspaper.
2. Color the whole surface of the paper with a crayon.

To use:
1. Place a sheet of paper on the desk.
2. Place your "carbon paper" colored side down on top.
3. Place a third sheet of paper on the paper.
4. Write or draw on the top sheet. Use a pencil or pen.
5. Lift up the top two sheets to reveal your carbon copy.

Extension:
- Try different-colored crayons for different-colored copies.
- Make two or three sheets of carbonpaper. How many copies can you make simultaneously?
- Color a sheet with several different-colored crayons to make a multicolored copy.

Today in 1977

Joe Greenstein, world famous strongman, died.

- His nickname was "the mighty atom."
- Although only (58.5 inches) 1.5 m tall he could bite through steel.
- At the age of 84, he bent a steel bar across his nose!

Word of the day

strong Having great power; from the Latin *stringere* (to bind tight).

Quote of the day

"My strength is as the strength of ten/Because my heart is pure."
Lord Tennyson

Imagine...

Problem: that new cereal you've been eating (with extra, extra iron) has had some weird side-effects. Like you've now got muscles of iron. Grant Kenny, iron man? A rusty has-been compared to your newfound strength! Being an iron-man has lots of advantages, too. The school bully runs away, your mom doesn't need to use the carjack for a blown tire, and you can hammer nails in with your little fingers. Then again, there are the disadvantages, like . . . . Are there any? Write about what happens when you become the world's latest iron person.

Activity of the day

Strong, Stronger, and Strongest
Use the clues to work out these nine strong words.

Strong								a strongly made chest
								a performer of feats of strength
								a fort or castle
								a burglar- and fire-proof room
								alcohol
								something you're good at
								determined
								swearing
								not made easily sick

Answers: 1. strongbox; 2. strongman; 3. stronghold; 4. strong-room; 5. strong drink 6. strong point; 7. strong-minded; 8. strong language; 9. strong stomach

Today in 1858

the Overland Mail stage reached St. Louis after 23 days and 4 hours on its first trip from San Francisco.

- John Butterfield of American Express organized the Overland Mail Co. and won the government contract to carry the mail.
- Wells, Fargo & Co., founded in New York by W. G. Fargo, carried mail between New York and San Francisco.
- Fargo consolidated with rival stagecoach companies in 1866 and became president of American Express in 1868 after a larger merger.
- Today it is possible to have a credit card issued by either or both Wells Fargo Bank and American Express.

Imagine...

Hmm. The bank doesn't usually address letters to you. But here it is. You open it. "Dear Sir or Madam (VERY personal!), Please accept this credit card as our present to you. You may spend up to $100,000 on it and never repay any money, as long as everything you purchase begins with the same letter as our bank's name does. Which bank? Ah!

So, tell how you'd spend $100,000. And everything must begin with a C.

Word of the day

credit An arrangement for a deferred payment of a loan or purchase; from Latin *creditum* (loan).

Quote of the day

"I don't trust a bank that would lend money to such a poor risk."
Robert Benchley (on being granted a loan)

Activity of the day

Answers: 1. Contains only even numbers; **2.** It's a palindrome (first eight digits are the reverse of the last eight digits.); **3.** Each four-digit number is twice the one before.; **4.** All are odd numbers.; **5.** The digits are ordered odd-even-odd-even.; **6.** Contains eight two-digit prime numbers; **7.** Double 1 = 2, double 2 = 4, double 4 = 8, etc. **8.** The sum of the first three four-digit numbers equals the last.; **9.** The sum of the four numbers is 9,999.; **10.** When converted to letter of the alphabet, they spell "credit card." (c = 3, r = 18, e = 5, etc.)

Credit Card Capers

Credit cards have 16-digit numbers, such as 4567 6002 0762 3535. What's unusual about each of these following credit card numbers?

1. 2884 4646 2228 8422
2. 1009 8423 3248 9001
3. 0537 1074 2148 4296
4. 1991 3357 9113 9711
5. 5238 1654 9858 1234
6. 1113 2317 3419 2931
7. 1248 1632 6412 8256
8. 1500 2534 4104 8138
9. 0088 5489 3774 0648
10. 003 1854 9203 1184

Today in 1924

Tutankhamen's treasures were photographed for the first time.

- Tutankhamen is known as the "boy king." He became Pharaoh at the age of 9 and died at 18.

- Tutankhamen's tomb was almost completely untouched by grave robbers and included chariots, weapons, and his coffin.

- When Lord Carnarvon, the dig's sponsor, died (along with his dog!) a few days after the opening, it was rumored the tomb was cursed. However, Howard Carter, the man who opened the tomb lived for another 17 years.

Word of the day

Pharaoh The title of the ancient Egyptian kings; from the Latin *Pharao* (great house).

Quote of the day

"I'm surprised that a government organization could do it that quickly."

Jimmy Carter (after being told it only took 20 years to build the pyramids)

Imagine...

You're the photographer following Howard Carter into Tutankhamen's tomb. What do you see? How do you feel, being in an unopened tomb? You set up your camera. What was that noise behind you? You look. Nothing. But, did that mummy move? Write about what happens next.

Activity of the day

Tut, Tut, Tut
King Tut, poor lad, was a sorry, confused boy (or so the story goes). Use the hieroglyphic translator to find out just why.

♩	🍓	🍇	📺	🏢	🚃	🚃	🚂	〰	🚂	🦀	🌲	•
a	b	c	d	e	f	g	h	i	j	k	l	m
👤	𓂀	🗡	🏛	🏢	✉	🏢	🦅	☥	🏛	🌸	🌼	🌹
n	o	p	q	r	s	t	u	v	w	x	y	z

Today in 1887

A. Miles patented the elevator.

- Early elevators were powered by steam engines.
- In 1980, a lift (elevator) fell 1.19 miles (1.93 km) down a shaft at the Vaals Reefs (South Africa) gold mine.
- The World Trade Center in New York has 244 elevators.

Word
of the day

elevator A cage that is moved mechanically in a shaft to move people from floor to floor in a building; from the Latin *elevare* (raise).

Imagine...

The elevator doors open and you step in to join the seven other occupants; a business executive with a briefcase, a fellow with a guitar, a young parent with a baby girl, a teenager with a nose-ring, and an elderly man carrying a small poodle. The elevator descends, then suddenly shudders and stops with the doors shut. There's silence for a second, and then the poodle barks. Write a story about what happens next.

Quote
of the day

"When I was little, my grandfather used to make me stand in a closet for five minutes without moving. He said it was elevator practice."

Stephen Wright

Activity
of the day

Alphabet Elevator

At the alphabet convention, letters using the elevator have to arrange themselves into words. Use the clues below and work out what words the letters made on each floor.

V, **E**, and **R** get in on the ground floor.
On the first floor, **O** joins them.
T gets in on the second floor
E's twin joins them on floor 3.
A hurries in on the 4th floor.
L gets in on the 5th floor—the elevator is full!
O and **E** get out on the 6th floor.
V and **R** get out on the 7th.
A leaves on the 8th floor.

	Clue
8	Allow
7	A story
6	To take a trip
5	A lift
4	Eat too much
3	To vote again
2	A person who votes
1	Above
G	Speed up an engine

Answers: G: rev, 1: over, 2: voter, 3: revote, 4: overeat, 5: elevator, 6: travel, 7: tale, 8: let

Today in 1823

Charles Macintosh invented a waterproof fabric.

- Soft natural rubber is used in "Macs" to keep them waterproof.
- In Great Britain, Macintosh is a synonym for raincoat.
- Charles Goodyear discovered that by mixing natural rubber with sulphur and heating it, the soft rubber would change into the more "elastic" rubber we use in tires.

Word of the day

macintosh A waterproof coat or cloak; named after Charles Macintosh.

Quote of the day

"Wear the old coat and buy the new book."
Austin Phelps

Imagine...

Spies are renowned for wearing trench-coats bulging with all manner of secret weapons, spy devices, communication equipment, and escape gear. Design your own spy coat. Show where all the secret compartments, pockets, and equipment are hidden. Describe how you used the coat on your last top-secret mission.

Activity of the day

anorak	macintosh
blazer	overcoat
bolero	parka
bomber	ski
bush	sports coat
duffle	topcoat
fur	windcheater
jacket	

Mystery Coat Word Search

What kind of coat goes on best when it's wet—and stays on best when its dry? Find each of these coats in the word search grid; then rearrange the missing letters to answer the question.

```
A  R  U  F  C        O  H  A  T  S
S  P  O  R  T  S  C  O  A  T  O  S  F  K
P  R  E  T  A  E  H  C  D  N  I  W  U
A  H  S  O  T  N  I  C  A  M  O  I  N  B
   D  T  T  A  B  O  R  V
   U  A  E  N  L  R  E  E
   F  O  K  O  A  E  B  R
   F  C  C  R  Z  L  M  C
   L  P  A  A  E  O  O  O
   E  O  J  K  R  B  B  A
   T  T  P  A  R  K  A  T
```

Answer: a coat of paint

Today in 1987

Costa Rican president Oscar Arias Sánchez was awarded the Nobel Peace Prize for finding ways to resolve conflicts in Central America.

- The Nobel Prize was established in 1901 by the will of Alfred Nobel, to be given for outstanding achievement in physics, chemistry, medicine, literature, and peace.
- In 1911, Marie Curie became the first person to be awarded a second Nobel Prize.
- The first Nobel Prize in physics went to W. C. Roentgen in 1901 for his X-ray discovery.
- Among the American writers who have won the Nobel Prize for literature are William Faulkner, Ernest Hemingway, and John Steinbeck.

Word of the day

prize Something offered or won as an award for superiority or victory; from Middle English *pris* (value, price, reward).

Imagine...

You find yourself a millionaire many times over. This year you are going to award prizes of $1 million to five deserving recipients. First, decide how you are going to choose the lucky five. Will you make the choices yourself, or will you choose a committee to make the choices? What will the criteria to be? Are you going to choose people who have excelled in certain fields of endeavor? Are there any restrictions? Will you name the prizes after yourself or, wishing to remain anonymous, perhaps, give them some other name?

Quote of the day

"The hunger for love is much more difficult to remove than the hunger for bread."

Mother Teresa, Nobel Peace Prize winner

Activity of the day

Imaginary Prize Awards

Using the list of criteria you developed in "Imagine . . .," find the five people who meet them. List their names and the reasons you chose them. If any of your choices are not people others might be expected to recognize, then be sure to fully identify each person so that others can better understand your selection.

Person	Reasons for Choosing

Today in 1838

a strangely engraved tablet was found in Moundsville, West Virginia. Baffling ancient language experts for 92 years, it was eventually deciphered by a teenager who realized it simply said "Bill Stump's Stone" in poorly-written English!

- The Ancient Egyptians engraved their tombs with a prayer and the name and family of the deceased.
- The First Emperor of China has the world's largest tomb at almost 1.2 miles (2 km) long by .6 mile (1 km) wide.
- Christopher Wren, the architect of St Paul's Cathedral in London has written on his tomb: "Reader, if you seek his monument, look around you."

Word of the day

epitaph An inscription on a tombstone in memory of the person buried there; from the Greek *epitaphion* (funeral oration or speech).

Imagine...

What would you like people to say about you when you're no longer alive? Write your own epitaph, describing what a wonderful person you are (or were). What were your achievements? What did you excel in? What brave feats did you carry out? What did you invent? make? win? perform? What will people miss about you?

Quote of the day

"Here lies Will Smith – and, what's something rarish,
He was born, bred, and hanged, all in the same parish."

Anonymous epitaph

Activity of the day

A Grave Set of Sums
Starting at the 12 o'clock position, write the answer to each problem in the next circle. If you return to the top with the answer of 12, you've worked them all out correctly!

x 6   ÷ 4
÷ 4   x 5
– 11   + 5
+ 17   – 6
11 ÷   8 +

Answers: 12 4 ÷ 3 × 5 = 15 + 5 = 20 – 6 = 14 + 8 = 22 11 ÷ 2 = 17 = 19 – 11 = 8 4 = 2 × 6 = 12

Today

is White Cane Safety Day in the U.S.

- White Cane Safety Day is celebrated to remind people about the abilities, rights, and responsibilities of the blind.

- Head injuries are the most common cause of vision loss.

- 90% of blind people can see the sun.

Word of the day

vision The ability to see; from the Latin *vis* (see).

Imagine...

You've bought fresh bread, flowers, a pet guinea pig, a painting, and a new CD as presents for five friends. Unfortunately, each friend has only one sense-either touch, taste, smell, hearing, or sight. Which present would you give to which person and why?

Quote of the day

"Painting is a blind man's profession. He paints not what he sees, but what he feels, what he tells himself about what he has seen."

Pablo Picasso

Activity of the day

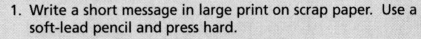

Braille Messages
Braille is a point system of writing for the blind in which patterns of raised dots represent letters and numerals. Try writing and receiving a Braille message.

1. Write a short message in large print on scrap paper. Use a soft-lead pencil and press hard.

2. Turn the paper over on top of a note card. Rub firmly over the top with a harder pencil to leave a print of the message (backwards) on the card.

3. Use a pin to prick holes around the lines of the message.

4. Turn the card over. Feel the holes.

5. Swap with a friend. Can you decode the message, using just touch?

Today

is annual sermon day in the church of St. Katherine Cree in Leadenhall St., London.

- The sermon is preached to fulfill a promise that John Gayer, former Lord Mayor of London, made in 1795. He was attacked by a lion on a visit to Arabia and prayed to be saved from the ferocious beast.
- When the lion went away without hurting him he left money so a sermon could be preached at St. Katherine's church each year on the anniversary of that day.

Word of the day

sermon A religious address or lecture; from the Latin *sermo* (talk).

Quote of the day

"About ten minutes."
Duke of Wellington (when asked what a sermon should be about)

Imagine...

Being a mythical Greek hero can have its downside sometimes, like being attacked by a three-headed hydra for instance. No sword's going to get you out of this one; in fact, Mighty Zeus, King of the gods, is your only hope.
"Mighty Zeus, if you get me away safely from this monster, I'll promise to do anything!"
"Anything?" thunders Zeus. "Anything!" you reply as the hydra gets closer. "Done!" says Zeus and he zaps the hydra with a well-placed lightning bolt. "Now, about our deal . . . ." So, what does Zeus get you to do? Don't forget, you said anything!

Activity of the day

What Wise Words?

Today's Sermon

"I've cut my sermon short today," said the pastor. "Just take these wise words to heart."
DOUN
TOOT
HERS
ASYO
UWO
ULDH
AVET
HEM
DOUNT
OYOU

Answers:
Do unto others as you would have them do unto you.

Today in 1933

The New York Museum of Modern Art hung Henri Matisse's painting "Le Bateau" upside-down. It wasn't corrected until December.

- Forgeries by Dutch painter Hans Van Meegren were so realistic that they hung in the Boymans Museum in Rotterdam for over 20 years before being discovered.

- Elmyr de Hory claims to have painted thousands of "masterpieces" in his lifetime and that up to two percent of the world's Picasso, Van Gogh, and Matisse paintings are actually his.

Imagine...

The large oil painting of the willow trees by the lake is your favorite in the whole art gallery. You love the way the bow of a small blue boat is peeking out from behind the branches. But when you gaze at the picture today, you notice the boat seems to be missing. But how can that be? Has the picture been replaced? Is it a forgery? Who should you tell? the museum guard? the curator? Who's going to listen to a kid anyway? Write about what you do and what happens.

Word of the day

museum A place for collecting and displaying objects with scientific, historical, or artistic value; from the Greek *Mouseion* (seat of the Muses, the nine goddesses who were the daughters of Zeus).

Quote of the day

"Skill without imagination is craftsmanship ... Imagination without skill gives us modern art."
Tom Stoppard

Activity of the day

Spot the Forgery

Look at the two pictures —the one on the left is the original, the one on the right a forgery. How many differences can you find between the two?

Scoring:
Fewer than 5: Are you for real?
Between 6 and 8: Forging ahead!
9 or more: No one pulls the wool over your eyes!

Answers: nails, frame, sky, tree, pin, hair, sweater, expression, freckles, land/water

Today in 1966

Elizabeth Arden, the founder of the Elizabeth Arden cosmetics company, died.

- The heiress to the l'Oréal cosmetic company (Liliane Bettencourt) is the richest woman in the world.

- Over 45 billion dollars is spent each year on cosmetics.

- Egyptian women used green paint made from malachite to darken their eyelids.

Word of the day

cosmetic A preparation that helps beautify; from the Greek *kosmetikos* (skilled in adornment).

Imagine...

As a top-notch lawyer, you've been asked to represent AniFree cosmetics in a court case. AniFree doesn't use animals to test their products on, but a lipstick they've been selling has caused lots of skin problems. Should companies use animals to test products for humans? How could you convince the judge? Write a list of arguments.

Quote of the day

"There is no cosmetic for beauty like happiness."
Countess of Blessington

Activity of the day

Cosmetics Word Search
Find the words listed below in the grid. What useful proverb can be made from the remaining letters?

blusher	lipstick
enamel	makeup
eyeliner	mascara
eye shadow	nail polish
foundation	powder
kohl	

```
N  R  L  F  P  B  E  W  E  M
A  E  I  O  O  R  N  O  A  A
I  N  P  U  W  E  A  D  L  S
I  I  S  N  D  H  M  A  H  C
P  L  T  D  E  S  E  H  O  A
O  E  I  A  R  U  L  S  K  R
L  Y  C  T  U  L  T  E  Y  A
I  E  K  I  I  B  S  Y  B  U
S  T  S  O  K  I  N  E  D  E
H  E  P  N  M  A  K  E  U  P
```

Answers: Beauty is but skin deep.

Today in 1872

the world's largest single mass of gold was discovered by Bernard Holtermann at the Star of Hope Mine, in New South Wales, Australia.

- The specimen was 3,000 ounces of gold.
- The rarest form of gold is a nugget. The largest known nugget, the Welcome Stranger, weighing about 156 lb. (70.8 kg) was turned up accidentally, just below the surface of the ground, by a wagon wheel in Victoria, Australia, in 1869.
- A gold strike by prospector Benny Hollinger (in eastern Ontario) led to Canada's becoming the world's third largest gold producer after South Africa and Russia.
- In 1935, Fort Knox was established in Kentucky to serve as a repository for U.S. gold bullion. The Army guards the gold.

Imagine...

Winter on the goldfields in the 1870s is never pleasant, and your last strike was months ago. Your clothes are threadbare and you can feel the rough path through your shoes as you trudge into town to spend your last few coins on a hot meal. Ow! Who put that rock there! Hold on— that rock is yellowish—could it be — GOLD??!!! Write a ballad (rhyming song) about the day you found the famous "_____ nugget" (Insert your name!)

Word of the day

Nugget a solid lump of a precious metal found in the earth; probably from British dialect *nug* (lump.)

Quote of the day

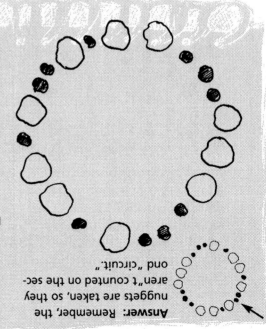

"Well, I don't know, but I've been told
The streets in heaven are lined with gold.
I ask you how things could get much worse
if the Russians happen to get up there first;
Wowee! Pretty scary!"

Bob Dylan, U.S. singer, songwriter (written in 1964, during the Cold War)

Activity of the day

Johnno, Jacko, and the Nuggets

"This is tricky," said Jacko to his mate Johnno. "We've got ten large nuggets of gold, and eleven smaller ones. How are we going to divide them up?"

"Well," mused Johnno. "What say I count clockwise around the circle and take each fifth nugget. When I've got ten, you can have the eleven left."

"That sounds pretty fair," replied Jacko.

But it wasn't. Johnno ended up with all ten big nuggets. Where did he start counting from?

Answer: Remember, the nuggets are taken, so they aren"t counted on the second "circuit."

Today in 1921

10,000 windows and 2,000 doors had been put into the house of Mrs. Sara Winchester in San Jose, California.

- Her house was added to continually over 38 years, as she believed she would die if she stopped building.
- The house eventually had over 160 rooms and eight stories, with thousands of feet of secret passages, and hidden hallways.
- Mrs. Winchester died in 1922 at the age of 85—the day of a strike by builders.
- Today the house is known as the Winchester Mystery House and is rumored to be inhabited by the spirits of dead construction workers who don't know to stop building the house. Oh, and Mrs. Winchester's ghost is said to be in the house, too.

Word of the day

window An opening in a wall that lets in light; from the Old Norse *vindr* (wind) and *auga* (eye).

Quote of the day

"The physician can bury his mistakes, but the architect can only advise his client to plant vines."

Frank Lloyd Wright

Imagine...

Write the guidebook for Mrs. Winchester's house. List the more unusual rooms, describe the secret passages, and include a site plan. Oh, and don't forget to mention those rumors of the ghost of the good lady herself, haunting the house armed with a hammer, saw, and architect's plan!

Activity of the day

House Math

What a house! Thousands of windows, doors, floors, and ceilings—very strange. Almost as strange as the house that—that what? Read the written numbers and then write the matching letter in the answer space. Read the answer vertically.

			Answer	
1	Seven hundred and fourteen		9307	A
2	Two thousand and four		111	B
3	Nine thousand, three hundred and seven		612	C
4	Double Three hundred and fifty seven		8759	F
5	Seventy-four		2004	H
6	Ten thousand take six hundred and ninety three		6065	I
7	Six hundred and twelve		74	J
8	Two thousand, four hundred and eighty one		2481	K
9	One hundred and eleven		242	L
10	Nine hundred and eighty		3512	M
11	Six thousand and sixty-five		90	O
12	Two hundred and forty-two		714	T
13	One hundred and two times seven		980	U

Answer: That Jack built

Today in 1879

the light bulb was finally invented by Thomas Edison.

- The average light bulb lasts for 750–1,000 hours.
- American Hugh Hicks has a collection of over 60,000 light bulbs.
- Edison formed several electrical companies that were merged in 1889 to form the Edison General Electric Company. In 1892, it became General Electric, now one of the largest companies in the world.

Word of the day

bulb The glass housing containing a filament that emits light when heated; from the Latin *bulbus* (a bulb shaped plant).

Imagine...

What if every time you had an idea, a light bulb actually lit up above your head (just like in cartoons). Write about a day in your class when everyone (including the teacher and class pets) has an "idea light bulb." What sort of light would appear for bad ideas? What kind of people would have fluorescent idea lights? Would your "idea light bulb" ever need replacing? What problems might it cause? What would a dim bulb mean?

Quote of the day

Q. "How many jugglers does it take to change a light bulb?"
A: "One, but it takes at least three light bulbs."

Activity of the day

Light Bulb Word Search

Find all these light bulb words in the light bulb. The letters that are left over will tell you how many lawyers you need to replace a light bulb.

Answer: How many can you afford?

Word										
bulb				I	E	T	T			
dark			H	N	L	H	E	V		
electricity		O	E	C	E	G	K	A	L	
filament	B	B	W	A	C	I	C	C	I	M
flashlight	U	A	H	N	T	L	O	U	G	N
glow	T	L	H	C	D	R	H	S	U	H	Y	T
incandescent	C	B	C	T	E	I	S	A	M	T	N	W
lamp	N	R	I	S	C	A	Y	O	E	O
light		O	W	C	I	L	U	M	L	
socket		T	S	E	T	F	A	G	A	
switch		F	N	Y	L	K	F			
torch			T	I	A	R				
tube			F	O	M	A				
vacuum			R	D	P	D				

Today in 1773

Captain James Cook received a present of a giant tortoise.

- An adult tortoise can weigh up to 1,907 lbs. (865 kg) and reach lengths of 8.2 feet (2.5 m).
- The tortoise was at least 190 years old when it died in 1966.
- The English National Tortoise Championship land speed record is 0.2 mph (0.45 km/h), set in 1977.

Word of the day

tortoise A land turtle with clawed, elephant-like limbs; from the French *tortue* (turtle).

Quote of the day

"Then it comes into view overhead, bigger than the biggest, most unpleasantly-armed starcruiser in the imagination of a three-ring film-maker: a turtle, ten thousand miles long."

Terry Pratchett

Imagine...

You have to write the tortoise chase scene for the upcoming movie *Turn Turtle and Run*. In the scene, both the good guys and bad guys are on tortoises. Describe the chase, including the near misses with other tortoises, the part where the bad guy leaps onto the good guy's tortoise, and the big crash at the end.

Activity of the day

Tortoise Trails

These four tortoises are trotting off to a juicy patch of grass. They're all waddling at the same speed, so which one will get there first? (Hint: Measure up!)

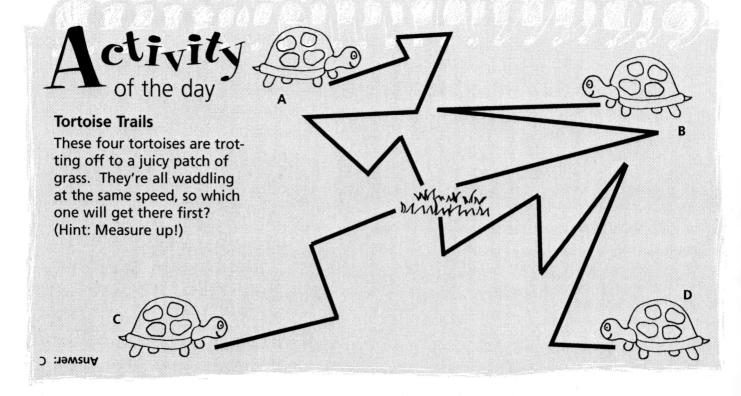

Today

is Chulalongkorn Day in Thailand.

- Chulalongkorn Day marks the anniversary of the death of King Rama V.
- It is marked with parades, the placing of flowers, and the burning of incense.
- King Chulalongkorn reigned for 42 years and one of his greatest achievements was the abolishment of slavery in the country.

Word
of the day

Thai A native of Thailand; in the Thai language, it means *free*.

Imagine...

The government has chosen you to nominate a special person to honor on October 23rd. Choose an admirable person and write down five reasons why you think this person should be honored. Suggest how the day might be celebrated.

Quote
of the day

"Naturally, if a fish leaves the water, it is unlikely to return."
(Old Northern Thai Proverb)

Activity
of the day

Chulalongkorn "C" Words
How many five-letter words beginning with "C" can you make from the letters in the word *Chulalongkorn?*

4—7: Good
8—12: Excellent
13 and over: Brilliant!

Answers: Here are 13. You may even think of a few more!: cargo; carol; chalk; chunk; churn; clang; cloak; clunk; Conga; cough; crank; croak; crook.

Today

is United Nations Day.

- The UN was established in 1945.
- U.S President Franklin D. Roosevelt first devised the name "United Nations."
- The United Nations is only able to spend the equivalent of 81¢ for each person in the world on health care, sanitation, agriculture, and food distribution (some $4.8 billion). World governments spend over $135 for each person (over $797 billion) on weapons and war.

Word of the day

united Acting together for a common purpose or belief. From the Latin *unire* (join together).

Quote of the day

"Katz's Law: Man and nations will act rationally when all other possibilities have been exhausted."

Imagine...

If you were in charge of the United Nations, what would you try to do for the world?

- Education?
- Food and housing?
- Medicine and health care for children?

Make a list of ten agenda items for the U.N.'s next world leaders meeting.

Activity of the day

Country	Population
Australia	18,235,600
Canada	30,286,000
France	58,317,450
Indonesia	195,280,000
Morocco	26,736,000
New Zealand	3,618,500
Panama	2,674,490
Peru	24,523,408

Counting Countries

Use the population chart opposite to answer the questions.

1. How many countries in the chart have a smaller population than Australia?
2. Which two countries together almost have as many people as France?
3. Which country has almost ten times as many people as Australia?
4. How many more people live in New Zealand than Panama?
5. How many more people does Indonesia need to reach 200 million?
6. How many more does Australia need to reach 20 million?
7. If all of Peru visited Australia on a vacation, what would Australia's population be?
8. If all of Australia visited France, what would Australia's population be?

Answers: 1. 2; 2. Morocco + Canada; 3. Indonesia; 4. 944,010; 5. 4,720,000; 6. 1,764,400; 7. 42,759,008; 8. 0

Today in 1955

the first household microwave oven was introduced by the Tappan company.

- The first home microwave ovens cost $1,200 and cooked eggs in 22 seconds and bacon in 90 seconds.
- Dr. Percy Spencer discovered the power of microwaves when he was testing a magnetron and the candy bar in his pocket melted.
- Early commercial microwaves weighed over 661 lbs. (300 kg), stood just under 5 feet (1.5 m) tall and needed water plumbing to cool them down.

Word of the day

Imagine...

So we have the microwave for nearly instant cooking of food. What else do we need to happen faster? How about instant freezing? instant seedlings? instant pets? instant washing? Turn on your instant idea machine, crank up the instant writing machine, and tell us all about it—good and bad.

Quote of the day

"I think it (a microwave) takes the soul out of food. Cooking is about ingredients being put together, and having time to amalgamate."

Delia Smith (chef)

Activity of the day

Mickey the Talking Microwave

It's not everyone who has a talking microwave. But just what is it saying? Turn this page upside-down to find out what Mickey is saying.

Challenge: Can you make up any more words using the digits on a microwave time display?

"07734." said the microwave as I entered the kitchen.

"Anything in the mail today?" I asked.

"57718."

"As usual!" I laughed. "Did anyone call?"

"7718."

"What did he want?"

"53045."

"Whoops. I should have returned those! Anyone else?"

"5508."

"She said she would. Whoops—I've dropped my icecream!"

"8075."

"You should talk".

"8078."

"Be nice!"

"3434."

Today in 1966

the U.S. and the USSR cooperated to free two gray whales from frozen Arctic waters.

- Gray whales are now only found in the north Pacific Ocean after being hunted to extinction in the north Atlantic Ocean.
- They grow to over 50 feet (15 m) in length. Each gray whale has a unique mottled pattern of gray, black, and white.
- They migrate each year from Mexico to the Bering Sea.

Word of the day

whale A large cetacean mammal that breathes through a blow-hole; from the Old High German *wal* (whale).

Imagine...

You're a female gray whale on your annual migratory journey. You're not a particularly fast whale (all those barnacles on you really slow you down!) and the journey has been tiring. You've just returned from the ocean floor after scooping up your morning meal. You surface through a flock of seagulls to see your only calf being hunted by a whaling ship. Write about what happens next.

Quote of the day

"A whale ship was my Yale College and my Harvard."
Herman Melville (author of *Moby Dick*)

Activity of the day

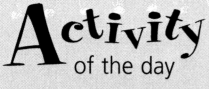

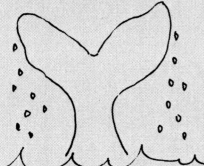

Free the Whale

Object of the game: Free the frozen whales
Equipment: Outside open area
Preparation: Choose two students to be the "ice." Divide the rest of the class into "whales" and "icebreakers."
To play: The ice players attempt to freeze the whales by touching them. The whales attempt to avoid the ice by running away. Frozen whales can be freed by two icebreakers touching them simultaneously.
Rules: Frozen whales cannot move. Icebreakers cannot be frozen.

The game ends when all the whales are frozen simultaneously (ice wins) or a pre-set time (two to three minutes) passes without all whales frozen (whales and icebreakers win).

Today in 1939

English comedian John Cleese was born.

- Cleese is best known for his role as Basil Fawlty in the farcical comedy series *Fawlty Towers*.
- He played the voice of the ape in *George of the Jungle* and Cat R Waul in *An American Tail*.
- His grandfather changed his surname from Cheese to Cleese when he joined the army in 1915.

Imagine...

Cleese's grandfather changed his name from Cheese. Would you like to change your surname? What would you change it to? Why? What if your name was once spelled a little differently (and funnier!) than it is now. (What might Mr. Boodie once have been named? Who might have changed it? Why? What difference might it have made?) Write a story where you have to change your surname because of problems with it.

Word of the day

farce A comedy based on ludicrously improbable events; from the *Latin farcire* (to stuff).

Quote of the day

"Loving your neighbor as yourself is practically . . . impossible . . . You might as well have a commandment that states, 'Thou shalt fly.'"
John Cleese

Activity of the day

Change of Name

It's not common knowledge, but a number of famous people started off with some quite strange names — the eleven people below, for instance. Who are they? Rearrange the letters! (Use the clues to help.)

1. OGEW Subh (U.S. President)
2. IV Peerlessly (still alive?)
3. DRJ Wadessmool ame (U.S. actor)
4. Cana Spindries (still mourned)
5. TJN Asnavee (red, white, and blue water)
6. NO Adman (a beautiful stranger)
7. PET Pramesas (what a racket!)
8. G Bastille (rich, rich, rich)
9. AEM Jockos (explorer)
10. ILO Nicknamed (Aussie movie star)
11. OW Stodgier (golfer)

Answers: 1. George W. Bush; 2. Elvis Presley; 3. Edward James Olmos; 4. Princess Diana; 5. Janet Evans; 6. Madonna; 7. Pete Sampras; 8. Bill Gates; 9. James Cook; 10. Nicole Kidman; 11. Tiger Woods

Today in 1886

the Statue of Liberty was dedicated.

- The original torch had an oil and charcoal fire in it.
- The statue was designed by French sculptor Frédéric Auguste Bartholdi and commemorates the friendship and ideal of liberty shared by both nations.
- The statue is over 148 feet (45 m) high, with each fingernail measuring 12.6 in. x 9.8 in (32 cm x 25 cm).

Word of the day

liberty Personal freedom; from the Latin *liber* (free).

Quote of the day

"Give me your tired, your poor,
Your huddled masses yearning to breathe free,
The wretched refuse of your teeming shore.
Send these, the homeless, tempest-tossed to me.
I lift my lamp beside the golden door."

Emma Lazarus (on the Statue of Liberty)

Imagine...

Imagine your school is going to erect a giant statue or monument at the entrance. What would it build? A giant statue of your principal? A giant coffee cup? A giant mathbook? A giant dunce's cap? Draw a picture of the monument next to your school. Write a poem or inscription to have on its base.

Activity of the day

Landmark Match-up

How's your LQ (landmark Quotient)? Try matching these famous landmarks to their country of origin.

Australia	**India**
Egypt	**Italy**
England	**Japan**
France	**USA**

Answers: 1 England; 2 France; 3 Italy; 4 Egypt; 5 USA; 6 England; 7 France; 8 Australia; 9 India; 10 Japan

Today in 1929

the Oscars were presented for the first time.

- Oscars are presented by the American Academy of Motion Picture Arts and Sciences.
- Each Oscar is a gold-plated bronze statuette.
- Titanic (1997) won 11 Oscars, equaling the record set by *Ben Hur* in 1959.

Imagine...

It's Oscar time! But these Oscars are the Ordinary School Children Award Ribbons. Decide who in your class will win:

- Most interesting contents of a lunch-box.
- Weirdest absence excuse of the year.
- Most stickers/stars/awards.
- Monitor of the year.
- Best reason for not completing homework.

Now make up your own!

Word
of the day

Oscar A statuette awarded for excellence in film-making; supposedly named after the Uncle Oscar of an employee at the Academy.

Quote
of the day

"I don't deserve this, but I have arthritis, and I don't deserve that either."

Jack Benny (on receiving an award)

Activity
of the day

Oscar Night

Here's an Oscars" night news report. Unfortunately, the reporter has Oscar fever and has used the word Oscar whenever she can. Can you sort it out by unscrambling the words?

Oscars night! In homes [OSCAR + S] the world families are watching the [OSCAR + ABDT]. Here in Hollywood, the excited audience claps as the [OSCAR + EHRT] plays the opening music and the evening's two [OSCAR + ENNNU] walk onto the stage.

The first awards are for [OSCAR + NOT] and it seems *The Simpsons* will win this year. Best [OSCAR + DKNTU] goes for the great music in *Roller* [OSCAR + ET]; the musical. *Worsel Gummidge*, starring Tom Cruise as the lovable [OSCAR + CERW] doesn't win an award, but his young [OSCAR + T] does. [OSCAR + EFH] Batman and the Riddler don't win either, and rumors say their [OSCAR + CNTT] won't be renewed.

Soon the night is over and the stars leave in their [OSCAR + PRSST], except for one actor who was taken to hospital after he tripped. He cried a lot, but everyone said he always [OSACR + ETV].

Answers: across, broadcast, orchestra, announcers, cartoons, soundtrack, coaster, scarecrow, co-star, arch-foes (tricky!), contracts, sports cars, overacts

Today in 1938

Orson Welles broadcast a radio drama based on HG Wells' *The War of the Worlds*.

- Over one million people tuned in to the broadcast.

- Listeners were convinced that Martians were really invading the U.S.A. and caused mass panic as they fled.

- H. G. Wells was partly inspired to write the original novel when the Italian astronomer Giovanni Schiaparelli reported seeing canals on Mars.

Word of the day

panic Sudden mass fear over anticipated events; from the Greek *panikós* (from the god Pan who caused terror).

Quote of the day

"I began at the top and I've been working my way down ever since."
Orson Welles

Imagine...

Oh no! Research by the city's building and safety department has discovered that your school is built 49 feet (15 m) too close to the street! The only solution is to lift up the entire school with huge hydraulic jacks and move it back. Write a fake news story about the situation. Look at some real news stories for ideas. Include an interview with building and safety department, the principal, and comments from the local board of education.

Activity of the day

Invasion: Earth!

The Martians are invading! They're fed up with seeing themselves portrayed on Earth TV as horrible two-headed monsters (when actually they're horrible three-headed monsters), and they're out for revenge. They've filled up their spaceship tanks with gas and headed here as fast as they can. But will they make it? Their tanks hold only 50 million kilometers worth of gas and Earth is . . . . How far away is Earth? Follow the maze to Earth and find out.

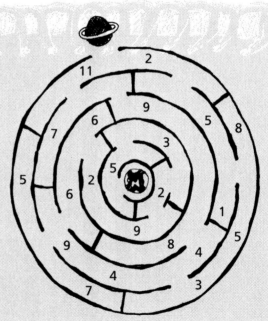

Answer: Whoops. Mars at its closest distance is 55 million kilometers. The poor old Martians are 5 million kilometers short.

Today in 1926

Erich Weiss, (better known as the magician Harry Houdini), dies.

- He took his stage name from the French magician Robert Houdin.
- Houdini broke several Australian aviation records when he visited there in 1910.
- His vanishing elephant trick was the world"s biggest illusion for several years.

Imagine...

Gilbert has accidentally picked up Marvellino, the 'Mazin' Magician's secret word. Trouble is, the word is not very magical sounding, and Gilbert doesn't know he's got it. Write about Gilbert's day and what happens when he uses the word "Marvellino" in his conversations with others. Will Gilbert realize what is happening? Will the 'Mazin' Magician get her magic word back? How?

Word
of the day

prestidigitator A conjuror. From the French *preste* (nimble) and the Latin *digitus* (finger).

Quote
of the day

"Any sufficiently advanced technology is indistinguishable from magic."
Arthur C. Clarke

Activity
of the day

Magic Word Search

So, do you know what happened when the magician"s wand became sick? Find all these conjuror-related words in the top-hat puzzle and the leftover letters will give you the answer.

abracadabra	magic
cape	presto
card	puzzle
conjure	rabbit
deception	sleight
disappear	trick
hat	vanish
illusion	wand

```
A A R B A D A C A R B A L
  H T E H P H A T
  S E C T U R E R
  I I E D Z C P I
  N K P N Z T P C
  A O T A L H A K
  V T I W E G S S
  W S O S R I I R
  E E N C U E D A
  D R A C J L R B
  E P I L N S L B
  E L U S O I O I
  M A G I C N S T
```

Answer: All the tricks were illusions.

Today in 1790

legislation was first introduced into British Parliament to actively protect and conserve water birds.

- The passenger pigeon, once found in massive flocks numbering millions of birds, was hunted to extinction in the wild by 1894. The last passenger pigeon (named Martha) died in captivity in 1914.
- Several kinds of Amazon parrots are in danger of becoming extinct due to loss of their habitat, poaching, or from being illegally collected for the pet market.

Word of the day

conserve To keep up and reserve for special use; from the Latin *servare* (to keep, guard or observe).

Quote of the day

"People can't change the way they use resources without changing their relations with one another .... How to conserve is usually a harder question than whether, or what, to conserve."

Hugh Stretton

Imagine...

Magpies Terrible creatures! Cawing away every dawn, awakening hard-working citizens from their sleep! Swooping on helpless little children and senior citizens! They ought to be shot! Wiped out! Completely eradicated. Hold on, surely they can't be that bad! After all, they contribute much to the environment. Write an impassioned letter to the paper saying why magpies should be protected, and conserved.

Activity of the day

Spot the Water Bird
Water birds are often well-camouflaged to protect them from predators, and there are ten well-hidden in these words. To find them, complete these "sums" by "subtracting" letters from the main word or words and unscrambling the remaining letters.

1. SUN DECK – ENS =
2. THRONE – T =
3. APPLIANCE – AP =
4. FRANKING-MACHINES – AACMNN =
5. CONTEMPORARY – EPY =
6. ICEBERG – CI =
7. BUTTERING – GU =
8. FRANCE – F =
9. REGRET – R =
10. SPELLING BOOK – EGK =

Today in 1950

author, journalist, playwright, and Nobel Laureate George Bernard Shaw died, aged 94.

- Shaw wrote over 50 plays, including "Pygmalion," later filmed as the musical *My Fair Lady*.

- He was well-known for his prolific letter-writing, and in his lifetime wrote thousands of letters to friends, acquaintances, public figures and newspaper editors.

- He wrote the play *How He Lied to Her Husband* in just four days after continuous rain kept him inside while on a vacation to Scotland.

Word of the day

play A dramatic work intended for performance by actors on a stage; from the Old English *plega* (exercise).

Imagine...

A grubby girl whose name is spelled with a "y" . . .

A blubbing boy who's lost his best friend . . .

A terrifying teacher with a secret . . .

A windy day in the abandoned old junkyard outside of town . . .

And a joke, a slug, and a crack in the wall . . .

Use one, use all, but don't take all day—start right now and write a play!

Quote of the day

"What really flatters a man is that you think him worth flattering."
George Bernard Shaw

Activity of the day

The Stage Directions Game

- You will need a large defined rectangular area (or a stage if you have one lying about).
- Practice the various stage directions before commencing the game.
- Remind students that "down" is towards the audience, "up" is away from the audience, and that right and left are the performers right and left when facing the audience.

To play, the 'director' calls out a stage direction. The last person to get to the location is out. Add additional directions such as "freeze" (everyone freezes), "curtain" (everyone lies down), "encore" (everyone bows).

Upstage right	Upstage center	Upstage left
Center stage right	Center stage	Center stage left
Downstage right	Downstage center	Downstage left

Audience

Today in 1957

Kudryavka the dog (nicknamed Laika), became the first living creature to orbit the Earth.

- Laika (Russian for "Barker") was a stray found on the streets of Moscow.

- Her spaceship was the 4 feet (1.2 m) long *Sputnik 2*, the second artificial satellite to orbit the Earth. It stayed in orbit for 163 days.

- It's thought that Laika died after around ten days, probably from an over-heated shield or from a leaking gas.

- Belka (Squirrel) and Strelka (Little Arrow) were the first two dogs to be successfully returned to Earth after a space flight.

Word of the day

Sputnik Name given to the first Russian satellites; Russian for *fellow-traveller*.

Quote of the day

"The noblest of all dogs is the hot dog; it feeds the hand that bites it."
Laurence Peter

Imagine...

Tell Laika's story, beginning from her puppyhood in a poor Russian household, her life on the streets of Moscow, her capture and training for her space flight, the launch, and the real story of what happened to her.

Activity of the day

Famous Dogs
Who are these famous dogs? Some are real, some are movie stars, and some are cartoons.

			S							"Come home!"
			P							A planet of a dog!
			U							He sits and waits here.
			T							"This doesn't look like Kansas!"
			N							Curse the Red Baron.
			I							Wallace's better half
			K							Famous Russian "muttnik"

Answers: Lassie, Pluto, Tuckerbox, Toto, Snoopy, Gromit, Laika

Today in 1939

the first car with air conditioning as an accessory was put on exhibition in Chicago.

- Older air conditioners contain the gas Freon, which is dangerous to the environment. Newer air conditioners use a friendlier gas with the lovable name of "R-134a."
- Some air conditioners are rated by their ton of refrigeration—the amount of heat needed to melt a ton of ice.
- More unusual car accessories include mini-bars, satellite TV, and, in one large (and well-equipped) vehicle, a small swimming pool.

Imagine...

Advertisements for cars aren't always what they seem. That "free air conditioner" may be little more than a gaping hole in the roof. "Free air" might just mean the tires are pumped up. Some standard features may sound more exciting than they really are—how about an "overhead roof" or "see-through" windows? Write an ad for a car with every accessory under the sun.

Word of the day

accessory A supplementary component; an added extra; from the Latin *accedere* (to go).

Quote of the day

"People can have it in any color so long as it's black."

Henry Ford (referring to the Model T Ford motor car]

Activity of the day

Shim-Sham 3000 Sports Car

Dear Customer,

Please find enclosed the brochure you requested on the Shim-Sham 3000 Sports Car. We've hidden the price in these ten sentences. Just find each number and write it in its space below.

1. All of our car sales staff are fully trained in removing cash from your wallet.
2. And for that feminine touch, there's perfumed radiator coolant!
3. On entering the Shim-Sham 3000, please buckle your tie-dye seat belt.
4. One satisfied customer said: "During golf I've often used the Shim-Sham 3000's sun-roof as an extra hole"
5. Our loop wool carpet is sheer luxury; it wouldn't be out of place in a palace.
6. The Shim-Sham 3000 sports even has four-on-the-floor: wheels that is!
7. Watch our lengthy film commercial; by the fifth reel you'll buy a car just to get out of here!

Answer: $49,152.73

$ ⬜⬜,⬜⬜⬜.⬜⬜
  1 2   3 4 5   6 7

Today in 1605

Guy Fawkes was discovered, along with barrels of gunpowder, beneath the Houses of Parliament in London.

- He planned to blow up the Parliament as a protest against harsh laws for Roman Catholics.
- Children in England remember the night by burning an effigy of Guy Fawkes (a "guy") and setting off fireworks.
- A 928-lb. (421-kg) firework (aptly named "Universe 1") was exploded in Japan in 1983. The exploding display was close to .6 mile (1 km) in diameter!

Word of the day

effigy A likeness of a person, especially in the form of sculpture; from the Latin *effigies* (to form or shape).

Quote of the day

"A desperate disease requires a dangerous remedy . . . one of my objects was to blow the Scots back again into Scotland."

Guy Fawkes

Imagine...

It's a cold, crisp, July night. Imagine a fireworks display, lighting up the night. Write a poem about the display. Start with a verse describing the night—what you're wearing, how you feel, the people around you, the preparations. Then describe the shapes, patterns, colors, and sounds the fireworks make. Finish with a verse about your reactions to the display. Give your poem an "explosive" title.

Activity of the day

Guy Fawke's Poem

Below are the words to a traditional poem that tells all about the Guy Fawkes story. Unfortunately, someone's made it more complicated than it really is. Put the words below back into the poem (one word for each underlined word or phrase) to make a more sensible (and rhyming) poem.

ever, fifth, forgot, gunpowder, gunpowder, no, November, plot, remember, remember, treason, treason

<u>Commemorate</u>, <u>recollect</u>, the <u>one before sixth</u> of <u>the eleventh Month</u>,

<u>A mixture of potassium nitrate, charcoal, and sulfur</u>, <u>treachery</u> and <u>conspiracy</u>.

We see <u>not one</u> reason why <u>a powder used in cannons</u> <u>dishonesty</u>

Should <u>at all</u> be <u>blanked from our minds</u>!

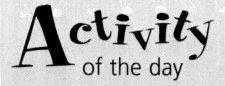

Answer: Remember, remember,
the fifth of November,
Gunpowder, treason, and plot,
We see no reason, why gun-
powder treason
Should ever be forgot.

Today in 2948 B.C.

(according to some Bible scholars) Noah was born.

- The Bible says that Noah lived for 950 years.
- Noah"s ark is recorded as being 300 cubits long by 50 cubits wide by 30 cubits high.
- A different flood story is recorded by the Cherokee people of the United States, in which a dog warns its master that "a great rain is coming that will flood the land."

Word of the day

ark A boat built by Noah to save his family and animals from the flood; from the Latin *arca* (chest).

Imagine...

Uh-oh. Its been raining for more than 40 days and nights, and there's no sign it's about to stop. With the water rising and time running out, you realize you must be a modern day Noah and take yourself and a bunch of animals into your hastily constructed ark. The trouble is, there's only room for five pairs of animals. Decide which five animals you're going to take (they can be from anywhere), write a list, and give reasons for each of your choices.

Quote of the day

"There is a tide in the affairs of men,
Which, taken at the flood,
leads on to fortune"
William Shakespeare (*Julius Caesar*)

Activity of the day

Animal Pair Word Search

With such wet weather, how did Noah's daughters keep their hair looking so neat? To find out, search for the pairs of animals (dove 1, dove 2) in the puzzle grid. The leftover letters give the answer.

```
1  E  F  F  A  R  I  G  T  H  E  W
E  S  Y  U  1  E  S  U  O  M  S  O
V  E  O  G  I  R  A  F  F  E  2  M
O  2  1  R  H  O  R  S  E  1  D  B
D  R  T  O  E  2  E  S  U  O  M  A
R  H  I  N  O  C  E  R  O  S  2  T
K  A  N  G  A  R  O  O  2  A  E  2
I  E     E  P  H  A  N  T  1  V  E
T  I  G  E  R  1  P  G  I  N  O  S
W  O  M  B  A  T  1  E  N  H  D  R
1  G  I  P  B  O  W  S     A  R  O
T  I  G  E  R  2  G  I  P  E  K  H
```

Dove 1	Giraffe 2	Mouse 1	Rhinoceros 2
Dove 2	Horse 1	Mouse 2	Tiger 1
Elephant 1	Horse 2	Pig 1	Tiger 2
Elephant 2	Kangaroo 1	Pig 2	Wombat 1
Giraffe 1	Kangaroo 2	Rhinoceros 1	Wombat 2

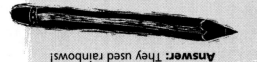

Answer: They used rainbows!

Today in 1885

the Canadian Pacific Railway was completed, joining east to west.

- The longest straight section of railway track in the world crosses the Nullarbor Plain in South Australia—478 km without a bend!

- Handpumped railcars are used by teams inspecting tracks. One team in Canada reached a speed of 20 mph (32 km/h) in 1982.

Word of the day

spike A very large nail; from the Middle English *spiker* (spoke).

Quote of the day

"RAILROAD, n. The chief of many mechanical devices enabling us to get away from where we are to where we are no better off."
Ambrose Bierce

Imagine...

As chief surveyor of the Canadian Pacific Railway, you were looking forward to the day when the team from the east met the team from the west in central Canada. Well, you were—except you've realised that due to a small error, they were going to miss each other by a country mile. What could you do? Put a huge kink in the line? Join up further along? Send the crews back to work? Write about how you discovered the error, how it happened, and what you did to fix it.

Activity of the day

Railway Words

Look carefully at these four word puzzles.
Can you work out what each says?

R Y A A I W L I W A A R Y	THESTtrainATION	 ticket	RAILWAY RAILWAY RAILWAY RAILWAY RAILWAY RAILWAY RAILWAY RAILWAY RAILWAY RAILWAY RAILWAY RAILWAY

Answers: Railway crossing, a train in the station, round trip ticket, railway line

Today in 1951

Yeti tracks were discovered on Mt. Everest in the Himalayas.

- There is no proof that Yetis actually exist. A supposed Yeti "scalp" was actually goat skin.
- Yetis are supposedly large, ape-like, hairy creatures. Stories of Yetis have been told for over 6,000 years.
- The famous climber Reinhold Messner claimed to have seen a Yeti in 1986.
- The U.S. has a similar "wild creature," called "Bigfoot" (or "Sasquatch").

Word of the day

Yeti Tibetan word for the Abominable Snowman; (*metoh kangmi* [supposed translation of a Tibetan phrase but probably an erroneous rendering of the Tibetin *mi t'om*, meaning man-bear, and *k'ang mi*, meaning snowfield man)

Imagine...

"It's true mom," said the young Yeti to his mother. "I saw some tracks today. Too small for one of us, they were in pairs, as if they walked on one set of legs!" Mrs. Yeti shook her head and stirred the broth. The child's imagination was so fanciful! Describe what happens when the young Yeti finally meets a real human (climber) and tells his parents about the encounter.

Quote of the day

"There is precious little in civilization to appeal to a Yeti."
Sir Edmund Hillary

Activity of the day

Yeti Words

Funny how no one's ever seen a Yeti. Guess it's the way they hide themselves: in the snow, in the mountains—and in lots of words, too! Add the letters below to the word "Yeti," and then use the definition to unscramble the word.

YETI+

GH	Ten times eight
NN	One hundred subtract ten
LM	At the right time
ADM	Not night
DFG	Unable to be still
BLR	Freedom
ARV	Lots to choose from
AGNP	A person from Egypt
GHW	Of great weight
LLOP	In a polite manner

Answers: eighty, ninety, timely, daytime, fidgety, liberty, variety, Egyptian, weighty, politely

Today in 1950

hailstones "the size of dinner plates" fell in England.

- One hailstone beheaded a sheep!
- A French church minister recorded finding hailstones with "the bust of a woman, with a robe turned up at the bottom like a priest's cope" inside them.
- A hailstorm in Bangladesh killed five people when hailstones over 28.6 lbs. (3 kg) in weight fell.
- Hailstones are made up of concentric layers of clear ice and compacted snow.

Word
of the day

concentric Having a common center; from the Latin *com* (with) and *centrum* (center).

Quote
of the day

"This thing that we call 'failure' is not the falling down, but the staying down."
Mary Pickford

Imagine...

It started as a steady rain on the school roof. It became a nightmare with hailstones the size of footballs punching their way through the classroom ceiling. Write about "hailstone havoc" and what happened when you tried to get home from school through the worst hailstorm ever to hit your neighborhood.

Activity
of the day

Hailstone Construction

Make a classroom hailstorm.

Every student will need a sheet of paper and colored pencils. Draw a small circle in the center of the page. Color it.

Students swap pages.

Draw a larger circle around the first. Color it in. Swap pages again. Draw another circle. Color it in. Continue until no more circles can be drawn.

Cut out the "hail-stones" and hang in the class.

Extension ideas: Paint rather than draw. Limit the colors (e.g., only blues and grays). Draw the hailstones in reverse order (large to small circle).

Today in 1969

Sesame Street premiered on PBS TV in the United States.

- Today is brought to you by the number 10 and the letter "S."
- Muppets were first seen on American television in 1954.
- *Sesame Street* is part of over 1,300 hours of educational TV broadcast each year by PBS. Some 64,000 schools across the world watch their PBS programs.

Word of the day

puppet A small person or animal-like figure with a cloth body and hollow head that is moved by the hand; from the Latin *pupa* (girl or doll).

Imagine...

Weird . . . . Your regular teacher has been replaced by a Muppet. And not just any muppet, but—but who? Ernie? Big Bird? Kermit? Oscar the Grouch? The Count? Write about your day and what happens. Do any other characters arrive?

Quote of the day

"Nobody creates a fad. It just happens. People love going along with the idea of a beautiful pig. It's like a conspiracy."
Jim Henson

Activity of the day

Sesame Word Search

What did Jim Henson make the original Kermit the Frog muppet from? To find out, locate each of the Sesame Street characters in the list below. The left over letters give the answer.

Bert, Big Bird, Cookie, Count, Elmo, Ernie, Grover, Guy Smiley, Kermit, Oscar, Snuffy, Telly, Willy, Zoe

```
K E H O T E O Z Y
E I I R S R S E B
R S E K E C L M I
M B N V O I A E G
I O O U M O R R B
T R M S F N C W I
G O Y L I F T I R
H U E E E R Y L D
G T E L L Y S L C
C O U N T O A Y T
```

Answer: His mother's coat

NOVEMBER 11

Today in 1572

Tycho Brahe discovered "Stella Nova," a new star in the constellation of Cassiopeia.

- The star wasn't actually new; it was a supernova that had only become visible when it exploded.

- Despite being a brilliant scientist, Brahe believed that the sun and the five main planets revolved around the Earth.

- The "Great Galaxy" in Andromeda can be seen without a telescope, but is over 2 million light years away.

Word of the day

supernova A star that explodes and becomes extremely luminous in the process; from the Latin *stella nova*: *stella* (star) + *nova* (new)

Imagine...

"Twinkle, twinkle, little star," you tunelessly hum to yourself as you adjust the focus on the telescope. Another night, another star. Gee, astronomical life sure can be boring . . . . But hold on—what's that! There shouldn't be a—well, not there anyway! What have you seen? Where is it and why is it there?

Quote of the day

"Twinkle, twinkle, little star,
"How I wonder what you are!
Up above the world so high,
"Like a diamond in the sky. "
Jane Taylor

Activity of the day

Constellation Word Search

Which famous constellation can't be seen in the Northern Hemisphere? To find out, locate each of the constellations below in the grid. The left over letters give the answer.

Aquarius	Libra
Aries	Pisces
Cancer	Sagittarius
Capricorn	Scorpio
Gemini	Taurus
Leo	Virgo

```
S U R U A T A U S T R
V I R G O A L I A S S
C A P R I C O R N O P
U A R B I L T H E R I
S A G I T T A R I U S
N S U I R A U Q A O C
S C O R P I O C R E E
O S R E C N A C S L S
G E M I N I S E I R A
```

Answer: Australia"s Southern Cross

Today in 1936

the first gardening program was broadcast in England.

- Flower bulbs were first introduced into European gardens in the 16th century.
- A *parterre* (along the ground) garden is designed to be seen from a raised position.
- King Nebuchadnezzar II built the Hanging Gardens of Babylon in around 600 B.C.

Word of the day

garden A plot of ground where plants are cultivated; from the Old High German gart (enclosure).

Imagine...

Plan your dream garden. It can be any size, any shape, any theme—money is no object! Will you have a vegetable section (where the veggies you don't like can't grow)? Flower beds in the colors and logos of your favorite sports team? A lawn as big as a football field? Or will you go super-small, a garden so tiny you have to be shrunk to visit? Hey, it's your garden—you decide!

Quote of the day

"God the first garden made, and the first city, Cain."
Abraham Cowley

Activity of the day

Garden Time

Make your own garden.
- Start with a Styrofoam plate (the sort that meat is packaged in).
- Fill the bottom with a layer of sand.
- Find small twigs, flowers, leaves, moss, rocks, and bark to arrange on the tray.
- Use a piece of aluminium foil for a pond.
- Make people out of modeling clay for your garden.
- What other garden features can you construct, e.g., a seat, lawn, bridge?

Extension:

Make a small garden in the bottom of a large plastic drink container. Cut the bottom off (at about 2-2.5 in [5-7 cm] from the bottom) using a sharp knife (with an adult's help). Fill with soil and plant some seeds. Put the top back on. Keep in a warm spot and water sparingly.

Today in 1850

Robert Louis Stevenson was born.

- Amongst his many books are *Treasure Island*, *Dr Jekyll and Mr. Hyde*, and *A Child"s Garden of Verses*.

- Stevenson was the first to use the phrase "The Land of Nod" to describe sleeping.

- Inscribed on his gravestone are the words, "Home is the sailor, home from the sea, and the hunter home from the hill."

Word
of the day

nod Be almost asleep; from the Old High German *hnoton* (to shake).

Imagine...

A famous scene in *Treasure Island* has Jim, the young cabin boy, hiding in a barrel of apples. Outside, the murderous pirates plot and scheme, unaware their plans are being over-heard. Where might you be to overhear a plot being hatched? In a cupboard at school? Under the kitchen table at home? Just around the corner of a dark alley? What did you hear? What will you do about it?

Quote
of the day

"For my part, I travel not to go any-where, but to go . . . . The great affair is to move."

Robert Louis Stevenson

Activity
of the day

Treasure Island Word Hunt
There are lots of words in the book Treasure Island—and there lot of words hidden in the words "Treasure Island," too. Because there are so many, we're making it easier for you—you only have to find five letter words—and they can't be plurals ending in "S."

Answers: Here are a few—
(there are over 400!)
adult, alien, arise, atlas, drain,
drier, easel, enter, erase, isles,
learn, lined, lunar, radar, rider,
rinse, risen, ruled, ruler, rural,
Santa, sinus, slate, slide, snail,
stand, stare, steal, tease ...

Today in 1896

cars in England were allowed to travel faster than 13.5 mph (22 km/h) for the first time.

- Before this time the Red Flag Act meant a flag had to be carried 43.5 miles (70 meters) in front of the vehicle to warn pedestrians and other road users. A lantern had to be carried at night.

- In 1985, a steam car called Steamin' Demon traveled at over 149 mph (240 km/h).

- In 1984, a Chevrolet was driven in reverse for over 8,694 miles (14,000 km) by Brian Keene and James Wright. They drove through 15 states in the U.S. and Canada.

Imagine...

Due to the ever-increasing road use and unemployment levels, Congress has re-enacted the Red Flag Act. Henceforth. no vehicle may travel faster than a walking pace and must have a duly appointed, official "red-flag carrier" walking in front of the vehicle at all times. Can you imagine what life would be like? Who would carry the flags? What would the cities and freeways be like during peak hour?

Word of the day

speedometer A measuring device that measures and displays a vehicle's speed; from the Latin *speti* (to be in time) and *meter* (measure).

Quote of the day

"Be wise with speed; A fool at forty is a fool indeed."

Edward Young

Activity of the day

Speeding Along

To calculate the average speed of a moving object, divide the distance traveled by the time taken. For example, a car travels 27 miles (44 km) in 2 hours. Its average speed is 27 ÷ 2 mph or 13.5 mph (44 ÷ 2 km/hour, or 22) km/hour.

Calculate the average speed of each of these moving objects.

1. A plane travels 915 miles (1,470 km) in 3 hours.
2. A snail travels 22 inches (55 cm) in 11 minutes.
3. A cyclist travels 60 miles (95 km) in 5 hours.
4. A race car travels 200 miles (320 km) in 2 hours.
5. A dad with a baby carriage travels 2000 yards (2,000 m) in 40 minutes.
6. The space shuttle travels 3 miles (5 km) in 10 hours. (Carefull!)

Why did the space shuttle travel so slowly?

Answers: 1. 305 mph (490 km/hour) 2. 2 in/min (5 cm/min) 3. 12 mph (19 km/hour) 4. 100 mph (160 km/hour) 5. 50 yards/min (50 m/min) 6. .3 mph (0.5 km/hour) It was being towed to the launch pad.

Today in 1492

Christopher Columbus first saw tobacco being smoked by the Arawak people.

- Tobacco was introduced to France by Jean Nicot (from whose name we get *nicotine*).

- Although tobacco smoking causes lung cancer and heart disease, usage in developing countries is still increasing by 2% each year.

Word of the day

tobacco Leaves of the tobacco plant dried and prepared for smoking; from the Spanish *tabaco* (a roll of dried tobacco leaves).

Imagine...

I think we'd got over our amazement at the aliens and their habits, long before they got over us. I still remember the time one of the bodyguards lit up a cigarette. Ruage suddenly rushed over and tore it from her mouth shouting "R"othl elt Rgol!" (stick of death). They just couldn't understand why we behaved the way we did. What else about Earth life might confuse aliens? Driving cars? Killing animals for food? Wars? Lipstick? Techno music?

Quote of the day

[To Sir Walter Raleigh] " I have known many persons who turned their gold into smoke, but you are the first to turn smoke into gold."
Elizabeth I

Activity of the day

Up in a Puff of Smoke
These chemicals and metals are all found in tobacco smoke:

1. carbon monoxide
2. formaldehyde
3. ammonia
4. carbon dioxide
5. aluminium
6. copper
7. lead
8. mercury
9. zinc

Use a dictionary or encyclopedia to research where else these chemicals and metals are used or found.

Answers: 1. A dangerous gas that comes out our car exhausts 2. Used to preserve dead bodies 3. Found in kitchen and bathroom cleaners 4. Exhaled by humans—contributes to global warming 5. Cans, cooking utensils, house frames 6. Electrical cables, coins 7. Batteries, cables (highly poisonous) 8. Thermometers, lights (also highly poisonous) 9. Paint pigment, soldering fluid, TV tubes

Today in 1978

a small island was first discovered north of Greenland.

- Kalaatdit Nunaat (Greenland) is the largest island in the world. (Australia is a continent.)

- Fraser Island (in Australia) is the world's largest sand island.

- The world's largest Island in a lake is Manitoulin Island in Lake Huron, Canada.

Imagine...

Take one blank sheet of paper. Draw an island. What island? Your island! Add a lake. A small mountain. A cliff. A forest. A swamp. A secluded beach. An island in the lake. A river or two. A small settlement of buildings. A waterfall. Now name all the features of your island. Use the names of friends, or pick a theme (your teachers, colors, or famous people). Now name your island.

Word of the day

island A small land mass surrounded by water; from the Old English *igland*: *Ig* (island) and *land* (land).

Quote of the day

"Oh! what a snug little Island, A right little, tight little Island!"
Thomas Dibdin

Activity of the day

World island Match

Here are the world"s ten largest islands, in order of area. Unfortunately, the actual numbers have got mixed up. Can you match them? (Remember, Greenland is the largest, Ellesmere Island the smallest.)

1.	Greenland	A.	828,800 sq km
2.	New Guinea	B.	230,988 sq km
3.	Borneo	C.	196,236 sq km
4.	Madagascar	D.	229,898 sq km
5.	Baffin Island	E.	743,325 sq km
6.	Sumatra	F.	507,451 sq km
7.	Honshu	G.	425,150 sq km
8.	Great Britain	H.	2,175,600 sq km
9.	Victoria Island	I.	217,290 sq km
10.	Ellesmere Island	J.	586,373 sq km

Answers: 1 H, 2 A, 3 E, 4 J, 5 F, 6 G, 7 B, 8 D, 9 I, 10 C

Today in 1973

the Danish rugby team Lindo lost 194-0 in an inter-club match.

- Rugby Union is said to have started in 1823 when William Web Ellis picked up the ball in a soccer game and ran with it.
- New Zealand beat Japan 106-4 in Tokyo in 1987.
- The All Blacks New Zealand rugby union team saw the new Rugby League demonstrated in England in 1905 and introduced it to Australia and New Zealand.

Word of the day

rugby A British form of football played with an oval ball; from Rugby School (in Rugby, England).

Quote of the day

"Nobody ever beats Wales at rugby, they just score more points."
Graham Mourie

Imagine...

Rugby union. Rugby League. Australian rules. Soccer. American gridiron. All different—but all a kind of "football." Even with all these "codes," there's still room for one more—yours! So, design a new type of football. It must have a ball that is kicked and you must score goals, but anything else goes. Shape of ball? You decide. Shape of field? You decide? Number of players and umpires, scoring, game length—all yours!

Activity of the day

Rugby League Table Test
Here's the final table for the Danish under-fives rugby league. If you know that a win is worth 2 points and a draw is worth 1 point, can you complete the table?

Team	Won	Lost	Drawn	Points
Herning	8	1	a)	17
Arhus	6	b)	c)	d)
Alborg	e)	f)	0	10
Odense	g)	6	0	h)
Kolding	3	6	i)	7
Helsinger	j)	7	0	k)

Answers: a) 1 b) 4 c) 0 d) 12 e) 5 f) 5 g) 4 h) 8 i) 1 j) 3 k) 6

Today in 1307

William Tell shot an apple off his son's head (or so legend has it!)

- Tell was ordered to shoot the arrow after refusing to bow to the cap of the local Canton (governor).

- He was imprisoned for telling the governor that he had intended killing him if his shot had not missed his son's head.

- In 1987, Harry Drake (of the U.S.) shot a crossbow arrow over 5400 feet (1,800 m).

Word of the day

arrow A projectile with a straight thin shaft designed to be shot from a bow; from the Latin *arcus* (bow or arch).

Imagine...

Your town is to host the next Olympic Games. The Opening Ceremony Committee wants to match the amazing burning arrow from the 1996 Olympics. In desperation they turn to you. Your task: ignite the eternal flame from a distance of 155 feet (250m). Make it different. Make it spectacular!

Quote of the day

"I shot an arrow into the air,
It fell to earth, I knew not where."
Henry Longfellow

Activity of the day

Shoot an Arrow in the Air

Here are ten words that all relate to "arrow": barb, bolt, dart, gauge, indicator, missile, needle, pointer, quarrel, sign
Seven of them also have the meanings listed below. Which words fit where?

Arrow		
		A disagreement or argument
		To rush from place to place
		A threaded metal road
		To autograph a document
		An instrument for measuring quantity
		A smooth-haired dog of Spanish origin
		A sharp object used in sewing

Answers: quarrel, dart, bolt, sign, gauge, pointer, needle

Today in 1895

the pencil sharpener was invented by African-American inventor Granville T. Woods.

- Lead pencils don't contain lead, but rather a mixture of graphite and clay (a mixture invented by Henry David Thoreau).
- The mechanical pencil (with its individual "leads") was patented in 1877.
- Pencil lengtheners were used in 1930s and 40s to extend the life of pencil stumps.

Word of the day

pencil A thin cylindrical pointed implement for writing; from the Old French *pincel*, from Latin *peniculus* (brush).

Quote of the day

"Do you know what breakfast cereal is made of? It's made of all those little curly wooden shavings you find in pencil sharpeners!"
Roald Dahl

Imagine...

Place: Your pencil case.
Time: Tonight:

There's a long ziiipppppp! as three pencils and a crayon stick their heads out. The coast is clear and the contents of your pencil case roll out on the desk. Yee hah! Party time! But what's that sinister shadow? Arrgh! It's the dreaded pencil sharpener! What happens next?

Activity of the day

Spot the Odd One Out
Someone's left some pencils in a jumble on the desk. They all look the same, but one is different from all the rest. Which one is it? Who might use it? (There's a clue in the first sentence!)

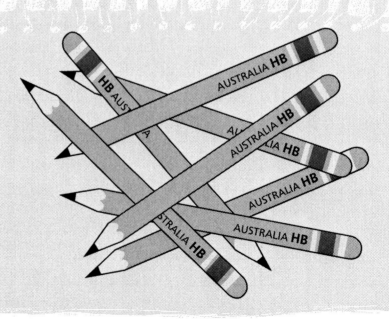

Answers: The one that with the eraser in the top left corner. Its writing runs in the opposite way to the others—it's a "left-handed" pencil.

Today in 1976

students at Cleveland High School in Queensland, Australia made a banana split nearly .9 mile (1.5 km) long.

- The recipe called for 11,333 bananas, 34,000 scoops of ice cream, 12 barrels of chocolate syrup, and 106 gallons (400 L) of whipped cream.
- Bananas contain 75% water.
- In 1973, a university lecturer ate 17 bananas in 2 minutes.

Imagine...

Required: A recipe for the world's largest . . . hamburger . . . stew . . . lemon pie . . . chocolate sundae . . . birthday cake . . . Swiss Bavarian triple decker strawberry mousse. Please give size, weight, cooking details, and calorie count.

Word of the day

banana Long, crescent-shaped, soft yellow fruit; from the Portuguese *banana* (er, a banana).

Quote of the day

"Time flies like an arrow. Fruit flies like a banana."
Lisa Grossman

Activity of the day

Banana Split
Split banana by removing the given letters.
Then add the extra letter in, and unscramble using the clue.

Extra points: Banana + ND = an item of headwear.

	ABN	L		Boy's name
	AAB	E		Girl's name
	ANN	R		A person of Arabia
−	AAN	D	=	A group of musicians
	AAN	K		The side of a river
	AAN	R		A farm building
	AAN	E		A small green building
	AB			A grandmother

Answers: Alan, Anne, Arab, band, bank, barn, bean, nana, Extra: bandanna

Today in 1763

the Montgolfier Brothers made the first flight in a hot-air balloon.

- The brothers were two of sixteen children.
- The idea for a balloon came as they watched a shirt dryby the fire.
- The sections of the balloon were held together with buttons!
- The first 'live' ascent was made by a sheep, a cockerel, and a duck.

Word of the day

ascend To travel up. From the Latin 'ascendere'. 'Ad' and 'scandere' (to climb).

Quote of the day

There's something in a flying horse,
There's something in a huge balloon;
But through the clouds I'll never float
Until I have a little Boat,
Shaped like the crescent moon.

William Wordsworth

Imagine...

'Hi and welcome to all our viewers joining us for the live telecast of this truly historic event. Yes, folks, today, just a few metres away from where I stand, the Montgolfier Brothers intend to launch a 'balloon' containing a number of real live animals! Let's cross to Jennifer in the studio who's going to explain just what a "balloon" is, and how it works...' Write an on-the-spot account (complete with interviews with the sheep, cockerel and duck) of the Montgolfier Brothers' famous first ascent.

Activity of the day

Patch the balloon
The Montgolfier Brothers' Balloon was made up of two different coloured stripes. Soon it got a few holes in it and had to be patched. The Brothers didn't want any patch to touch a stripe of the same colour, or another patch of the same colour. What's the least number of colours they could use?

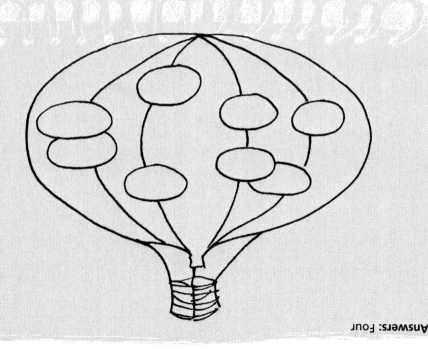

Answers: Four

Today in 1718

the notorious Blackbeard, the pirate, was hanged.

- Blackbeard's real name was Edward Teach (or Thatch).
- To scare his enemies he would weave wicks of burning gunpowder into his huge beard.
- Records show he captured some 45 ships in his career.
- In his final battle, he received 5 musketball wounds and more than 20 sword cuts.

(b) X

Word of the day

pirate Someone who robs at sea; from the old Greek *peiratés* (attempt or assault).

Imagine...

"Ooh arr, Jim lad! Shiver my timbers and ooh arr again! Well, me hearties, I be Blackbeard, the darkest-hearted buccaneer ever to sail the Spanish Main. Aye, I could tell you a story or two! Ships laden with gold . . . buried treasure . . . cut-throat crews . . . ah—nostalgia! But the best tale—well, it all began the day I thought I'd scare a bunch of sailors by weaving burning wicks in me beard . . . ooh arr!" Finish the story of what happened to Blackbeard.

Quote of the day

(e) X

"It is, it is a glorious thing to be a Pirate King."
W. S. Gilbert

Activity of the day

(c) X

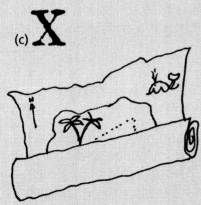

Find the Treasure

There are five Xs on this page. Which one marks the spot where Blackbeard has buried his treasure? Follow the directions below and see!

1. Start from the top left-hand corner.
2. Walk 13 paces east then 23 south.
3. Head 8 paces to the west then 4 1/2 paces north.
4. Turn to the east.
5. Walk 6 paces. Turn a quarter turn to the right.
6. Take five paces forward. Turn a half circle.
7. Walk forwards 14 paces.
8. Dig!

(d) X

P.S.: A pace = 1 cm; north is the top of the page.

Extension: Make up instructions to reach one of the other Xs. Try them on a friend!

NOVEMBER
23

Today in 1948

the zoom lens was patented by Dr. Frank Gerard Back.

- The first lenses were glass bowls of water.
- Roger Bacon constructed the world's first telescope with lenses in the 13th century.
- Lenses are classified as concave or convex. Convex lenses bow out, concave lenses bow in. (Like a cave!)

Word of the day

lens A transparent optical device used to change the path of light rays; from the Latin *lentil* (shaped like a lentil bean).

Quote of the day

"The camera cannot lie.
But it can be an accessory to
untruth."
Harold Evans

Imagine...

"Sandy's family had money. Lots of money. So, of course, when we went on the class camping trip, Sandy had the best camera. A brand new megapixel digital camera, with the most amazing zoom you've ever seen! Sandy let us try it, of course—especially when Tom asked. We zoomed in on an ant nest—little critters everywhere. But then we zoomed in on the Queen ant. Boy, oh, boy—that was one thing we never expected to see!" Write about the amazing thing they saw.

Activity of the day

Make a Lens

Convex lenses: Fill a clear, clean glass with clean, clear water. Put the glass down on the desk and look sideways through it. Light rays are bent as they reflect off objects in the classroom and pass through the glass. How is the image different from the object?

Concave lenses: Fill a bucket or ice cream container 3/4 full. Place an empty glass part way into the water. Place an object behind the glass and observe it through the top of the glass.

Extension: The words *concave* and *convex* are used with mirrors as well as lenses. Find a shiny spoon and hold it up to your face with the back towards you. What happens to your reflection? What happens if you turn it around? Which way is convex and which way is concave? How is the image different from the object?

Today in 1504

Castile's (Spain) Isabella died at the age of 53 after a 30-year reign in which she financed the voyages of Christopher Columbus in his efforts to find the New World.

- Among Columbus' discoveries was Watling Island in the Bahama group.
- Another island, Martha's Vineyard off the southern coast of Cape Cod, Massachusetts (U.S.), was settled in 1642.
- James Cook, an English explorer, explored the coasts of Australia and New Zealand and in 1776 rediscovered the Sandwich Islands. He was killed by natives on the Hawaiian Islands.
- The Dutch navigator Abel Tasman discovered the Australian island of Tasmania (separated from the mainland by Bass Strait) in 1642.

Imagine...

You look at the names of places on a map of the state you live in and realize that, based on your knowledge of the area (history, topography, etc.), you could do a better job of naming the mountains, lakes, deserts, rivers, villages, cities, etc., Prepare a map of the state/area you are using for your renaming project. Label places with the "old" names and then add your "new" names below.

Word of the day

discover To be the first to find, learn of, or observe; from the Latin *dis* + *cooperire* (to cover).

Quote of the day

"I asked the captain what his name was
And how come he didn't drive a truck
He said his name was Columbus
I just said, "Good luck.""

Bob Dylan, U.S. singer, songwriter

Activity of the day

Tasman's Diary

Abel Tasman's surname occurs 15 times within this passage from his diary. Each time it has been scrambled and embedded in a longer word. Can you find them all?

Dear Diary,

This dawn finds me in good health, though not my ship. The mainmast (along with the mainstay) broke in last night's storm and my best craftsman claims he is unable to repair it. We continue to play cat-and-mouse with the English ships. I have made arrangements with the soldiers and men-at-arms to be ready if they should try to board us. My navigator has consulted the astronomical charts and fears we are lost. Personally, I feel he is overly dramatizing events. The craftsmanship of our compass (and the bar-magnets within it) is second to none. Food is in good supply. The bantams are breeding, and the men's stamina for catching fish near inexhaustible. Before retiring I'll feed the pet Dalmatians, check on the basket-making, and see what our cook is making of the manta rays he has caught. So, as I lower the gas-mantle, I bid you diary, adieu.

Abel Tasman

Answers: mainmast, mainstay, craftsman, cat-and-mouse, arrangements, men-at-arms, astronomical, craftsmanship, bar-magnets, bantams, stamina, Dalmatians, basket-making, manta rays, gas-mantle

Today in 1881

the wind-up car was patented. Sales began in spring of the following year but were soon wound up.

- In 1995, Trevor Bayliss invented a wind-up radio. It uses a gear box to power a radio for 40 minutes from 20 seconds of winding.

- Baygen, a company selling products based on his invention, also sell a wind-up flashlight.

- Apple Computer Company has experimented with a wind-up laptop computer.

Word
of the day

clockwork Any mechanism of geared wheels that is driven by a coiled spring; from the Medieval Latin *clocca* (bell).

Quote
of the day

"The angels all were singing out of tune,
And hoarse with having little else to do,
Excepting to wind up the sun and moon,
Or curb a runaway young star or two. "
Lord Byron

Imagine...

It got very cold last night when your wind-up electric blanket wound down. Having a hot shower this morning won't help either. Your father says he'll only keep winding the hot-water heater for another five minutes. The spring's almost wound down on the refrigerator, too—there's a job for tonight! You rip the top off the can of beans. One thing about this wind-up world are your muscles; all that winding has left you looking like a bodybuilder! What else might have to be wound up? Write about your wind-up morning . . . afternoon . . . and night.

Activity
of the day

Clockwork

Five numbers are missing off this strange clockface. Can you work them out?

Hint: 1+ 1 = 2

PS: L = 50 (in Roman numerals)

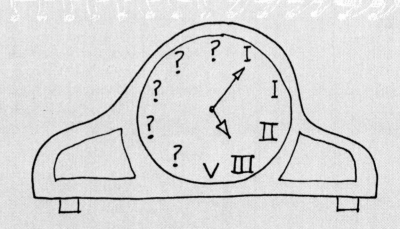

Today in 1864

young Alice Liddell read the first copy of *Alice in Wonderland*, complete with 37 illustrations by its writer.

- The author, Charles Dodgson, wrote under the pen name of Lewis Carroll.
- Carroll was a mathematician at Oxford University.
- Alice was the daughter of his friend Henry Liddell, a dean of Christ Church.
- Alice's cat Dinah even appeared in the story.

Imagine...

The Mad Hatter is inviting everyone in Wonderland to his next Mad Hatter's Tea Party and you've been asked to draw up the seating plan. First write up the guest list— And if you value your head, make sure you invite the Queen of Hearts! Then decide just who is sitting next to whom. Should Tweedledee and Tweedledum be separated? (They do fight so.) Would the Walrus enjoy sitting next to the Cheshire Cat? And just where will the White Rabbit sit? (Hint: A copy of *Alice in Wonderland* would be useful!)

Word
of the day

porpoise Plan. As in "Said the Mock Turtle: Why, if a fish came to me, and told me he was going on a journey, I should say 'With what porpoise?'" from *Alice in Wonderland*

Quote
of the day

"What is the use of a book," thought Alice, "without pictures or conversations?"
Lewis Carroll

Activity
of the day

Wonderland Word Search

What's this bottle—"Drink me"? No, "Solve me!" Find all the characters listed in the word grid and the leftover letters will spell out the name of a Wonderland identity with a very annoying habit.

							T	C	F	
Alice							W	H	L	
Baby							E	M	A	
Carpenter							E	U	M	
Caterpillar					R	D	D	I	D	
Cook		W	A	L	E	N	U	C		
Dinah	D	A	L	E	L	G	C	A	R	
Dodo	I	L	L	D	D	O	H	R	E	
Dormouse	N	R	I	E	E	E	E	P	T	
Duchess	A	U	P	E	E	C	S	E	T	
Flamingo	H	S	R	E	W	I	S	N	A	
Hatter	O	K	E	S	T	L	H	T	H	
Rabbit	D	O	T	I	R	A	E	E	C	
Tweedledee	O	O	A	Y	B	A	B	R	A	
Tweedledum	D	C	C	R	A	B	B	I	T	
Walrus	D	O	R	M	O	U	S	E	T	

Answer: Cheshire Cat

Today in 1914

Miss M. Allen and Miss E. Harburn became England's first policewomen.

- Chicago did not allow policewomen to patrol the streets until 1974.
- Shanghai (China) introduced a special squad of female officers in 1997 to counter "increasing female illegal activity."
- 92% of U.S. police officers are male.

Word of the day

truncheon A policeman's club; from the Latin *truncus* (trunk).

Quote of the day

"When constabulary duty's to be done,
A policeman's lot is not a happy one.

W. S. Gilbert, from *The Pirates of Penzance*

Imagine...

The success of Shanghai's female officers at arresting female crooks has sparked interest around the world. England is introducing a special squad of teenagers to counter "increasing teenage illegal activity." Canada is introducing squads of grandparents to counter "over-sixties crime." The U.S. in addition to its canine units, has decided to adopt another kind of animal to help fight crime? What kind of animal is it and what will this new unit be trained to do?

Activity of the day

On the Beat

Out on the beat at 7 A.M., Police Officers Betty and Bernice pick up a trail. A brazen thief has stolen multiples of seven! Fortunately, the thief has dropped some along the way. So, follow the trail of sevens until you exit the city block—and catch the thief!

	↓						49	
	7	21	49	70	77	50	14	56
49	15				28			70
	35	84	42	48	35	70	84	23	77
				20			21		70
49	14	63	56	42			14		56
	17			35	29	22	35	42	55
	77		56		48			49	70
35	27	35	77	35	28				77
		48			14	7	14	28

Today in 1968

children's author Enid Mary Blyton died.

- Enid Blyton, author of more than 700 books for children, was born in South London on August 11, 1897, the eldest of three children.

- *The Secret Seven* were real children who had started a Secret Seven Club and through their publisher father asked Enid Blyton to write about them.

- By the 1950s, Enid was one of the four most-read authors in the world.

Word of the day

author Someone who writes books or stories.
From the Latin "auctor" (promoter or originator).

Imagine...

A previously unpublished Enid Blyton manuscript has been found in a dusty chest in a forgotten attic in a tiny rose-covered cottage in England. The book (*The Not So Secret Six and the Completely Un-mysterious and Empty Envelope*) is sure to be a bestseller and you've been asked to write the summary on the book jacket. So, write away. Who is in the Not So Secret Six? (They must be British names!) Do they have a pet? Where do they meet? Why was the envelope empty? Who is the stranger at the bus stop?

Quote of the day

"Criticism from over-12s doesn't really count."
Enid Blyton (attributed)

Activity of the day

All in a Name

How many words (of five letters or more) can you make from Enid Blyton's name?
Score:
Over 5: Big Ears is impressed.
Over 10: Noddy is nodding.
Over 15: Even Mr. Plodd would be proud!

Answers: beyond, blend, blind, blonde, boiled, boned, ebony, inlet, intend, lined, linen, ninety, olden, tiled, tinned, toiled, toyed, yield (and more...)

Today in 1944

the U.S. Congress passed a Federal Highway Act to establish a new U.S. National System of Interstate Highways.

- An arterial network of 40,000 miles was planned to reach 42 state capitals and to serve 182 of the 199 U.S. cities with populations above 50,000.

- In Australia, this day in 1969 marked the completion of a track standardization program of the Trans-Australian Railway. There was a golden spike ceremony at Broken Hill in New South Wales. The road included a 29-mile stretch of continuously welded track—the longest such stretch of track in the world.

Word of the day

transport To carry from one place to another; convey; from Latin *transportare*: *trans* (trans-) + *portare* (to carry).

Quote of the day

"I have found out that there ain't no surer way to find out whether you like people or hate them than to travel with them."

Mark Twain, from *Tom Sawyer Abroad*

Imagine...

Your family is planning an automobile trip throughout the United States. However, there are some limitations. You will be going to no more than five different states and traveling for only two weeks. Choose two to five states that you would like to visit and plan your route. List the specific places—national parks or forests, cities, amusement parks, etc., that you want to see. Tell what you expect the various places to be like, what you hope to experience there.

Activity of the day

Hitting the Road

Using the information from your "Imagine . . .," do some further trip planning. Assume that the cost of a motel/hotel will be $100 per night, that your family of four will spend approximately $100 per day on meals, and that gasoline costs will average $1.50 per gallon (You'll need to know about how many miles for your round trip.). Remember that some of the things you want to see and do will also involve spending money. How much will your family have to budget for this trip? Write out your figures; make a vacation budget.

Today in 1954

a woman in Sylacauga (Alabama, U.S.) became the first woman to be hit by a meteorite.

- A 59-ton meteorite was found in Africa in 1920.
- Barringer Crater is believed to have been created when a two-million ton meteor crashed in the Arizona desert in 25,000 B.C.
- Meteorite ALH84001 (a "Martian" meteorite) is thought to show evidence of early life on Mars.

Imagine...

On some days you're lucky. Some days— some days a train runs through your front room. Or a runaway bull makes believe it's a hood ornament on your brand new car. Or the lotto machine throws a fit after delivering all your lotto numbers. Or maybe you get hit by a meteorite. Write about your unluckiest day, ever.

Word of the day

meteor A meteoroid that has entered the earth's atmosphere; from the Old Greek *meteoros* (high in the air).

Quote of the day

"I'd like to be buried Indian-style, where they put you up on a high rack, above the ground. That way, you could get hit by meteorites and not even feel it."

Jack Handey

Activity of the day

Meteorite Muddle

It's amazing what you can find hidden inside a meteorite. Well, the letters of the word meteorite anyhow . . . . The black squares are the letters not used in the answer. Unscramble the remaining ones to find the answer.

Clue	M	E	T	E	O	R	I	T	E	
Woody plant with trunk and branches										
To remove the edges										
Mysterious										
Deserve										
100 cm										
Aquatic mammal with gnawing teeth										
Clock that measures a time interval										
A section of a school year										
Far away										
Whitish insect that feeds on wood										

Answers: tree, trim, eerie, merit, metre, otter, timer, term, remote, termite

Today in 1929

bingo was invented by Edwin S. Lowe.

- He created the game after watching children play a game in which they yelled out "beano".
- The British Army calls bingo "housey-housey." The British Navy call it "tombola".
- Over 15,000 people played a huge game of bingo in Canada in 1983. One game had a payout of over $100,000!

Word of the day

bingo A game in which numbers are randomly selected and players cover the corresponding numbers on their cards.

Imagine...

Your younger brother is being a real pain today. He thinks you repeat yourself all the time so he's made up a bingo card with your "favorite phrases" on it. Then, as he hears each one, he crosses it out. You managed to get a look at the card before he got his ear free of your grip and he's only got one more to cross off before he's got a line. "I'll wipe the floor with your head," you yell out from the kitchen. "Bingo!" he shouts back. There's a sparkle of colored light beams and an elfin-looking creature appears on the table. "Bingo?" it says . . . . Write about what happens next.

Quote of the day

"The generation of random numbers is too important to be left to chance."
Robert R Coveyou

Activity of the day

C	B	L
A	H	V
Q	M	G

D	U	M
E	R	W
J	Z	H

E	D	N
I	S	P
K	X	J

F	Y	P
O	T	G
L	R	K

Letter Lotto

You'll need these:

a book

copies of the four Letter Lotto cards.

plastic counters (six each)

Answers to extension:
1. Put more 'common letters' on an individual card.
2. Once six counters are on the card they must make a row or line.

To Play:

One player is the caller.

The caller calls out the letters from the first sentence of the book, one by one.

If players have that letter, they cover it on their cards.

When a player has three covered letters in a row, that player calls out "bingo!"

The first to call "bingo" is the new caller.

Extension:

1. What letters should be on a card so you win more often?

2. Why does each player only need six counters?

Today in 1901

King Camp Gillette patented the razor blade.

- In the first year he sold only 51. Two years later he was selling 250,000 a year.
- The electric shaver was introduced in the 1930s by Jacob Schick.
- Early shaving implements included clamshells, bones, and rocks.

Imagine...

Razor blades are fine when your facial hair only grows a couple of inches a month. Not so useful if it were growing an inch a minute. Then you'd have to use—scissors? Hedge clippers? Circular saw? Lawnmower? Write about what happens when men's beards and mustaches really begin to grow, and grow, and grow!

Word
of the day

razor An instrument with a sharp blade used in cutting hair; from the Old French *rasour* (to raze or shave).

Quote
of the day

"With five or six faces in front of a mirror it sometimes becomes a problem just which one to shave."

Denis Glover (discussing overcrowding on Navy ships)

Activity
of the day

How sharp are you today?
You can change blunt into sharp in 13 steps! Read each clue and then change just one letter of the previous answer to make the new word.

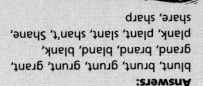

B	L	U	N	T	
					the main force of a blow
					a low, pig-like noise
					let have
					$1000
					a heated iron
					has no taste or flavor
					empty, not written on
					a straight length of wood
					to put seeds in the ground
					not level
					abbreviation of "Shall not"
					boy's name
					to give out a fair portion
S	H	A	R	P	

Today in 1586

Sir Thomas Herriot introduced potatoes to England.

- Potatoes are native to the Peruvian Alps.

- Potatoes are members of the nightshade family of plants. They are edible tubers—an underground edible stem.

- Potatoes have been known to grow up to 17.6 lbs. (8 kg) in weight.

Word of the day

potato An edible tuber, native to South America. From the Spanish *batata* (potato).

Quote of the day

"Good mashed potato is one of the great luxuries of life and I don't blame Elvis for eating it every night for the last year of his life."

Lyndsey Bareham

Imagine...

Quick and easy today. Write a list—20 uses for a potato (other than eating it). One point for each item. Two points if your teacher laughs when you read it out loud. Three extra points if you thought of it and nobody else did. Need ideas? How about an all-natural softball . . . doorstop . . . pencil holder . . . music instrument (tuber).

Activity of the day

Grow a Spud

You'll need these:

- ❧ a potato
- ❧ a knife
- ❧ a paper towel
- ❧ a saucer

Look at the potato. Cut off a section (carefully!) that has a number of "eyes" (small dents). Fold the paper towel in four. Place it on the saucer. Dampen with water. Place the potato section on the paper towel.

Over the next few weeks: Keep the paper damp. Observe the potato. What grows? From where? Keep a record (measure the height) and make observational sketches of the changes that take place.

Extension:

Use the left over potato for potato printing. Cut (carefully again) a design in the surface. Dip in paint then press onto paper.

Today in 1935

the game of Monopoly was launched by Parker Brothers.

- The game was invented by Charles Darrow.
- More than 150 million sets of Monopoly have been sold.
- The original game had street names from Atlantic City.
- The Canadian version has a beaver token.
- A completely edible chocolate edition of the game has been produced.

Word of the day

monopoly Exclusive control or possession of something; from the Greek *monopolion* (to sell).

Imagine...

Go to jail. Go directly to jail. Do not pass go. Do not collect $200. Nah. Too depressing. Too upsetting. We need happy cards! Positive cards! Create five new positive, uplifting (and wealth increasing) cards for Monopoly. Or, if you're in a bad mood, make five really depressing ones. Or five of each!

Quote of the day

"Monopoly is a terrible thing, till you have it."
Rupert Murdoch

Activity of the day

Build a Board Game

Stage 1: Design the game

1. Start with a theme for your game. Here are some ideas: A jungle trek, round-the-world race, underwater exploration, party time, find a pet.
2. Choose a shape for your board (square, round, novelty) and the design of your players' tokens (counters, matchsticks, small shapes, toys).
3. Decide how your players will move: by rolling dice, picking up cards, following instructions on the board, a mixture of all of these.

Stage 2: Make the game

1. Construct your board.
2. Mark the "squares" and number them (make sure they're big enough for the tokens!)
3. Decorate, following your theme.
4. Make the instruction cards.
5. Write out your rules.

Stage 3: Play the game

Play the game with some friends. Does the game "work"? What can you improve? Are the rules fair? Do they make sense? What might you change?

Today in 1791

Wolfgang Amadeus Mozart died.

- His full name was Johann Chrysostom Wolfgang Amadeus Theophilus Mozart.

- He was playing the keyboard at three and composing minuets at five.

- Mozart composed over 600 pieces in his life including variations on the tune "Twinkle Twinkle Little Star" (which he knew as "*Ah! vous dirai-je maman*").

Word of the day

composer A person who creates music professionally. From the Latin *componere*: *com* (with) and *ponere* (to put).

Quote of the day

"The sonatas of Mozart are unique; they are too easy for children, and too difficult for artists."

Artur Schnabel

Imagine...

Mozart was a child prodigy, able to play and compose music from a very early age. Imagine you are amazingly gifted in some area. (If you already are, imagine you're amazingly gifted in another area!) What "gift" would it be? Musical ability (like Mozart)? Spellbinding athletic ability? Mental ability? Artistic ability? You decide. Then write about the ways in which your life would be different—for better or worse.

Activity of the day

Placing a dot after a note increases the note by half its value.

Mozart Music Math

The chart shows how many beats each note is worth in 4/4 (or common) time. Can you work out the sums below?

o	♩	♩	♪	♪
4	2	1	1/2	1/4

1. ♩ + ♩ + ♪ + ♪ + ♩ =

2. ♪ + ♪ + ♪ + ♪ + ♪ + ♪ + ♩ + ♪ + ♪ + ♪ + ♪ =

3. ♩ + ♩ + ♩ =

4. ♪ + ♪ + ♪ + ♪ + ♪ + ♪ + ♪ + ♪ =

5. ♩ + ♪ + ♪ + ♩ + ♪ =

6. ♩. + ♩. + ♩ =

7. o. =

8. Write o in 3 notes.

9. Write ♩. in 2 notes.

Today in 1897

the world's first taxicab company began operation in London.

- The cabs were electric powered and traveled at 8 mph (13 km/h).
- Mexico City has a fleet of over 60,000 taxis.
- Delhi scrapped 600 fifty-year-old motorbike taxis in 1998 in an effort to clean up air pollution in the city.

Imagine...

It's been a long day in the old black-and-yellow taxicab. You started at 5 A.M., as the sun rose through the greasy fumes this city laughingly calls fresh air, and it's now past 6 P.M., and you're not finished yet. The traffic's been terrible and the fares have been pitiful. Your first passenger of the Day was a shocker—rude and ignorant, and they just got worse from there. Go on, tell us all about it. The passengers, the traffic, the other cabs. . . . Your day of taxi-driving misery.

Word of the day

taxicab A car driven by a person who takes passengers in exchange for money; short for "taximeter cab."

Quote of the day

"You'd better beat it. You can leave in a taxi. If you can't get a taxi, you can leave in a huff. If that's too soon, you can leave in a minute and a huff."

Groucho Marx

Activity of the day

Taxi Ride

You've been lecturing on ancient transportation systems at the city museum, but it's time to return home. So you call for a taxi.

1. Turn left onto East terrace.
2. Take the second street on your right.
3. Take the next right and then left.
4. Turn at the next right and pick up passenger.
5. Turn right, cross the intersection and stop. Pick up passengers.
6. Turn right, then left.
7. Turn right then right again. Cross the next intersection and stop.

Questions:

1. How many people end up in the taxi?
2. How did you leave town?

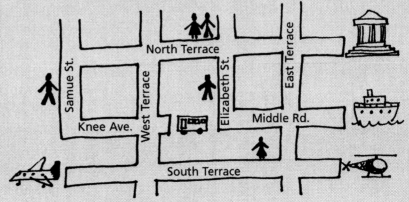

Today in 1761

Madame Tussaud was born.

- She founded her famous London wax museum in 1835.
- She started her modeling career making death masks of prisoners who were executed by the guillotine.
- Over 100 of the wax models were exhibited in Melbourne in 1997.

Word of the day

wax Fat-like material, but less greasy, harder, and more brittle. From Old English *wæx*.

Quote of the day

"If you think we're wax-works," he said, "you ought to pay, you know. Wax-works weren't made to be looked at for nothing. No-how!"
Lewis Carroll

Imagine...

The moon is waxing whitely over Madame Tussauds as you make your rounds for the night, the midnight rounds in fact. All seems peaceful. The wax statues stand, sit, and lie in their frozen poses, and the only sound is the click of your shoes on the floor. Except—what is that noise? You shake your head to get the wax out of your ears. It's a slopping, slithering, sliding sound. And it's coming from the chamber of horrors . . . . Write about what happens next.

Activity of the day

Groovy Wax-Crayon Patterns

You'll need these:
- old crayons
- scissors
- paper
- newspaper

1. Place several sheets of newspaper on the desk.
2. Holding the crayons lengthwise, cut (carefully) some small grooves into the sides of the crayons. Pick up any pieces that fall to the ground.
3. Use the cut edges to create patterns by rubbing them on the paper.
4. Swap "groovy" crayons with friends and use them in your design.

Today in 1934

weekly airmail started between Australia and the United Kingdom.

- In 1918, the first U.S. airmail stamps were issued as regular service began between Washington, D.C., and New York. The 24-cent stamps showed a biplane in flight, but some of the stamps were accidentally printed with the plane inverted and the faulty stamps became rare collectors' items.
- In 1921, two-way weekly airmail service between Cairo and Baghdad began in June. The Royal Air Force reduced the time it took a letter from London to reach Baghdad to between five and ten days. Before the airplane, the time was 28 days.
- In 1929, an airmail letter crossed the United States in 31 hours at a cost of 25 cents for 3 ounces.

Imagine...

Jacques, while on a vacation in Western Australia, posted an airmail letter to his sister Jeanne in France. It traveled by train to Adelaide and by plane to Sydney. After the letter was transferred to a jet, bad weather caused a flight-plan change. As a result, the letter crossed the Pacific to land in San Francisco before flying over the Rockies to land in New York City. The Atlantic was wild with storms, which ceased only as the plane dropped into Paris. So, now that you know where the letter went, it is your job to describe what it might have seen along the way—as if it were in a first-class seat and not inside a dark postal bag.

Word of the day

par avion By airplane.

Quote of the day

"Consider the postage stamp: its usefulness consists in the ability to stick to one thing till it gets there."
Josh Billings

Activity of the day

Stamp Forgery

How many differences can you find between the original and fake stamps below?

Original **Fake**

Answers: 1. Stamp value. 2. Tree is reversed. 3. Sea gull missing. 4. Coconuts have fallen. 5. Footprints. 6. Extra shark. 7. One less perforation on right side. 8. The sun has moved. 9. A bottle. 10. Torn corner.

Today in 1884

ball-bearing roller skates were patented by Levant Richardson of Chicago.

- Early roller skates were wheeled frames that clamped onto shoes.

- Roller derbys are races between teams wearing roller skates.

- Roller blades were invented in 1979 by Scott and Brennan Olson, two professional hockey players.

Word
of the day

roller A revolving cylinder; from the Latin *rotulus* (wheel).

Quote
of the day

"Too bad Lassie didn't know how to ice skate, because then if she was in Holland on vacation in winter and someone said 'Lassie, go skate for help,' she could do it."

Jack Handey

Imagine...

For some unknown reason, your principal has decided that tomorrow will be Roller Skating Day. Every teacher, student, and visitor to the school must wear roller skates. For the whole day. It all seemed to be going fine until the canteen manager collided with the second grade teacher while carrying four dozen pies. Then the groundskeeper tried to mow the lawn while wearing some very sleek in-line blades. Then things went really crazy. Write about the "Roller Skating Day of Chaos!"

Activity
of the day

Roller Riddle

The word is round and the answers can all be found in the letters of the words *roller skate*.

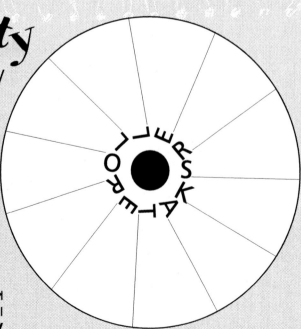

R: Thorny flowering plant
O: These trees have acorns.
L: Not the winner!
L: The smallest amount
E: To remove pencil marks
R: Give an account of
S: Skeleton like
K: Bird of prey
A: Take into custody
T: Famous nun, Mother _____
E: Religious holiday

Answers: rosella, oaks, loser, least, erase, relate, skeletal, kestrel, arrest, Teresa, Easter

Today in 1896

Alfred Nobel, the inventor of dynamite, died.

- He invented dynamite while trying to find a way to make nitroglycerine safer to handle. (His brother Emil had died in an explosion.)
- During his lifetime, he was awarded over 350 patents, including ones for synthetic rubber and leather and artificial silk.
- Nobel prizes are awarded each year with money from his trust account. The first Nobel prize was awarded on the anniversary of Alfred Nobel's death in 1901.

Word of the day

dynamite A strong explosive; from the Greek *dynamikos* (powerful).

Imagine...

We'd been mining the quarry for a few years . . . . Barry would set the charges, and then Shirley would check them. We'd run the wires out a safe distance and attach the detonator. The battery would be wired in, we'd check the area then- Boom! Down would come a couple of hundred tons of gravel. But this last blast-well, after we saw what was left behind in the cliff wall, no one was interested in the rocks . . . . Write about what was there, and what happened next.

Quote of the day

"He who was prepared to help the escaping murderer or to embrace the impenitent thief, found, to the overthrow of all his logic, that he objected to the use of dynamite."

Robert Louis Stevenson

Activity of the day

Dynamite Crossword

Will you take the cryptic or quick clues to solve this blast of a puzzle?

D Y N A M I T E

Cryptic
1. One date mixed with tea, say, will cause to explode. (8)
2. Desmond, in brief, and an ancient city damage beyond repair (7)
3. Is this inventor missing a bicycle alarm? (5)
4. B is first, last to give explosion (5)
5. Comb can"t see, say, and begins with the sound of an insect for explosive device (4)
6. To set, to set alight, an explosive substance (9)
7. To cause to explode because tennis game's not on (3-3)
8. Out of slow tread English burst outward (7)

Quick
1. Cause to explode (8)
2. To damage beyond repair (7)
3. Inventor of dynamite. (5)
4. An explosion (5)
5. An explosive device. (4)
6. A type of dynamite (9)
7. To cause to explode; or to leave on a journey (3-3)
8. To burst outward with a loud noise (7)

Answers: detonate, destroy, Nobel, blast, bomb, gelignite, set off, explode

Today

is National Noodle-Ring Day in the United States.

- Other kinds of pasta include macaroni, manicotti, spaghetti, lasagne, and ziti.

- Traditional Italian pasta is made from semolina.

- Marco Polo is thought to have introduced pasta to Italy after his journeys to the Far East.

- The Greek god Vulcan is said to have invented a spaghetti-making machine.

Word of the day

noodle A ribbon-like strip of pasta; from the German *nudel* (paste with egg).

Quote of the day

"A little more of the possible was every instant made real; the present stood still and drew into itself the future, as a man might suck for ever at an unending piece of macaroni."

Aldous Huxley

Imagine...

Hey! It looked like an ordinary packet of alphabet soup. You boiled the water, tipped it in, and stirred vigorously. While you waited for it to cool, you looked out the window, deep in thought. When would Mom be back? She was taking her time at the shops . . . . You looked down into the soup bowl. "Any moment now" was spelled out by the letter-shaped noodles. What? This bowl of soup could read minds and predict the future? Write about how the bowl of clairvoyant noodles changed your life.

Activity of the day

Spot the Spaghetti

Match the pasta description to the picture!

Capellini: "angel hair"

Conchiglie: shells

Farfalle: bow ties

Fusilli: "twisted spaghetti"

Wide egg noodles: curling ribbon

Rigatoni: large, grooved

Rotini: spirals and twists

Ruote: wheels

Answers: 1. rotini 2. capellini 3. farfalle 4. conchiglie 5. ruote 6. wide egg noodles 7. rigatoni 8. fusilli

Today in 1976

Walter Stolle completed a 17-year, 402,000-mile (646,818 km) bicycle ride around the world.

- Tandem bikes usually have two seats; a Belgium "tandem" (weighing over a tonne) had seats for 35 riders.
- The bicycle's ancestors include the hobby horse, the Macmillan bike and the velocipede .
- Kirkpatrick Macmillian was the first person to be fined for dangerous cycling; he ran over a small child.

Imagine...

"Budget cuts," explains the teacher. "There's not enough money to hire a bus for the school fieldtrips. So we've hired a-well, we've hired a bike." "A bike?" we all chorus. "It's got 35 seats—enough for all of us!" she says. "A bike?" we repeat. You put up your hand. "What kind of class fieldtrip would it be on a bike?" Describe it!

Word of the day

bicycle A two-wheeled vehicle propelled by foot pedals; from the French *bi* (two) and *cycle* (from the Greek *kyklos* meaning circle).

Quote of the day

"Own only what you can carry with you; know language, know countries, know people. Let your memory be your travel bag."
Alexander Solzhenitsyn

Activity of the day

Bicycle Word Search

Lots of bits make up a bike—and they're hidden "wheely well."

Find:

air, bell, bicycle, BMX, chain, gears, handlebar, light, mirror, mudguard, oil, pedal, pump, seat, spoke, sprocket, tube, tire, valve, and wheel

Today in 1843

6,000 copies of Charles Dickens' *A Christmas Carol* were sold.

- Charles Dickens invented the phrase "Merry Christmas."

- At the age of 12, Dickens had to work as a shoe polisher to earn money for his family.

- He wrote several articles under the name of Boz.

Word of the day

carol Joyful religious song celebrating the birth of Christ; from the Greek *choraules*. *Choros* (chorus) + *aulein* (to play a reed instrument).

Imagine...

Ebenezer Scrooge was visited by the Ghost of Christmas Past, the Ghost of Christmas Present, and the Ghost of Christmas Future. Write about three of your Christmases; one that's gone, the one you're about to have, and one you'd like to have in the future.

Quote of the day

[In a lecture on Dickens] "One would have to have a heart of stone to read the death of Little Nell without laughing."
Oscar Wilde

Activity of the day

Christmas Carol Crossword

Test your Christmas carol (and song) knowledge.

Answers: crib, holly, French, kings, sixth, bobtail, mouse, Tannenbaum, bells, corncob, manger, herald, Noel, Wenceslas

C				"Away in a manger, no ___ for a bed
H				"Deck the halls with boughs of ..."
R				Type of hen in the "Twelve Days of Christmas"
I				"We Three ..."
S				The last day of the 12 days of Christmas
T				The horse in "Jingle Bells"
M				What wasn't stirring the night before Christmas
A				German "Oh Christmas Tree"
S				"I heard the _____ on Christmas Day"
C				Frosty the snowman"s pipe was a ...
A				"Away in a ..."
R				"Hark, the . . . angels sing"
O				"The First ..."
L				"Good King ..."

Today in 1929

the world's first miniature golf course was opened in Chattanooga, Tennessee, by Garnet Carter.

- Most golf courses have 18 holes; the Chattanooga course had only six.
- Themes for miniature golf courses include Fantasia, nursery rhymes, and a pirates' cove.
- In 1912, a golfer made a short 387-ft.(118 m) hole a very long one after she hit the ball into a river and took 166 strokes to get it into the hole.

Imagine...

Yep, you heard the man right. He wants a new miniature golf course based on a TV show. That's right, a TV show. Let's say the show was The *Simpsons*. You'd have to hit a ball over Marge's hair, roll it around Homer's stomach, and finish with a chip-shot through Brat's hair. So, get to it! Decide on the TV show theme and then write about the nine holes, using lots of imagination.

Word of the day

golf A game played on a large open course with 9 or 18 holes. Scottish.

Quote of the day

"Although golf was originally restricted to wealthy, overweight Protestants, today it's open to anybody who owns hideous clothing."
Dave Barry

Activity of the day

Miniature Golf

Make a miniature golf course on your school playground.

You'll need:

newspapers

tennis balls

ice-cream containers

assorted pieces of furniture equipment, and junk.

Directions:

1. Design your course. Use the containers (on their sides) as the "holes." Mark off each hole with jumpropes or twine. Add obstacles, such as tables and chairs, to make the hole more difficult. Use marker cones to "channel" the ball towards the hole.

2. Roll up the newspapers, tape them together, and use as golf clubs.

3. Make score sheets to tally the number of "strokes" needed to complete a hole.

4. Play the game. Select a starting tee. What's the least number of strokes you get around the course in?

Today in 1964

Canada adopted the maple leaf flag.

- The flag was designed by Canadian Jacques St. Cyr.
- Its official heraldic description is "Gules on a Canadian pale argent a maple leaf of the first."
- The largest flag flown from a flagpole is in Brasilia, Brazil. It's 230 feet x 62 feet (70 m x 100 m) in size.

Word of the day

vexillology The study of flag; from the Latin word "*vexillum*" (flag).

Quote of the day

"November's sky is chill and drear,
November''s leaf is red and sere . . ."
Sir Walter Scott

Imagine...

You're designing the new national flag. You don't have too many rules to follow, except for these:

No animals

No stars

No red or blue

Hmm, does that make it difficult enough?

Activity of the day

Flag Quiz

Each answer in this flag quiz is spelled out in International flags. Use the answer from one to help you with the next.

1. A rectangular piece of cloth of distinctive design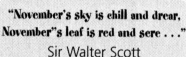

2. Pirate flag: A jolly

3. Long, decorative flag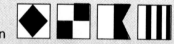

4. A flag flown by a ship to show its nationality

5. A long, tapering flag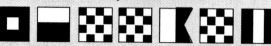

Answers: flag, roger, banner, ensign, pennant

Today in 1911

Roald Amundsen started home after becoming the first person to reach the South Pole.

- The South Pole is actually 1,615 miles (2,600 km) from the South Magnetic Pole.

- Amundsen was once trapped in the Antarctic ice for over a year. He survived by eating seal meat.

- In May of 1926, he crossed the North Pole in an airship.

Word of the day

pole One end of the earth's axis. From the Greek *"polos"* (pivot).

Imagine...

What would you do if you were trapped in Antarctica for a year? Would you eat seal meat? (How do you cook it, for a start?) What would you do to pass the time? What games might you invent to stave off boredom? What might you write in your diary? ("Monday, October 2nd. Had seal for tea last night . . .") Record your diary entries for one week of the year you were trapped in the Antarctic.

Quote of the day

"Great God! this is an awful place."
Captain Robert Scott (talking about the South Pole)

Activity of the day

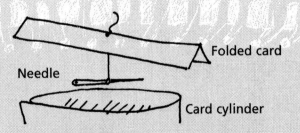

Needle — Folded card — Card cylinder

Compass Construction

Make your own compass and rediscover the poles.
You'll need:
a long needle
8 in. (20 cm) of thread
8 ½ x 11 in. (21.5 x 28 cm) tagboard
a magnet
transparent tape

Directions:

1. Stroke the needle with the magnet at least 25 times (in the same direction) to magnetize it.

2. Tie the thread around the middle of the needle.

3. Cut a 1 1/4-in. (3-cm) strip off one side of the card.

4. Roll the rest of the card into a cylinder.

5. Fold the strip in half lengthwise.

6. Push the needle through the center of the strip to make a hole.

7. Place the strip over the cylinder.

8. Pull the thread through the hole until the needle is suspended.

9. The needle will line up north-south.

10. Use a map to determine north.

11. Write the compass directions on the outside of the cylinder.

Today in 1903

at 10.35 AM, the Wright brothers made the first sustained motorized aircraft flight.

- They stayed in the air for a grand total of 59 seconds. They traveled 840 feet (256 m).

- Early European aircraft used ideas from Australian inventor Lawrence Hargreaves.

- Samuel Pierpont almost became the first person to fly. Problems with his launching catapult allowed the Wright Brothers to take the honors.

Word of the day

aviation Travel via aircraft; from the Latin *avis* (bird).

Quote of the day

"The airplane stays up because it doesn't have the time to fall."
Orville Wright (on how planes fly)

Imagine...

History records the firsts, but rarely the seconds and almost never the "almost-but" . . . . Imagine you were an "almost—but":

Almost the first to fly, but . . .

Almost the first to reach the North Pole, but . . .

Almost the first person to balance an Indian elephant on your head, but . . . .

Write about what stopped you.

Activity of the day

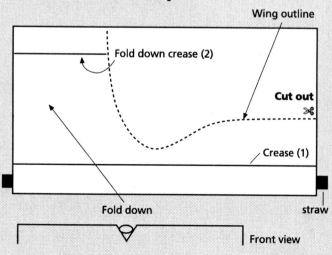

Wing outline

Fold down crease (2)

Cut out ✂

Crease (1)

Fold down   straw

Front view

Paper Plane

Make a paper aircraft.

You'll need: paper, transparent tape, scissors and a straw (optional)

1. Fold a sheet of paper in half.

2. Draw the outline of the wings from the diagram.

3. Cut out the section indicated.

4. Fold down the two wings at crease (1).

5. Fold down the wingtips at crease (2).

6. Insert a straw inside crease (1). A small piece of tape will keep the wings together.

Test your paper aircraft's flight capabilities.
Which way is the "front"? Try throwing it both ways.
Does the aircraft fly better with the wingtips up or down?
What other modifications can you make?

Today in 1719

Mother Goose's *Melodies for Children* was first published in Massachusetts, U.S.

- The publisher was Tom Fleet, who'd collected the stories and nursery rhymes from his mother-in-law, Elizabeth Foster Goose. Over 100,000 copies were sold.

- Charles Perrault published *Tales of Mother Goose* 20 years earlier in 1699, but in French. The tales included "Sleeping Beauty", "Red-Riding Hood", and "Puss in Boots".

Imagine...

Imagine you are editing the book nursery rhymes and you want to give it a new twist. How about combining the nursery rhymes? You can take a character from one and place it in the situation and setting of another. What if it was Humpty Dumpty who ran up the clock? Or, what if it was Little Miss Muffet who jumped over the moon? Use your imagination and perhaps a book on nursery rhymes to get you started.

Word of the day

nursery A room or place equipped for children, overseen by a nurse or nanny; from the Latin *nutrire* (nourish).

Quote of the day

"Round and round the garden
Like a teddy-bear
One step, two steps
Tickly under there!"
Nursery rhyme

Activity of the day

Nursery rhyme headlines

Some nursery rhymes are thought to be based on actual events, such as "London Bridge is Falling Down" and "London's Burning." See if you can match these nursery rhyme titles to the imaginary newspaper headlines reporting the events.

1. As I was Going to St. Ives

2. Baa Baa Black Sheep

3. Bye, Baby Bunting

4. Hey Diddle Diddle

5. Jack and Jill Went Up the Hill

6. The Grand Old Duke of York

7. Hickory, Dickory, Dock,

8. Hot Cross Buns!

A. "I wrapped my baby in dead animal fur"

B. Army maneuvers put soldiers in no-man's land

C. Brother and sister injured in shocking irrigation mishap!

D. Cutlery elopes as cattle boosted into orbit

E. Direct marketing proves hit for wool growers

F. Easter treats prove no dearer bought in bulk

G. Time runs out for rodents

H. Traffic jam blocks highway!

Answers: 1. H, 2. E, 3. A, 4. D, 5. C, 6. B, 7. G, 8. F

DECEMBER 19

Today

is the beginning of Saturnalia.

- Saturnalia was a mid-winter festival celebrated in ancient Rome.

- It honoured the god of the harvest, Saturn.

- Saturnalia became part of Christmas celebrations when Pope Gregory announced that Christmas Day would be celebrated on December 25.

Word of the day

festival A day or period of time set aside for feasting and celebration; from the Latin *festivus* (feast).

Quote of the day

"Good King Wenceslas looked out,
On the Feast of Stephen,
When the snow lay round about,
Deep and crisp and even."
John Mason Neale

Imagine...

One part of the Saturnalia celebrations was the choosing of a mock king. The king was usually a slave and was allowed to rule for the duration of the holiday. Imagine a Saturnalia-style festival in your school. You have been chosen by the principal to "rule" for a whole day. What decisions would you make? What rules would you pass? Would it matter that you would only be principal for the day? Write about your time as the mock principal.

Activity of the day

December Festivals

December gets pretty busy what with Christmas, Saturnalia, and all the other festivals. There are 10 celebrations for December listed below. Use an encyclopedia or other reference source to find out the date of each festival and then enter it onto the calendar.

1. Boxing Day
2. Capricorn star sign begins
3. Christmas Day
4. Christmas Eve
5. Holy Innocents day
6. Kwanzaa
7. New Year's Eve
8. Saturnalia
9. St Nicholas's day
10. St Stephen's Day

December

1	2	3	4	5	6	7
8	9	10	11	12	13	14
15	16	17	18	19	20	21
22	23	24	25	26	27	28
29	30	31				

Answers: (1) 26th (2) 22nd (3) 25th (4) 24th (5) 28th (6) 26th (7) 31st (8) 19th (9) 6th (10) 26th

Today in 1803

One of history's greatest real estate deals, the Lousisiana Purchase, took place.

- The U.S. bought the 825,000 square miles of territory from France for $15 million.-Less than $20 per square mile.
- The Lousiana Purchase doubled the area of the United States.
- All or part of 15 U.S. states were formed from this territory.

Imagine...

You could make a big purchase, a really big purchase. Tell what this really big purchase is and why you're going to make it. Make sure you include lots of details about your really big plans for this really big purchase.

Word of the day

territory The land and waters under the jurisdiction of a nation, state, ruler, etc.

Quote of the day

" . . . the fertility of the country, its climate, and extent promise in due season important aids to our treasury, an ample provision for our posterity, and a wide spread for the blessings of freedom and equal laws."
President Thomas Jefferson

Activity of the day

Label the States

All or part of 15 states were carved from the area of the Louisiana Purchase. Can you identify them? Use reference materials to help.

1. _____
2. _____
3. _____
4. _____
5. _____
6. _____
7. _____
8. _____
9. _____
10. _____
11. _____
12. _____
13. _____
14. _____
15. _____

Answer: (b)Answers: 1. Montana, 2. North Dakota, 3. Minnesota, 4. Wyoming, 5. South Dakota, 6. Nebraska, 7. Iowa, 8. Colorado, 9. Kansas, 10. Missouri, 11. New Mexico, 12. Texas, 13. Oklahoma, 14. Arkansas, 15. Louisiana

DECEMBER
21

Today

the sun is at its greatest distance from the equator

- For people who live in the Northern Hemisphere (like the U.S.), it is the first day of winter and the shortest day of the year.
- For people who live in the Southern Hemisphere (like Australia), it is the first day of summer.
- In the Arctic Circle, the sun will not appear at all today!
- In Antarctica, the midnight sun will keep people awake!

Word of the day

hemisphere Any of the halves of the earth.

Quote of the day

"Don't worry about the world coming to an end today. It's already tomorrow in Australia."
Charles Schultz

Imagine...

Write a winter and a summer poem. Down the left side of your paper, write the word WINTER and below that, write the word SUMMER. Begin the first line with a word that begins with W and the second line with a word that begins with I. Continue until you have a six-line poem. Do the same for your summer poem. Remember to think about the seasons you are writing about.

Activity of the day

Air conditoner
Beach
Boots
Campsite
Coat
Cold
Fireplace
Hot
Hot chocolate
Ice skates
Mittens
rollerblades
Sandals
Sled
Snow
Snow cone
Snow skis
Sunny
Surfboard
Water skis

Winter or Summer?
Read the words and decide which season they belong to.

Winter	Summer

Answers: Winter (boots, coat, cold, fireplace, hot chocolate, ice skates, sled, mittens, snow, snow skis)

Today

maybe one of the days of the Hannukkah celebration.

- Hanukkah is a Jewish holiday that is observed during mid-winter.
- Jewish people celebrate the time when their ancestors rebelled against a Syrian king and retook the temple of Jerusalem.
- When they retook the temple, they only had enough oil to light their lamp for one day but amazingly, it stayed lit for eight days.
- Each day during Hanukkah, one candle is lit on the eight-branch menorah.
- During Hanukkah, people work during the day and sing, play games, and exchange small gifts at night.

Word of the day

Hanukkah A Jewish festival in early winter that commemorates the rededication of the temple of Maccabees; from Hebrew *hanukkah*.

Imagine...

To have a lamp remain lit for eight days was amazing. Write about something you think is amazing.

Quote of the day

"Praised are You
Our God, Ruler of the Universe,
Who made us holy through your commandments
and commanded us
to kindle the Hanukkah lights."
The first Hanukkah Blessing

Activity of the day

Poppyseed Candy
Poppyseeds are used frequently in candies and cookies.

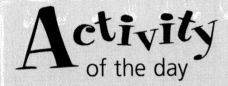

SHALOM
HAPPY HANUKKAH

Ingredients:
¼ cup (100 g) poppy seed
½ cup (120 mL) honey
2 tablespoons (30 mL) chopped nuts

Directions:
Places ingredients in small saucepan and bring to a boil over medium heat. (Be sure to have an adult help you with this.)

Boil steadily, while stirring, for 8 minutes until mixture starts to brown.

Remove from heat.

Spread mixture on a greased plate.

Cut into squares while still hot.

The candy will be chewy when cool. Enjoy!

Answer: (b)

Today in 1986

Dick Rutan and Jeana Yeager were the first pilots to travel around the world without stopping to refuel.

- Their trip in the Voyager, designed by Bill Rutan, began on December 14th from Edwards Airforce Base in California's Mojave Desert.
- They spent the next 216 hours flying 24,986 miles around the globe.
- 24,986 miles is equal to 40,202 kilometers. On this day in 1975, the Metric Conversion Act was passed in the U.S. declaring that the International System of Units (the metric system) would be the U.S.'s basic system of measurement. The law was never put into use.
- Today the U.S., Liberia, and Myanam are the only countries that do not use the metric system.

Word of the day

metric system A decimal system of weights and measures in which the gram, meter, and the liter are the basic units of weight, length, and capacity.

Quote of the day

"You are limited only by what you can dream."
Dick Rutan

Imagine...

You were one of Voyager's two pilots. Write about the things you would do that would keep you from becoming bored.

Activity of the day

Tables of Linear Measure

To convert:	Multiply by:
inches to millimeters	25.4
inches to centimeters	2.54
feet to meters	0.305
yards to meters	0.914
miles to kilometers	1.609

To convert:	Multiply by:
millimeters to inches	0.039
centimeters to inches	0.394
meters to feet	3.281
meters to yards	1.094
kilometers to miles	0.621

Try this: Which system of measure do you like? For a week, try using the metric system if you are accustomed to the U.S. system and the U.S. system if you are accustomed to the metric system. How did you do? Which system do you prefer? Would you be able to switch systems easily or would it be like learning a foreign language?

Today

is Christmas Eve.

- In France, after midnight, people invite over family and friends and eat a large meal. Pere Noel fills shoes with presents and candy.
- In South America, the midnight service is called "Mass of the Rooster," named after the rooster that announced the birth of Jesus.
- In Sweeden, a gnome, who lives under the floor of a house or barn, brings presents.
- In America, Santa Claus arrives on his sleigh pulled by eight reindeer, slips down chimneys, and leaves presents under the Christmas tree.

Word
of the day

eve The evening or day before a holiday; from the Old English *aefen* (evening).

Imagine...

You are Santa for a day . . . or a Christmas Eve. Write your itinerary for the night before Christmas.

Quote
of the day

"Twas the night before Christmas and all through the house, . . ."
From *The Night Before Christmas*

Activity
of the day

A Scrambled Christmas
Can you unscramble these words that are associated with Christmas?

etre _____   nmaails _____

anlecds _____   eblls _____

tasrs _____   sreawth _____

aoittepnsis _____   rcoals _____

goscktin _____   ifgts _____

atsna acusl _____   ttnvaiiy ecsne _____

oisemtlte _____   luye olg _____

Answers: 1. tree, 2. candles, 3. stars, 4. poinsettias, 5. stockings, 6. Santa Claus, 7. mistletoe, 8. animals, 9. bells, 10. wreaths, 11. carols, 12. gifts, 13. nativity scent, 14. Yule log

Today

is Christmas Day.

- On this day, Christians believe, Jesus was born.
- All around the world people who celebrate this day exchange gifts, get together with friends and family, and think of peace on earth.
- Many countries have their own special holiday symbols and customs.

Word of the day

Christmas Holiday celebrating the birth of Jesus Christ; from *Christ* and *Mass*.

Quote of the day

"Glory to God in the highest and on earth, peace, good will to men."
The Bible, Luke 2:14

Imagine...

You choose to celebrate Christmas in a special way that doesn't involve buying gifts. What things can you give that don't cost money? For example, you might make something for someone or volunteer your time to a worthy cause. What would you do?

Activity of the day

Merry Christmas
Learn to say "Merry Christmas" in different languages.

France	Joyeux Noel		Norway	God Jul
Italy	Buone Feste Natalizie		Poland	Boze Narodzenie
Spain	Feliz Navidad		Germany	Froehliche Weihnachten
Holland	Vrolyk Kerstfeest		Puerto Rico	Felices Pascuas
Ireland	Nodlaig Mhaith Chugnat		Japan	Meri Kurisumasu
Denmark	Glaedelig Jul		China	Kung His Hsin Nien

Today

begins the seven days of Kwanzaa.

- Founded by Dr. Maulana Karenga, this cultural festival celebrates African and African-American heritage.
- Each of the seven days of Kwanzaa represents a different life value. This day emphasizes unmoja, or unity.
- Kwanzaa is celebrated by lighting red, green, and black candles set in a kihara, a candleholder that symbolizes the seven principles.
- On the seventh day, special handmade gifts are opened and a special meal is served.

Word of the day

Kwanzaa *Matunda ya kwanza* meaning *first fruits*; (Dr. Karenga added the extra "a" so that the word Kwanzaa would be seven letters long, with each letter representing one of the seven principles or values

Imagine...

You are part of a group writing a report on the seven principles of Kwanzaa (unity, self-determination, group effort, group cooperative economics, creativity, purpose, and faith). Choose one of these celebrated values and write what it means to you and why.

Quote of the day

"Kwanzaa organizes people, gives them a chance to ingather, and to reinforce the bonds between them, and to focus on positive cultural values and practice."

Dr. Karenga

Activity of the day

A Gift of Special Meaning

Create a gift of special meaning for someone in your family. Think about what is important to that person before you make that special gift. For example, if your sister likes to read, make her a bookmark. Promise your parents you'll do a certain chore. Help your mother by cooking a special meal (or at least help her to prepare one).

KWANZAA

DECEMBER 27

Today in 1571

Johannes Kepler, the father of modern astronomy, was born.

- Kepler believed that planets move in an oval or ellipse-shaped orbits around the sun.
- Also born on this day in 1822 was Louis Pasteur, the father of modern medicine.
- The French chemist/bacteriologist discovered that disease could be caused by various bacteria. This laid the groundwork for research in sterilization and the prevention of infection.
- Pasteur lent his name to "pasteurization," a process he discovered while trying to make milk safe to drink.

Word of the day

pasteurization The method of checking and destroying bacteria in milk by heating liquid to a specified temperature for a specific period of time; after Louis Pasteur who discovered the process.

Quote of the day

"Change only favors minds that are diligently looking and preparing for discovery."
Louis Pasteur

Imagine...

Johannes Kepler and Louis Pasteur were remarkable scientists. Wouldn't it be great to be known as the father of . . . of . . . of something? What would you like to be known as the father of? Write about it and tell why.

Activity of the day

Scientist Match Up

Can you match up these scientists to what they study? Can you think of any more to add to this list?

1. Astronomer	prehistoric life through the study of fossils
2. Biologist	composition and properties of substances
3. Botanist	plants
4. Chemist	birds
5. Entomologist	earthquakes and related phenomena
6. Geologist	starts, planets, and heavenly bodies
7. Horticulturist	insects
8. Ichthyologist	fish
9. Ornithologist	all living things
10. Paleontologist	growing flowers, fruits, and vegetables
11. Physicist	physical structure of the earth
12. Seismologist	property and changes of matter and energy

Answers: 1. F, 2. I, 3. C, 4. B, 5. G, 6. K, 7. J, 8. H, 9. D, 10. A, 11. L, 12. E

Today in 1869

chewing gum was patented.

- Dr. William Finley Semple, a Mt. Vernon, New York dentist, invented chewing gum.
- During World War II, Semple's gum was only given to soldiers in the armed forces overseas.
- In 1946, Wrigley Company introduced spearmint gum to the public. Juicy Fruit and Doublemint came in 1947 and Big Red Cinnamon arrived in the 1970s followed by Hubba Bubba Bubble Gum.

Word of the day

chewing gum Chicle or other gummy substance flavored or sweetened for chewing; chicle is a gum-like substance made from the milky juice of the sapodilla tree.

Imagine...

It's time to take chewing gum a step further. But what will that be? You have been given creative license to develop a new chewing gum product. Will you simply invent new flavors? If so, what will they be? Will you combine gum with other candy to produce a completely new kind of treat? Think of some catchy names for your new product.

Quote of the day

" . . . a combination of rubber with other particles . . ."

Dr. William Finley Semple, inventor of chewing gum

Activity of the day

The Biggest Bubble

Gather some friends together and practice blowing bubbles. See who can blow the largest bubble. Then make a bar graph and record the names of your friends and the size of each friend's largest bubble blown. Use a ruler to measure the diameter of the bubbles.

Bubble-blower's Name

Size of Bubble Blown

Today in 1800

Charles Goodyear was born.

- Goodyear developed and patented a process called vulcanization, which made India rubber less sticky and able to withstand high temperatures.
- Although he held many patents concerning rubber, they were infringed upon by opportunists, and he died penniless.
- He was incarcerated in both the U.S. and France for his debts. In a Paris prison, he was awarded the Cross of the Legion of Honor for his inventions.

Word of the day

rubber Elastic substance produced from the milky sap of various tropical plants.

Quote of the day

"Life should be estimated exclusively by the standard of dollars and cents. I am not disposed to complain that I have planted and others have gathered the fruits. A man has cause for regret only when he sows and no one reaps."

Charles Goodyear

Imagine...

You've just invented a super, dupe bouncy rubber. What do you suggest it be used for? What will using this rubber do for the average ball or even the pogo stick?

Activity of the day

Rubber, Rubber, Everywhere!
Take a look around your house. Find and list all the things made from or with rubber. Don't forget to check out your toys!

Rubber in My House

_____ _____ _____

_____ _____ _____

_____ _____ _____

_____ _____ _____

_____ _____

Today in 1865

Rudyard Kipling was born in Bombay, India.

- Although he wrote poems and novels for adults, he earned international acclaim for the stories he wrote for children.
- The Jungle Book, Kipling's, most popular work was about Mowgli, a boy who is raised by wolves, and grows up in the jungle.
- In Riki-Tikki-Tavi, a mongoose saves a family from a cobra. In this story, jungle animals talk to each other.

Imagine...

When Rudyard Kipling began to write for children, he used events from his childhood. What can you write from your childhood? Can you use animals to help tell your story?

Word of the day

childhood The period from infancy through puberty.

Quote of the day

"If you could talk to the animals . . . ."
Dr. Doolittle

Activity of the day

What Did You Say?
Can you match up each animal with the sentence it might say?

1.	Bee	A.	"I'm quite the sly one."
2.	Cow	B.	"I'll never forget you!"
3.	Dog	C.	"I'd stick out my neck for you."
4.	Elephant	D.	"I've never jumped over a moon."
5.	Fox	E.	"I don't monkey around."
6.	Giraffee	F.	"I'm the king around here."
7.	Gorilla	G.	"Oh, I am very busy."
8.	Hyena	H.	"I promise not to laugh."
9.	Lion	I.	"You're barking up the wrong tree."
10.	Owl	J.	"I'm the wise one."

Answers: 1. G, 2. D, 3. I, 4. B, 5. A, 6. C, 7. E, 8. H, 9. F, 10. J

Today

is New Year's Eve.

In many cultures, it is a time to leave behind differences with the passing year so that the new year will be better.

- Celebrations around the world include fireworks displays at the stroke of midnight.
- On this day in 1879, Thomas Edison first demonstrated his electric incandescent light bulb to the public.
- This glass globe and filament was the result of over 1,000 attempts.

Word of the day

filament A very slender thread-like part; the fine metal wire in alight bulb which is made incandescent by an electric current.

Quote of the day

"Those were steps on the way. In each attempt I was successful in finding a way not to create a light bulb. I was always eager to learn, even from my mistakes."

Thomas Edison (when asked if he ever considered giving up on the light bulb)

Imagine...

You have been given the responsibility of planning your city's New Year's Eve festivities. And money is no object! Write about the night's events.

Activity of the day

Types of Light
Use the definitions to complete these words with that are types of lights.

					L	I	G	H	T	
					L	I	G	H	T	a portable light powered by batteries
					L	I	G	H	T	an electric light
					L	I	G	H	T	a light with a reflector and lens, at the front of a car
					L	I	G	H	T	a small, dim light kept on at night
				L	I	G	H	T		a tall light that illuminates the street
					L	I	G	H	T	a light used to illuminate an home's entryway
					L	I	G	H	T	a lamp that casts a broad beam of light
				L	I	G	H	T		a set of signal lights at intersections that regulates traffic

Answers: flashlight, lamplight, headlight, night light, street light, porch light, floodlight, traffic light

Today in

Make Your Own

DATE:

Imagine...

Word of the day

Quote of the day

Activity of the day